APRIL BLOOD

ALSO BY LAURO MARTINES

The Social World of the Florentine Humanists
Lawyers and Statecraft in Renaissance Florence
Violence and Civil Disorder in Italian Cities, 1200–1500
(editor)
Not in God's Image: Women in History from the Greeks to the Victorians
(with Julia O'Faolain)
Power and Imagination: City-States in Renaissance Italy
Society and History in English Renaissance Verse
An Italian Renaissance Sextet: Six Tales in Historical Context
Strong Words: Writing and Social Strain in the Italian Renaissance

APRIL BLOOD

FLORENCE AND THE
PLOT AGAINST THE MEDICI

LAURO MARTINES

For my very dear Camilla,
wonderful friend,
vital spirit,
with much love,
LAURO

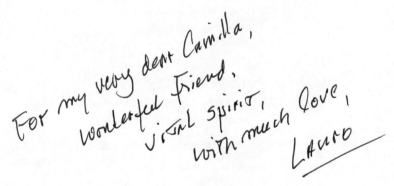

JONATHAN CAPE
LONDON

Published by Jonathan Cape 2003

2 4 6 8 10 9 7 5 3 1

Copyright © Lauro Martines 2003

Lauro Martines has asserted his right under the Copyright, Designs
and Patents Act 1988 to be identified as the author of this work

This book is sold subject to the condition that it shall not, by way of trade or otherwise,
be lent, resold, hired out, or otherwise circulated without the publisher's prior consent
in any form of binding or cover other than that in which it is published and without a
similar condition including this condition being imposed on the subsequent purchaser

First published in Great Britain in 2003 by
JONATHAN CAPE
Random House, 20 Vauxhall Bridge Road,
London SW1V 2SA

Random House Australia (Pty) Limited
20 Alfred Street, Milsons Point, Sydney,
New South Wales 2061, Australia

Random House New Zealand Limited
18 Poland Road, Glenfield,
Auckland 10, New Zealand

Random House (Pty) Limited
Endulini, 5A Jubilee Road, Parktown 2193, South Africa

The Random House Group Limited Reg. No. 954009
www.randomhouse.co.uk

A CIP catalogue record for this book is available from the British Library

ISBN 0–224–06167–4

Papers used by The Random House Group Limited are natural, recyclable
products made from wood grown in sustainable forests; the manufacturing processes
conform to the environmental regulations of the country of origin

Maps by Reginald Piggott

Set in 11¾pt on 14½pt Centaur by
Palimpsest Book Production Limited, Polmont, Stirlingshire
Printed and bound in Great Britain by
Biddles Ltd, Guildford & King's Lynn

For a delightful laity, friends in London
and why not for my enemies too
heralds of will and energy

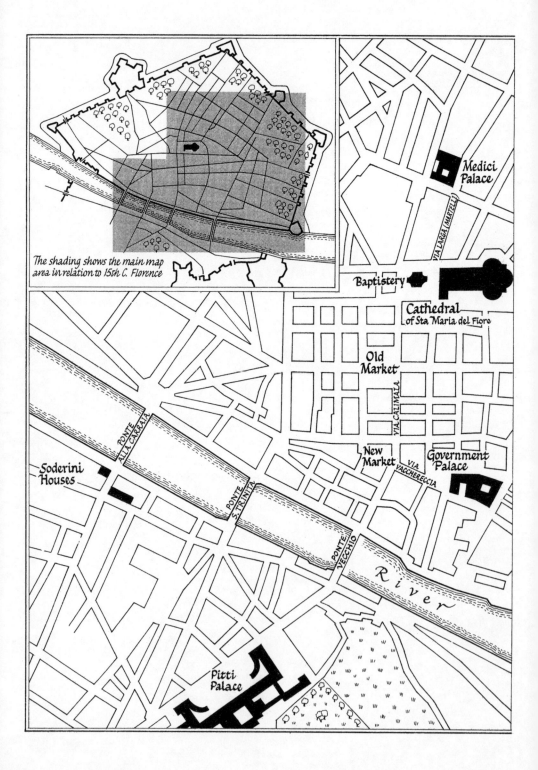

The shading shows the main map area in relation to 15th C. Florence

Medici Palace

VIA LARGA (MARTELLI)

Baptistery

Cathedral of Sta Maria del Fiore

Old Market

VIA CALIMALA

New Market

VIA VACCHERECCIA

Government Palace

Soderini Houses

PONTE ALLA CARRAIA

PONTE S. TRINITA

PONTE VECCHIO

River

Pitti Palace

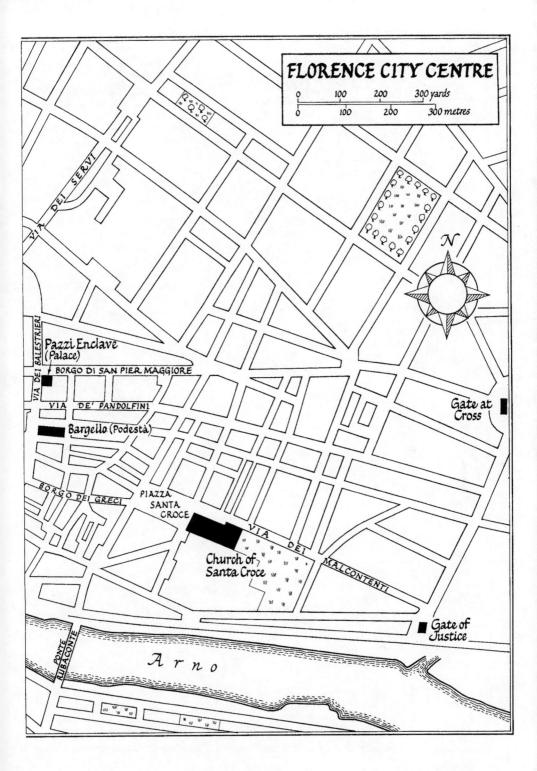

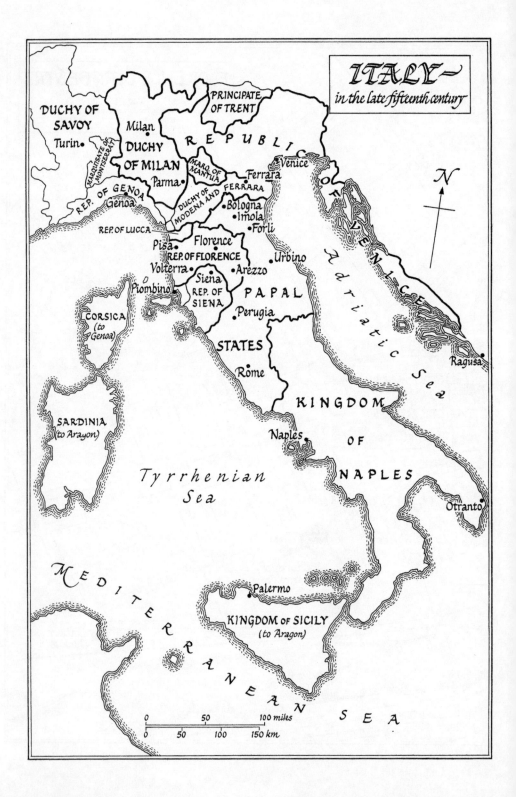

ITALY
in the late fifteenth century

DUCHY OF SAVOY

Turin•

Milan•

DUCHY OF MILAN

Parma•

MARQUISATE OF MONTSERRAT

REP. OF GENOA

Genoa•

REP. OF LUCCA

PRINCIPATE OF TRENT

REPUBLIC

MARQ. OF MANTUA

Ferrara•

Venice•

DUCHY OF MODENA AND FERRARA

Bologna•
•Imola
•Forlì

Pisa•

Florence•

REP. OF FLORENCE

Volterra•

•Arezzo

•Urbino

Piombino•

Siena•

REP. OF SIENA

PAPAL

Perugia•

CORSICA
(to Genoa)

STATES

Rome•

SARDINIA
(to Aragon)

KINGDOM

Naples•

OF

NAPLES

OF VENICE

Adriatic Sea

Ragusa•

Otranto•

Tyrrhenian Sea

Palermo•

KINGDOM OF SICILY
(to Aragon)

MEDITERRANEAN SEA

N

0   50   100 miles

0   50   100   150 km

CONTENTS

ACKNOWLEDGEMENTS

I BEGAN TO THINK about 'the Pazzi Conspiracy' some twenty-five years ago, but was reluctant to write about it, because it carries a strong whiff of sensationalism. Why, after all, had no 'real' historian ever written a book on the famous plot to murder the Medici? And there the matter rested until three years ago, when my friend and agent, Kay McCauley, urged a reconsideration. Now at last the climate for the bloody tale felt right; historical perceptions had changed; the possible terrors of politics speak more plainly; and a picture soon fell into place for me. *April Blood* owes its existence to Kay McCauley, and I have thanked her many times.

Much of the book's underpinning is drawn from a rich scholarship, fully acknowledged in notes at the end of the book. It is also the product of labour in the state archives of Florence, mingled with years of tinkering and reflection. I should add that the translations are mine.

Other debts remain. On the Sunday of the April Conspiracy, Lorenzo the Magnificent, along with a few of his companions, retreated into the north sacristy of the Florence cathedral and locked its bronze doors, to save him from the knives of his would-be assassins. Here properly, therefore, I want to thank a dear friend in Florence, Margaret (Peggy) Haines, the world's leading authority on the sacristy. In April 2001, she spent part of an afternoon there with me, talking about the remarkable wealth of its art work; and I was able to mount the stone stairs up to the gallery of the organ loft, from where I could look down, as Sigismondo della Stufa had done more than five centuries before, when he set eyes on the bleeding corpse of Lorenzo's younger brother, Giuliano.

Finally, I should be wanting in gratitude if I failed to acknowledge the cherished support of my two editors: in London, Will Sulkin of Jonathan Cape (Random House UK) and in New York, Peter Ginna of the Oxford University Press.

Lauro Martines
London

[xiii]

The Medici Family

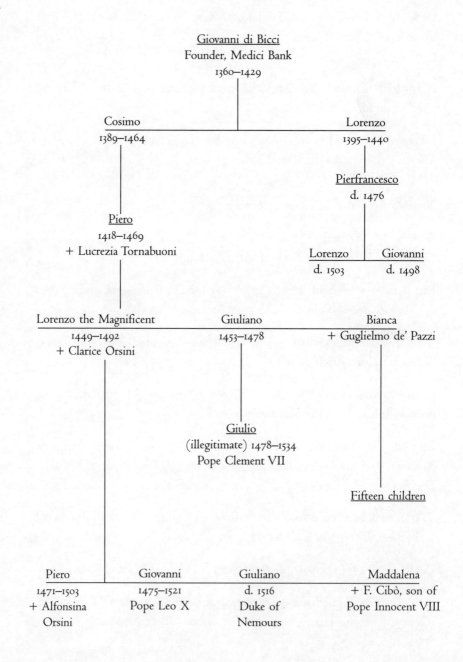

Giovanni di Bicci
Founder, Medici Bank
1360–1429

Cosimo
1389–1464

Lorenzo
1395–1440

Pierfrancesco
d. 1476

Piero
1418–1469
+ Lucrezia Tornabuoni

Lorenzo
d. 1503

Giovanni
d. 1498

Lorenzo the Magnificent
1449–1492
+ Clarice Orsini

Giuliano
1453–1478

Bianca
+ Guglielmo de' Pazzi

Giulio
(illegitimate) 1478–1534
Pope Clement VII

Fifteen children

Piero
1471–1503
+ Alfonsina
Orsini

Giovanni
1475–1521
Pope Leo X

Giuliano
d. 1516
Duke of
Nemours

Maddalena
+ F. Cibò, son of
Pope Innocent VIII

The Della Rovere Family
(of Pope Sixtus IV)

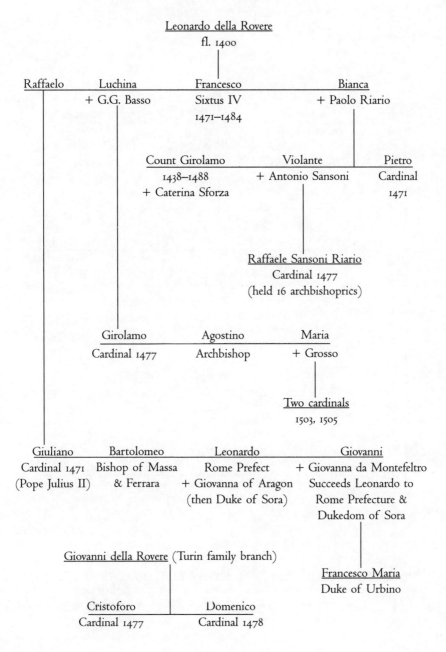

Leonardo della Rovere
fl. 1400

Raffaelo   Luchina   Francesco   Bianca
+ G.G. Basso   Sixtus IV   + Paolo Riario
1471–1484

Count Girolamo   Violante   Pietro
1438–1488   + Antonio Sansoni   Cardinal
+ Caterina Sforza   1471

Raffaele Sansoni Riario
Cardinal 1477
(held 16 archbishoprics)

Girolamo   Agostino   Maria
Cardinal 1477   Archbishop   + Grosso

Two cardinals
1503, 1505

Giuliano   Bartolomeo   Leonardo   Giovanni
Cardinal 1471   Bishop of Massa   Rome Prefect   + Giovanna da Montefeltro
(Pope Julius II)   & Ferrara   + Giovanna of Aragon   Succeeds Leonardo to
(then Duke of Sora)   Rome Prefecture &
Dukedom of Sora

Giovanni della Rovere (Turin family branch)

Cristoforo   Domenico   Francesco Maria
Cardinal 1477   Cardinal 1478   Duke of Urbino

The Pazzi Family

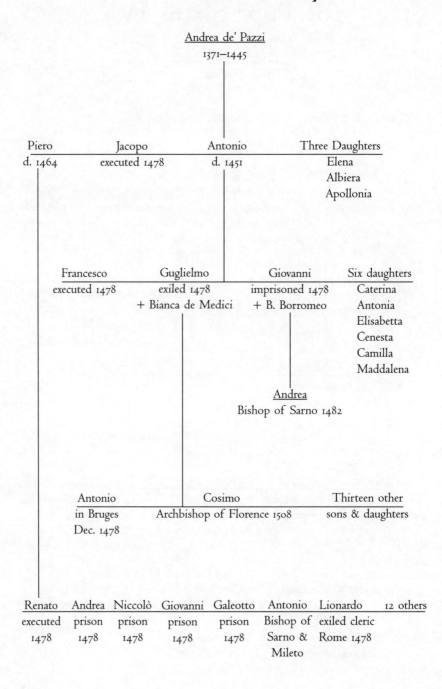

Andrea de' Pazzi
1371–1445

Piero	Jacopo	Antonio	Three Daughters
d. 1464	executed 1478	d. 1451	Elena
			Albiera
			Apollonia

Francesco	Guglielmo	Giovanni	Six daughters
executed 1478	exiled 1478	imprisoned 1478	Caterina
	+ Bianca de Medici	+ B. Borromeo	Antonia
			Elisabetta
			Cenesta
			Camilla
			Maddalena

Andrea
Bishop of Sarno 1482

Antonio	Cosimo	Thirteen other
in Bruges	Archbishop of Florence 1508	sons & daughters
Dec. 1478		

Renato	Andrea	Niccolò	Giovanni	Galeotto	Antonio	Lionardo	12 others
executed	prison	prison	prison	prison	Bishop of	exiled cleric	
1478	1478	1478	1478	1478	Sarno &	Rome 1478	
					Mileto		

Personaggi

Medici:

Lorenzo the Magnificent: quasi-lord of Florence, 1469–92
Giuliano: Lorenzo's brother, murdered, April 1478
Cosimo: Lorenzo's grandfather, top man in Florentine state, 1434–64
Piero ('the Gouty'), Lorenzo's father, unofficial head of state, 1464–69

Pazzi:

Messer Jacopo: banker, merchant, leading plotter
Francesco: banker, merchant, leading plotter, Messer Jacopo's nephew
Guglielmo: Francesco's brother, also Lorenzo de' Medici's brother-in-law
Renato: first cousin to Guglielmo and Francesco

Others:

Francesco Salviati: Archbiship of Pisa, leading plotter
Count Girolamo Riario: Lord of Imola and Forlì, Sixtus IV's nephew, plotter
Montesecco, Count of: soldier in service of Pope and Count Girolamo, plotter
Pope Sixtus IV (1471–84): covert backer of the plot
Cardinal of San Giorgio (Raffaele Sansoni Riario): student, nephew to Sixtus IV
King Ferrante of Naples (1458–94): covert backer of the plot
Duke Federigo of Urbino (d. 1482): covert backer of the plot
Bernardo Bandini Baroncelli: Florentine banker, probable Pazzi employee, plotter

Jacopo Bracciolini: classical scholar, tutor to the Cardinal of San
  Giorgio, plotter
Poliziano: classical scholar, poet, Lorenzo's protégé, author of a booklet
  on the plot

Prologue

O<small>N A SUNDAY</small> in April 1478, in the cathedral of Florence, a band of conspirators tried to murder the two heads of the Medici family: Lorenzo the Magnificent, unofficial head of state, and his younger brother Giuliano. Known as 'the Pazzi Conspiracy', the plot failed, and in reprisal a bloodbath followed. Thus my title *April Blood*.

Here was a tale of men driven by demonic energies; of a proud and brilliant young politician and poet, the 'Magnificent' Lorenzo de' Medici; of a pope who could not keep himself from heaping the wealth and offices of the Church on his own nephews; an archbishop who was ready to found his career on murder, a shrewd king of Naples, hired professional soldiers, and a talented Florentine family of enormous wealth – the Pazzi. The plot, however, was also a hinge for the history of Florence, with a lively republic on one side of the turn, stretching back to the thirteenth century, and on the other, after 1478, an incipient principality or 'tyranny'. But the swing itself, with its blood and immediate consequences, pivoted on an anxious and layered episode – cruel, framed by a High Mass, resounding, and with a tragic note for the human spirit.

If sounder reasons were needed for a book on the Conspiracy, there is also the fact that the opening burst of events in the cathedral was overtaken, within a day or two, by the pressing interests and voices of Italy's five great states (Map 2). For the Medici had strong political ties with the Duchy of Milan and its ruling Sforza family, and Lorenzo looked to the Sforza as protectors and patrons. Florence also had an alliance with the Republic of Venice, which bound the Venetians, in any emergency, to come to the military aid of the Florentine Republic.

In a startling discovery, however, it now emerged from behind the scenes that the two big powers to the south of Florence, the Papal State and the Kingdom of Naples, were deeply implicated in the assassination plot. Pope Sixtus IV and King Ferrante were pursuing political aims in central Italy, all along Florence's frontiers; and if the ebbing Republic of Florence could be shored up against the power of a budding Medicean lordship, then their goals would be more readily attainable. In these weavings, the two rulers had also enlisted the help of two Florentine neighbours, the tiny Republic of Siena and the Duke of Urbino, one of the foremost mercenary captains of the day. The result of the April Plot was to be the Pazzi War, or War of the Pazzi Conspiracy: nearly two years of armed conflict, incendiary words, and refined treachery.

The Italian Renaissance was not alien to political violence, especially since explosive anger and tumults against authority may be the fruit of the vital energies or alert stance of a people. The shape of early-modern Italy was cut and cast in the late Middle Ages (*c.* 1050–1350), in a cluttered sequence of uprisings and wars against German kings and emperors, popes, feudal magnates, and outside invaders. By the end of the fourteenth century, the Italian peninsula had hardened into its classic arrangement of independent powers: Venice, Milan, Florence, the papacy, and the kingdom of Naples, each with its constellation of subject lands and cities. Lesser or little states, such as the lordship of Ferrara, or the dwarf republics of Lucca and Siena, survived nervously beside their bigger neighbours; and the great port of Genoa lay under the rule of Milan. It was a setting that nourished the art of diplomacy and the gradual rise of the resident ambassador, soon to become a standard feature of the diplomatic process.

Yet rivalry for lands, troops, and leadership endured; the call to arms was common, if not inevitable; ruthless political genius and strong nerves were prime necessities; so too were discretion and reason; and marriage as an instrument of politics became policy. All these, in varying measures, entered into the April Plot, the ensuing Pazzi War, and Lorenzo de' Medici's more domineering achievements of the 1480s.

In regular revenue and the possible numbers of its professional soldiers, Florence was the weakest of the peninsula's major states, despite the city's many bankers and exceptional position as a capital of finance. War, therefore, could be especially hard on Florentines and their 'bourgeois' republic. But the city, as is well known, was neither weak in spirit nor in cultural energies.

Here was Machiavelli (b. 1469), growing up in a political milieu whose tensions would carry Florence toward an explosive renewal of its republican freedoms in 1494–95. He was a witness to the intense controversies – reactions against Medicean domination – of that troubled decade, and they would leave their stamp on the conceptual language of his political writings. Meanwhile, in what seemed a more routine world, Verrocchio, the Pollaiuolo brothers, and other Florentine artists were pursuing their work for private patrons and religious houses. Two or three years after the April Plot, Botticelli produced his *Primavera*, a sparkling picture with recondite references for an elite of connoisseurs. The serenity and elevated tone of many religious pictures of the period, such as by Ghirlandaio and Botticelli, containing the portraits of contemporaries, were arguably exercises in transcendence for patrons: works that constructed moments of surpassing personal peace or perfection, in stark opposition to the brutal strains of politics and the scramble for place and favour. The poetry of the age, including Lorenzo de' Medici's, has hymns to the country against the ambitions, greed, and moral dirty work of the city.

Though all these matters will loom silently along the edges of this history, I shall not be able to broach them. But we may for a moment here have a glimpse of the ubiquity of politics in Florence, and its imprint on high culture, by noting that it made continuous contact with the revival and study of classical letters ('humanism'). In the hunt for professorships at the University of Florence/Pisa, writers and scholars had to court political patrons and get them to intervene. Appointment to the city's top secretarial offices, strictly reserved for literary men and intellectuals, also required the intervention of politicians. Humanists translated classical writings from Greek into Latin, or Latin into the vernacular, very often by working on commission for rich and influential citizens. They dedicated unsolicited translations and their own writings to the leading men in government and politics, while also looking about for classical works that would appeal to wealthy merchants, bankers, politicians, and neighbouring princes. In this sense, they were striving to popularise parts of the classical syllabus, hoping to disseminate select voices from the ancient world – Quintilian, Livy, Plato, Plutarch, Pliny, and so forth.

But after Cosimo de' Medici's return from political exile in the autumn of 1434, no Florentine family was ever again to match or even approach the Medici in their mounting harvest of dedications, translations, and poetic accolades. In the office of promoting and flattering, the seductive power of literature gathered round them. As they seized power, they came to expect praise and then, by their bearing, to require it, though in a glide that also aroused political loathing. So it happened that to have a pen out for hire in such a setting, as Poliziano did (Figure 1) in his *Memoir of the Conspiracy*, forced writers and scholars into a traffic of ideas and degrees of partisanship. Whether or not they themselves directly engaged in political violence, they moved almost constantly in its shadows.

In the bulk of recent historical work on Renaissance Florence, politics has been much played down or even ignored, as if there were something so nasty and ignoble about it, or just plain grey, that the less said about it the better. 'Base and dirty' it may have been, but never grey, and we push it aside at the risk of missing the key point of departure for understanding the history of Italian Renaissance cities. Small, packed, observant, industrious, and sharply circumscribed by city walls (Venice by water), each of them was an arena for politics: a space in which the power of the state was omnipresent.

Here, every resident was touched, and touched daily, by decisions that had been made in a government palace never more than a few hundred metres away from most citizens. The sights and sounds of that authoritative presence were everywhere – in trumpeting heralds, uniformed guardsmen, court summonses, resounding official bells, grand arrivals and departures, and the livery of rushing officials and messengers. In addition to the property taxes and 'forced loans' paid by citizens, all contracts and comestibles carried a tax; dress of the more expensive sort was regulated by law; every night brought curfews; torture was common; capital punishment was knowingly turned into a public spectacle; and the intrusiveness of government couriers put much of the private business of families into the eyes or ears of neighbours. With an admixture of the teachings of late-medieval Christianity, this urban arena was the crucible for the making of social and individual identities, no less than for the formation of art and ideas.

✳ ✳ ✳

Fig. 1 Detail from Domenico Ghirlandaio, *The Confirmation of the Rule of St Francis*, depicting Poliziano on the stairs looking up to the black-haired Lorenzo.

Since Pope Sixtus will figure strongly in the key chapters, readers should know that the pope was not only the acknowledged head of Western Christendom and the Vicar of Christ on earth in theological terms, but also the supreme head of a secular state, in a region that straddled the Italian peninsula from Rome to the Adriatic. In this incarnation, he was much like any other Italian ruler, flanked by government officials, law courts, police magistracies, and tax collectors, in addition to having armies and diplomats under his control.

Of the importance of cardinals, who will also have a place in this story, suffice it to say that they sprang usually from the ranks of the eminent urban, feudal, and princely families. They were the electors of the pope and were themselves appointed by popes. When a cardinal was not already rich in his own right, it was the business of the pope to see to it that the man's ecclesiastical income enabled him to live in style, to command a train of servants, and to dispense patronage. Every region, every city, sought the Roman advocacy of one or more cardinals, in efforts to obtain a never-ending stream of favours, ranging from the right to tax priests and friars to the winning of lawsuits in Rome, not to mention the search for ecclesiastical place by clerics back home. Cardinals were the magnates of the Church.

My expression 'Lord Priors', to be used throughout the book, refers to Florence's governing council: the *Signoria*, *Signori*, or lords. They were a body of eight priors and a Gonfalonier of Justice, the head of state, chosen to serve in office for only two months. The city thus, surprisingly, had six changes of government per year. But the system normally provided remarkable stability, owing both to the habit of almost daily consultation with the most experienced members of the political class, and to the close involvement of citizens, who could entertain the hope or the expectation of rotating through the top offices.

The larger consquences of the Pazzi Conspiracy are matter for deeper reflection and my concluding pages.

CHAPTER ONE

Conspiracy

Revenge

'THE DISH OF revenge', they say in France, 'is best eaten cold.' And Lorenzo de' Medici finally ate the last of his in April 1488, exactly ten years after the sensational attempt to kill him in Florence at High Mass. In the town of Forlì, some fifty miles away and to the north-east, across mountainous country, one of the prime conspirators against him, and the only one still alive, was slashed to death in the government palace and his naked corpse was thrown down into the central square, to be gaped at and violated by angry citizens. He was Count Girolamo Riario, Lord of Imola and Forlì, a nephew of the late Pope Sixtus IV.

The assassins wrote to Lorenzo a few days later, complimenting themselves on wreaking vengeance for him. But he was not the engineer of the deed, despite the fact that, working through agents and diplomats, he had made a point of following the Count's every significant move for ten years. He had paid to sow discontent in his lands; he had a hand in three previous attempts on the Count's life; and he had laboured to thwart his ambitions by means of Florentine diplomacy. So as the first top man in Florence to get the news from Forlì, he was bound to be the first in rejoicing. The taste for vengeance was a virile duty in Renaissance Italy, and Lorenzo, though an outstanding poet and connoisseur, was not so delicately constituted as to balk at brutal revenge. He was also a political boss.

With its cluster of about 8000 or 9000 souls, Forlì was very different from spirited Florence, with a post-plague population of five times as many. But the ways of assassination – poison, strangulation, or a steel blade – were the same. And when dealt out to public figures, or for reasons of state, death was often a theatre of ignominy, with bodies hanged from the windows of government buildings or cast like carrion into central squares. In cities where the tight community and the individual were closely joined, punishment for capital crime against the prince or the public good had to be bloody and had to be seen to be so.

Count Girolamo was tumbled by the foe of many a government: taxes and the need for ready cash. The head of a mini-state in the Romagna of the popes, the most volatile part of Italy, this petty ruler had even been forced to pawn his wife's jewels in Bologna and far-off Genoa. He was seen by many as a man who had risen from nothing, in having come from relatively modest circumstances and an obscure village near Genoa. His uncle, Pope Sixtus IV (d. 1484), had all but made him in a day by putting Imola and Forlì – autonomous fiefs in papal territory – into his hands, and then by clinching a marriage for him with the fourteen-year-old Caterina Sforza, a bastard daughter of the Duke of Milan, Galeazzo Maria, himself assassinated in 1476.

These slippery circumstances added more risk to the dangers of the neighbouring Apennine mountains, a stronghold for bandits and unruly lords, who often threatened the security of Romagnol rulers and were the main cause of Count Girolamo's greatest expense: a small body of guardsmen and an extra company of 100 soldiers. But the treachery of passion could prevail against even these. When his fiscal agents, two brothers from the Orsi family, as well as two of his captains, fell out with him in heated quarrels over money, the four resolved to kill him, expecting that popular discontent would erupt in their favour, especially because one of their principal motives was the spur of a hated land tax, to be directly imposed on the class of landowners. But first there were the immediate spurs. On being pressed one day for back wages by one of his soldiers, the Count had shouted, 'Get out of my sight or I'll have you hanged.' To which the captain had replied, 'O My lord, one hangs thieves and traitors, and I am not that sort. I deserve to die sword in hand, like any other brave man at arms.'

As local noblemen, the two Orsi brothers enjoyed the privilege of 'the gilded key', meaning that they had the right to call on Riario without invitation or preliminaries. So, having made their plans, they went to his palace just after dinner on Monday, 14 April 1488, and finding him with a few servitors in the ornate Hall of Nymphs, one of the two men who had entered greeted Riario with the thrust of a short sword (*squarcina*). The victim's cry and rush to scurry under a table, to protect himself, brought two other men into the hall to help finish him off, as his terrorised attendants fled. Other conspirators joined in and now, nine in all, with some of them posted down below at the base of the palace staircase, they repelled the late arrivals who sought to stand up for Count Girolamo and his family. A little later, as though performing a well-known ritual, two men stripped the dead Count of his clothing and threw his body down into the principal piazza, where a crowd quickly collected to hail the deed and offer kisses to the conspirators. Once Caterina Sforza Riario and her children, who had been in another part of the palace, were taken prisoner, a mob sacked the building and an immense fortune, most of it in jewels, vanished.

Five days later, now worried, nervous, and casting about for help, the 'tax farmers' (fiscal agents), Checco and Ludovico Orsi, addressed a letter to 'Our Magnificent and Most Revered Lorenzo [de' Medici]', written in part, they say, 'to satisfy our debt [to you]'. They go on to ask for his advice and to offer their version of the gruesome assassination. Remembering that 'this Nero [Count Girolamo]' had 'the impudence to smear his hands with the blood of your lofty house', they rehearse his sins, noting that he had no regard for God or the saints, and that he had been 'a drinker of the blood of poor men'. Lorenzo replied with such speed that within two days, on 21 April, his secretary, a certain Stefano from the Florentine fortress of Castrocaro, had already met with the Orsi brothers. Stefano drafted a letter to his master, describing his meeting with them and recounting the particulars of the assassination. The people of Forlì, he writes, were happy about the Count's death. All wanted the Church to take over the reins of government there, and all said that they would rather have their bodies hacked up into quarters than let the city fall back into any other hands. He had assured the Orsi that Lorenzo would offer them his complete support, including the promise to defend their good name and actions to Pope Innocent VIII, Florence's closest ally. In fact, in that very year, Innocent was to become father-in-law to Lorenzo's third daughter. Stefano also quotes the words of one of the brothers: 'I am the slave of the Magnificent

Lorenzo, together with all my family, and if I should never in my life do anything else, I am content to have avenged the innocent blood of his brother.'

Lorenzo gave no written support to the Orsi brothers in his own hand: conspire in cloak-and-dagger doings he might, but to offer proof of it was, in a phrase of the period, 'another pair of sleeves'.

Ten days later, whipped up with fear and on the point of flight, the Orsi again wrote to Lorenzo; it was a plea for military aid; but being a political animal to the roots of his being, and his revenge now achieved, Lorenzo did not make a move. Uneasy about Milan–Sforza designs, neither he nor Pope Innocent, for all the Church's claims to Forlì, dispatched troops to support the Forlivesi and to enforce the rule of the papal governor. A small army from Milan and Bologna was already on the outskirts of Forlì, with orders to take it back for the widow, Caterina Sforza Riario, who had gained cunning access to the Rivaldino fortress at one end of the city and was safely billeted there. Threatening to bombard Forlì with rounds of artillery, and having already damaged a few houses, she saved the city from a savage sacking at the hands of the approaching army, blame for which would have been pinned to her. Now, however, she also would have her revenge, if only in part and not yet as a cold dish. Lorenzo de' Medici, meanwhile, was kept fully informed.

Frightened by the prospect of a murdering, pillaging, fornicating army, the Forlivesi had swung completely around in their loyalties and were ready to support anyone who would save them. This meant Caterina. And as if whisked in by ghosts, some of the objects that had been stolen from the sacked palazzo reappeared. The jewels, however, would not again be seen, for on the night of 29 April, two weeks after their assassination of the Count, the Orsi brothers and their closest collaborators fled from the city with the best of the loot.

When Caterina took possession of Forlì on 30 April, her eldest son, the ambitiously named Octavian, was the first to parade around the main square. Next, speaking the symbolic language of power, she entered the city in triumph, attended by noblemen in armour and magnificent dress, and riding between two files of soldiers posted along her route. Terror gripped the men who had most compromised themselves with the two tax farmers and who had failed to flee. That day Caterina's mercenaries drew blood. The houses of the Orsi, of the soldiers Pansecchi and Ronchi, and of others were looted and burned. A series of massacres followed on 1 and 2 May, terminating in the principal square, which seemed to be turned into 'a bloody lake'. Andrea, the eighty-five-year-old father of the Orsi brothers, was made to witness the total destruction of his house, swiftly levelled by 400 men. Then, tied to a plank and the tail of a horse, he was dragged around the government square three times, his face pressed to the ground. Later, he was quartered; his intestines were thrown about in the piazza, 'and one of those dogs of a soldier', the chronicler Cobelli reports, 'grabbed the heart, cut it out . . . put it up to his mouth, and bit into it, and I, seeing this, fled.'

The significance of such symbolic cannibalism will come forth in a later chapter. In the course of the blood riot, as though to compensate for the butchery, Caterina had Count Girolamo's body disinterred and done up to lie in state for three days in the church of San Francesco. Hours after the Count's assassination, in the watches of the night, a friar had gone out to collect the lone body from the piazza. He was connected, ironically, with the religious confraternity whose mission it was to comfort and pray for those on their way to the gallows.

What the mere facts as related above do not reveal is that both Lorenzo de' Medici and Pope Innocent had another most particular reason for applauding Riario's removal from the scene. Once the frank keeper of a mistress, though not (it was said) after he had taken holy orders, the Holy Father was also an unholy father and grandfather: he had sired a family, and Lorenzo had given his daughter Maddalena in marriage to Innocent's son Franceschetto. The Pope thought about creating a small state for that son by handing him the governments of Imola and Forlì, and possibly even of Faenza; but pursuing this hope had promised to be impossible during the lifetime of Count Girolamo, who looked both to Venice for military help and, through his wife Caterina, to the powerful intervention of her uncle, the Lord of Milan, Ludovico Sforza. Now, however, with Girolamo suddenly out of the way, the Pope could seek to invest Franceschetto with the two cities that were, after all, his nominal feudal territory as head of the Church. And Lorenzo, ever mindful of the Medici name and of 'our house', as he loved to call it, seemed ready to assist Innocent in this enterprise. Maddalena would then be 'Countess' of Imola and Forlì. He would indeed have liked this, but without a papal presence, and somehow without Innocent; for no patriotic Florentine really wanted the might of the Church to be exercised in the Church lands that bordered on Florentine territory. Lorenzo, therefore, dragged his feet, but meanwhile Florence grabbed the Castle of Piancaldoli in the province of Imola.

Seven weeks after the murder of Count Girolamo there was another assassination on a similar scale. Lorenzo de' Medici's chief dependant in the Romagna was stabbed to death in an ugly tangle of interests that opposed Florence, Milan, the Church, and Venice. Galeotto Manfredi, lord of the neighbouring town of Faenza, was a violent man who did not bother to conceal his adulterous roisterings from his wife Francesca, a proud lady from the ruling Bentivoglio family of Bologna. Feigning illness one day, and with her father's likely connivance, she summoned Galeotto to her bedroom, where he was promptly assaulted and murdered by four servitors, three of them having been hidden under her splendid bed. Her marriage to Galeotto had been brokered by none other than Lorenzo himself, who had used Faenza as a base for his operations against Count Girolamo.

An Age of Conspiracy

IF THE LANDS of Romagna were a hospice for mercenaries and conspirators, the rest of Italy was no safe haven. Explosive political violence could be infectious, particularly in regions and in cities where rulers were insufficiently dug in. Machiavelli himself was to point this out. The plot against the Medici was sprung a mere sixteen months after the assassination of the Duke of Milan (December 1476), in an era which, stretching back to the Roman conspiracy of Stefano Porcari (1452–53), has been called 'the Age of Conspiracies'.

When compared to the Milanese assassination, the dramatic attempt against Lorenzo and Giuliano de' Medici highlights the obstacles to political murder in a Florence that was still a republic, however perverted its direction. Yet owing to the republican claims and religious venues of the two plots, the Florentine conspirators were surely aware of echoes of Milan's 'tyrannicide' in their own attempted *coup*. The links between the two conspiracies were almost too obvious to be singled out by contemporaries, especially as the murdered lord of Milan, Galeazzo Maria (Figure 2), was the son of the great upstart general, Francesco Sforza, who had helped Cosimo de' Medici, Lorenzo's grandfather, to tighten the family's hold on Florence by posing a continual outside threat.

The Milanese events underline the pent-up rage that could be generated by authoritarian government in Renaissance Italy, while also revealing the fact, interestingly, that until about 1500 physical access to the lord of a city was easily had by most members of the local aristocracy. The bare facts of the Milanese case were these.

Just before the commencement of High Mass on the day after Christmas, 1476, the Duke of Milan was murdered by three men: Giovanni

Fig. 2 Piero del Pollaiuolo, *Galeazzo Maria Sforza.*

Andrea Lampugnani, Gerolamo Olgiati, and Carlo Visconti. Each had different reasons for wanting to plunge daggers into Galeazzo Maria Sforza, whose infamy for vice and barbarous cruelty was deplored even by his own father. May it be argued that a man – Galeazzo Maria – who spared no expense to hire some of the finest musicians of the age, in order to satisfy his love of music, could not possibly be a monster? Not at all. Though probably false, there was a strong, persistent rumour about that Galeazzo Maria had poisoned his mother: such was his reputation. Reports disclose that he bought girls and wives at will, got his fill of pleasure ('violavit virgines; aliorum uxores accepit'), and then passed them on to his courtiers. A priest who innocently predicted that the Duke would have a short reign was starved to death. On another occasion, stricken by amorous jealousy, the Duke had a certain Pietro da Castello's hands lopped off; he had another man, Pietro Drago, nailed alive to his coffin; and on his orders, executioners put a poacher to death by forcing him to swallow, fur intact, a hare.

In keeping with the upper-class fashion of the day, Galeazzo Maria was given a good grounding in Latin and tutored in some of the Latin classics, but this exposure to 'humanism' – as the programme of classical study came to be called – did little to humanise him. Understandably, therefore, a week or so after his assassination, his widow, Bona of Savoy, knowing her man, dispatched an urgent letter to a contact in Rome, the canon Celso de Maffeis, listing the late Duke's sins (robberies, wholesale violence, injustice, carnal vices, simony) and voicing agitation over the state of his immortal soul. Having already consulted canonists and theologians, she pressed Maffeis to seek a plenary remission of Galeazzo Maria's sins from Pope Sixtus IV, in return for princely donations to religious houses, charity for virgins, and other forms of material restitution. Moreover, she alleged, her husband *had* begun to feel contrition, but any such continuity had been brutally truncated by his murder.

Let's consider the plotters.

Carlo Visconti was drawn into the plot to kill Galeazzo Maria by the call of family honour. A well-connected government secretary, employed in Milan's Council of Justice, he had a sister who seems to have been deflowered by the priapic Duke.

It appears that the Duke had also given hints (or so it was bruited) of an erotic interest in Giovanni Andrea Lampugnani's wife, but this remains no more than a suspicion. Recognised as the leader of the conspiracy, slightly lame and with an explosive temper, Giovanni Andrea hailed from a family of jurists and high government officials – Milanese nobility. On occasion, for one job or another, he had also served the Duke and had access to the court. His murderous feelings, however, stemmed mainly from a sharp quarrel with the mighty Bishop of Como over a rich parcel of lands and houses that had been let to the Lampugnani brothers by the former abbot of Morimondo, a rich old abbey out in the country. When Morimondo passed suddenly into the possession of the new Bishop of Como, this high cleric, Branda da Castiglione, a notorious spender and a powerful official in Galeazzo Maria's court, repudiated the lease and the brothers were 'chased out' of the properties in question. Despite Lampugnani entreaties, the Duke refused to intercede or even to call the case into an appropriate tribunal for a hearing. Giovanni Andrea's anger turned into a criminal passion.

The youngest of the assassins, Gerolamo Olgiati, twenty-three years old, seems to have acted purely out of republican ideals, and he also was born into an esteemed family of government functionaries. His study of republican Rome under the guidance of the gifted Cola Montano, a Bolognese humanist, and reading of the Roman historian Sallust on the Catilinarian conspiracy, had fired the young Olgiati with a yearning for glory and the desire to liberate his *patria*, a dream that called for an act of tyrannicide. The conspirators were also moved by the recent memory of Milan's vibrant Ambrosian Republic, which had fought for three years (1447–50) to resurrect the communal liberties of the thirteenth century.

Knowing all about Galeazzo Maria's habits and movements, the conspirators decided to strike on the day of the martyr, Santo Stefano, hence in the church of Santo Stefano on the day after Christmas, a Thursday, 1476. Meeting there that morning before Mass, they prayed for the saint's protection. Giovanni Andrea led them in prayer and the others repeated his words. In one account, they also prayed that the saint be not offended by seeing his church spotted with blood, since it would all be for the good of Milan and the Milanese people.

The 26th dawned as an intensely cold day, and that morning the Duke was jumpy, having had odd forebodings, as is often alleged in the chronicles of such events. Down to nearly the last minute, before setting out to attend High Mass at Santo Stefano, he had doubts about whether or not to go forth, and would have preferred to hear Mass in his urban citadel (*castello*); but his chaplain and singers had already gone on to the church and the Bishop of Como was for some reason unable to perform the service. That morning too, as was customary at Christmas and other high holidays, a number of great noblemen and ambassadors were in attendance at court, and most of them seem to have favoured staying in the castello, owing to the frightful cold outside. Putting a sudden end to his dithering, the Duke emerged from his quarters, found and placed himself between the Ferrara and Mantua ambassadors, taking each by the arm, and walked out of the castello with them, while the rest of the court followed. Once outside, they hurried to their horses, mounted, and rode the short distance through the city to Santo Stefano, which was already crowded with noblemen, ladies, and lesser folk. Ordered to attend, several of the Duke's married mistresses were also present. Out of a sense of decency, however, and to avoid scandal, the historian Corio, a witness, refused to name them.

A different company was also in attendance: about thirty friends of the conspirators. They had been urged to show up at Santo Stefano that morning in order to lend their moral support, they believed, to Giovanni Andrea's unusual decision to accost the Duke, with an eye to getting his recognition of the Lampugnani claim to the disputed Morimondo estate. Most of upper-class Milan, in short, was well aware of the Lampugnani case. Of the plot itself the assembled friends were otherwise in complete ignorance.

Wearing hidden breast armour, Olgiati, Visconti, and Giovanni Andrea were gathered around the Point of the Innocents, a legendary abutting stone in the middle of Santo Stefano, supposedly bearing some of the stains of the blood of the Innocents. When the Duke reached that part of the church, with the Bishop of Como in the train behind him, the three men stepped forward and Giovanni Andrea went down on one knee before the surprised Sforza prince. There was a brief exchange of words and next, suddenly lunging as he stood up, our man stabbed the Duke in the groin and then the breast. Moments later Olgiati and Visconti, followed by Giovanni Andrea's servant Franzone, also struck him with their daggers and a sword on the chest, back, throat, shoulders, and forehead. One witness claimed that Franzone boldly plunged his hands into the flowing blood. Before dying, the Duke had just enough time to utter something like 'Io sono morto' (I'm dead) and 'By Our Lady!'

Pandemonium erupted, just as it would in the Florence cathedral sixteen months later. The Mantuan ambassador even thought he saw six assassins rather than four. People rushed headlong out of the church, fearing that others too would be murdered, one of the Duke's soldiers having also been killed and another wounded. Despite his limp, Giovanni Andrea rushed across to the women's side of the church, got entangled in a flow of cloth, apparently fell, and was caught and killed there by a guardsman. But his companions got away. In a matter of minutes, the church of Santo Stefano was vacant and strangely silent, the abandoned body of Galeazzo Maria Sforza, with its fourteen wounds, still lying there in a waste of blood. Knowing that secrecy and treachery often governed the conduct of politics, courtiers and ambassadors feared that other armed and disguised conspirators were also in the church that morning, ready to assault anyone who dared to move in favour of the slain prince. Whereupon the terrified court fled, including – possibly ordered to do so – the Duke's guardsmen. They retreated to the castello and to one of the big Sforza palaces.

Since the conspirators seem to have given no serious forethought to their own safety once the murder had been committed, the plot emerges as a rather primitive affair. Milan nursed strong feelings against Galeazzo Maria's reign, but Giovanni Andrea and his cohorts had little, if any, evidence that the people of Milan would rise up in their defence. There were surely some citizens about who cherished the memory of the city's Ambrosian Republic and its desperate, recent struggles against the machinations of princes, Milanese noblemen, Venice, and the great soldier Francesco Sforza. Now, however, the realistic hope of any return to a republic had vanished, above all because the late republican experience (1447–50) had pushed aside and outraged the nobility. So far as we can tell, the three men made no arrangements to stir up the populace or citizenry. They were isolated: so driven by hatred for the Duke and by a fantasy republicanism, that they must have imagined a consequent miracle. Their imaginings would end in an awesome exhibition of justice.

The Duke's body was soon borne away. But in a spectacle of grotesque entertainment, replayed in Florence in 1478, Giovanni Andrea's body was seized upon by boys, pulled jeeringly out into the streets, and dragged through the city, pelted with stones, beaten, and slashed with knives. It was then pulled along to his house to be hung upside down, next to a prominent window. Taken down the next day and by now headless, the corpse was again dragged through the streets. The authorities had removed the head, saving it for a later ritual. In an exercise of traditional symbolism, the sinning right hand was also cut off, burned, and nailed to a column in a central square. A poem of the day claims that a few people ate bits of Giovanni Andrea's heart, liver, and hands. Whatever was left of the corpse was finally fed to pigs.

In view of Christian doctrine concerning the soul, confession, last rites, and proper burial of the body in consecrated ground, the tearing up of a corpse was a scandalous spurning of the accepted order of things. Yet it was certainly condoned by police and magistrates, if not actually encouraged, in the angry belief that Giovanni Andrea's murder of the Duke was so horrific as to call for punishment even in death and beyond the grave.

The ducal government's frenzy for revenge and 'justice' held the promise of horror for the others as well. Late on 27 December, a day after the Santo Stefano orgy, Giovanni Andrea's overly-loyal servant Franzone was seized, tortured, and forced to name all the conspirators. He was identified by the Lampugnani colours on his stockings. On Sunday, 29 December, Carlo Visconti was caught, betrayed by a frightened relative who was also a ducal councillor. Tortured, he confessed and was condemned. Gerolamo Olgiati was not finally taken until 30 December, exposed in his case by several people, among them his own father. In an impassioned letter to the Duchess, the elder Oligiati, needing an outburst and seeking to protect himself, declared that in view of the atrocity of the crime, if this 'arch-traitor [my son] . . . had been offered to me a thousand times over, I would have considered it a favour to inflict the penalty of death on him with my own hands.'

Olgiati, Visconti, and Franzone were executed in the castello before dawn on Thursday, 2 January, 1477. Mounted on the so-called wheel, one of the most agonising of all the instruments of death, each was torn in half from groin to neck while still alive – not the sort of detail which historians like to ponder, though it says something about the morality of the age, about attitudes toward the body, justice, and the sense of sin. Next, to make a public show of justice and stern government, the torn body parts were carted out to the city's seven great gates, where a bloody half was affixed to each of five of them. The last half was then divided and each of these parts was put up on the other two gates: arm and shoulder on the Porta Cumana and the leg and foot on the Porta Nuova. The four heads, Lampugnani's included, were pinned with lances to the upper part of the Broletto belltower. All the parts remained in place until the stench required their removal; but the withered heads long remained in view and were still there in the 1490s.

Given the primal importance of the propertied family in Renaissance Italy, with its identity-giving powers, there was to be a reign of terror for relatives too. For guilt and dishonour were still seen as partly tribal, so how could the authorities look upon other family members as utterly blameless? On the day of the murder, apart from Giovanni Andrea's house, two other Lampugnani mansions were sacked by mobs, and for days to come many other properties were also threatened. Some members of the lineage even tried to claim that the assassin was not a Lampugnani, that he was an imposter; and the bearers of that proud surname spent all that winter and spring trying to establish their innocence. More than another half-dozen Lampugnani men were arrested. One, Bernardino, was put to death; and two others who had been in Santo Stefano on the tragic day swore that if they had known of the plot, they would have denounced that 'traitor' (Giovanni Andrea) 'and eaten him and his companions with their own teeth'. Princivalle, a brother of the traitor, lost his military post and was exiled first to Florence, then to Mantua.

Gerolamo Olgiati's horrified father just managed to hold on to the family properties, but he was banished post-haste to Turin. For the well-born especially, exile could be a devastating penalty, because it cut them away from friends and their vital roots, from daily confirmation of their identities, from their regular sources of income, and imposed a kind of quasi-death or half-life. Eight other men, known friends of the conspirators who had also been at the scene of the murder, were hanged on 8 January. Although directly implicated in the concealment of the assassins, three priests escaped death, owing to their clerical status and to the murdered Duke's widow, Bona of Savoy, who seems to have softened the demand for vengeance in their case, because she was anxious about her late husband's soul.

The Santo Stefano protagonists had been spurred on by ideas, as well as by deep personal resentment, and Bona's advisors would have loved, just then, to pounce on a man who had been banished from Milan some eighteen months earlier: the humanist educator Cola Montano, an implacable enemy of Galeazzo Maria Sforza, often seen as the one who had inspired the conspirators with murderous ideals by intoxicating them with the glory and virtues of Roman republicanism. Elements of this claim filtered through their confessions, especially those of the dreamer Olgiati. But since the plot was slowly concocted in the summer or autumn of 1476, and the conspirators admitted that the humanist had left Milan long before, never to be seen by them again, Cola's innocence seemed all but palpable. Reluctantly, therefore, Milan found Cola innocent at the time, but he was wise enough not to return.

Five years later, ironically, laying hands on Cola Montano fell to the lot of Lorenzo de' Medici's spies and the Medicean regime. Travelling south from Genoa to Rome in February 1482, Cola was secretly followed, seized in Florentine territory near Porto Ercole, and taken directly to Florence (12–15 February). Arrested with incriminating papers, he was charged with having been at the centre of a plot to assassinate Lorenzo the year before and, worse still, found to be in the pay of the Florentine lord's mortal enemy, Count Girolamo Riario. Tortured, Cola confessed to a secret pattern of sustained activity against Florence and Lorenzo, and was hanged a month later from the windows of the city's main criminal court, the Bargello.

One fine particular of the Cola Montano story points to a telling feature in the ways of princely government.

In about 1462, the enterprising Cola, come from a village in the mountains near Bologna, turned up in Milan, where he started a school for the study of classical Latin rhetoric and successfully attracted talented youths from the upper ranks. Winning favour and then the patronage of the Duke of Milan, he obtained a major teaching post in 1468 and four years later, in a partnership with several other men, founded one of Milan's earliest printing houses. A strong personality in a literary world riven by keen jealousies, Cola made enemies; those enemies had friends at court; his luck turned; and in 1474 the Duke too was turned against him in an obscure dispute that landed him briefly in prison. Summoned abruptly to Pavia in May 1475, there, before the whole court, he was accused by the Duke of 'corrupting' the wife, sons, and daughters of a certain count. The name was suppressed in our source, Cola's Florentine confession. Although firmly denying the charge, the humanist was again jailed and then banished from Milanese territory; but first – and this is the fine particular – he was publicly whipped while mounted on the shoulders of a soldier. What he failed to add in his confession, it being perhaps too obvious, was that he had been whipped with his buttocks bared. Public punishment of this order was meant to be a stinging humiliation, and Galeazzo Maria was just the sort of ruler to inflict the shaming penalty, even if it was more often reserved for wayward prostitutes. Was Cola Montano whipped until blood broke through the skin, as usually happened in these cases? No wonder he felt an everlasting hatred for the Duke.

The Roman conspiracy of Stefano Porcari (1453) ended with a lesser show of blood than the butchery at Milan and Forlì, but here also there was an echoing Florentine connection.

Born to a line of Roman noblemen, though into a household that had seen better times, Stefano Porcari passed in his adolescence to the care of the Florentine merchant Matteo de' Bardi. He received the rudiments of a classical education and became an outstanding speaker with a taste for high rhetoric. Later, he would serve for a year in Florence (1427–28) as *Capitano del Popolo*, one of the city's leading judges and police magistrates. Here he entered into close contact with a lively circle of humanists, most of them held in thrall by the study of antiquity and much taken with the élan and liberties of the ancient Roman republic. They longed to see Florence in this image. Already a republican, Porcari was emboldened by his Florentine experience, and in speeches delivered there as Capitano, afterwards much transcribed and passed around, he declared 'that Florence seemed to him the ideal of a perfect civil and political life, and that the grandeur, beauty, and glory of the Florentine Republic dazzled and bewildered him'.

At the time, the high office of itinerant short-term magistrate was a standard feature of Italian life, and Porcari served in other cities as well, including Bologna, Siena, Orvieto, and Trani. After 1435, he visited England and northern Europe, and given his republican leanings, he would not have failed to make a stop in Venice.

Like many other educated Italians of his day, Porcari resented the influence of clerics in affairs of state. In 1447, after the death of Pope Eugene IV, he gave public voice to this view in Rome, when he announced at a rally that it was a disgrace for the people of Rome, the legatees of the ancient Romans, to live 'under the heel of priests', so many of whom were foreigners. In effect, he appeared to call for a revolt against the papacy, but got away with this incitement because of political conditions in Rome at that moment. Tolerantly employed by the next pope, the humanist Nicholas V, he now came under the watchful eye of the Roman Curia, and when implicated in a tumult at Piazza Navona, during the Carnival games of 1451, he was banished from the city. Both appreciating and fearing the man's abilities, Pope Nicholas endowed him with a handsome pension, but exiled him to Bologna and there put him under the surveillance of the humanist Cardinal Bessarion. But Porcari could not be placated: he was determined to turn Rome into a republic, just as Olgiati in Milan, and others in Florence, would long for a revived republic.

Already in touch with Roman collaborators, Porcari stole out of Bologna at the end of December 1452, and riding at breakneck speed was in Rome on Tuesday, 2 January, completing in four days a journey that more often took eight to ten. Once at home, working with a circle of close relatives, he pulled the conspiracy together, collecting men, arms, and money. With the help of 300 to 400 men, the group planned to strike on Saturday, 6 January (Epiphany), to stir up confusion and panic by setting fire to the Vatican stables, to take pope and cardinals by surprise at High Mass, to seize the famous urban fortress, the Castle of St Angelo, and to proclaim a free republic. Although the point does not appear in Porcari's confession, contemporaries claimed that the conspirators had resolved, if necessary, to kill the pope and all the cardinals. Moreover, to win 'the people' over to their cause in the ensuing panic, some of the conspirators had been ready to encourage random crowds to sack the papal treasury, the great mansions of the cardinals and curial officials, and even the wealth of the big foreign merchants and bankers, in what would have been a local mutiny against the rich and powerful outsiders.

But the conspirators did not move fast enough and were too many, despite concealing the true plan from most of their armed men. The Curia probably picked up rumours of the plot even before Porcari bolted from Bologna. Late on Friday morning, therefore, the day before the intended strike, a company of 100 papal soldiers encircled the main house of the conspirators, lying just off the Piazza della Minerva. About seventy armed men lurked inside and there was a stand-off. The papal commander was determined to avoid open combat and all scandal. He hoped to arrest and bring them all swiftly to justice. During the afternoon, however, in a few skirmishes, most of the besieged men and all the ringleaders escaped, though at least a half-dozen men were killed. That night, his hiding place betrayed, Porcari was finally captured. There were more arrests in the following days, but four of the leaders managed to escape from Rome, getting as far as the frontiers of Tuscany, Città di Castello, and even Venice, where they were caught and put to death. Questioned, Porcari made a full confession; and on 9 January, clad entirely in ceremonial black, this would-be Tribune of the People was hanged from the battlements of the Castel Sant' Angelo. That day, too, another twelve men were put to death on the Capitol. More executions took place two days later. All the properties of the conspirators were confiscated, and in two cases their widows were forced to enter convents. Most of the armed men, however, misled by the ringleaders about the true aims of the conspiracy, were spared.

Horror and anger swept through the Curia. Pope Nicholas was driven to be pitiless with the principal conspirators, because their conspiracy had promised to attract some local support by exploiting the undertow of antipathy between native Romans and the rule of the privileged outsiders in clerical garb. Often a violent city, owing to the droves of armed retainers in the service of cardinals and neighbouring feudal noblemen such as the Orsini, Colonna, and Savelli, Rome was no venue for the speeches of armed republicans.

Such speeches were better saved for the republic of Florence, where Stefano Porcari had picked up his political ideals, but where the Medici were now making a sustained assault on its republican institutions – the real story behind the April Plot against Lorenzo the Magnificent and his brother Giuliano.

CHAPTER TWO

Social Climbers

Marriage

IN CASTING HIS influence over the Florence of his day, the young
Lorenzo de' Medici turned himself into the city's premier marriage
broker: he became the godfather, so to speak, of its upper-class
marriages. These family alliances were ventures in politics; men with
status in public life were usually seeking more of the same; with the
result, in Lorenzo's case that, after 1469, politics was to demand far more
of his time and patronage than art or literary interests.

Let's see what the business of marriage was all about.

It began with the assessing of girls, a job usually done by the parents
and relatives of men who were ready for marriage, especially in the ranks
of the propertied classes. In return, parents who could afford 'honourable'
dowries for their daughters kept an eye out for the movement and inquiries
of interested parties, who might be looking around to find a match for
a son or nephew. A girl's body, build, face, skin, hair, movements, carriage,
dress and general appearance were all studied and weighed. She was meant
to be a bearer of children, a hinge in the transfer of property from one
generation to the next.

If she had reached the point of scrutiny, of being closely examined,
then she had already passed the first hurdle. Those looking at her had
decided that her family were acceptable, that they might even represent
a step up the social ladder for the house of the possible fiancé. If the
girl turned out to be satisfactory in physical terms, then only the critical question of the dowry would remain. The two families must reach
an agreement on this: her father or guardians on the amount of capital
to be paid out to see her suitably married, and his on the sum that they
would consider honourable, fair, or even profitable. If old blood agreed

to have a daughter marry down, they disbursed less for her: social rank could thus be converted into something like money. The fact that brokering and negotiations had reached the dowry stage signified that the girl's family were satisfied with the name and domestic connections of the man in question.

Men, however, were not assessed in the manner indicated. They were not studied in churches, or at rare private gatherings, as if at a fair, where they might be chosen or rejected by probing eyes. And if the like occasionally happened, as perhaps it did, the telling evidence has not survived. The passive stance – the position of being assessed – belonged to women, and their guardians knew it.

In 1467, like any other rich Florentine *bourgeoise* of her day, Lorenzo de' Medici's mother, Lucrezia Tornabuoni, performed the job of girl assessor for the family, though the task on this occasion was unusual, because in seeking a match for Lorenzo, the family were looking away from Florence for the first time. They had gone all the way to Rome, strongly attracted by a possible link with the greatest of the Roman nobility, the Orsini. Petty princes, leading soldiers, and well-placed clerics, the Orsini had powerful military and papal ties; and unlike the Colonna at that moment, their great rivals, they had a cardinal. The Medici desire for a strong Roman and curial connection went back to the astute Cosimo (d. 1464), Lorenzo's grandfather, who had already realised, by the late 1450s, that the position of their house in Florence wanted outside buttressing in the world of military and Church magnates. The fact that Lorenzo was only eighteen years old in 1467, and that his father Piero was very ill, indeed often bedridden, attested to the urgency felt by the family. It was unusual for Florentine men to marry so young. In his social class, twenty-five years of age was closer to the average mark.

When Lucrezia went to Rome in 1467, to size up the possible bride, she stayed with her brother Giovanni, head of the Roman branch of the Medici Bank. On 28 March, never truly at home with a pen, this author of religious poems dictated a letter to her ailing husband back in Florence, and her brother took down the dictation. She tells him:

> Thursday morning, on the way to St Peter's, I met my lady, the sister of the cardinal, Maddalena Orsini, with her daughter, who is about

fifteen or sixteen years old. She [the girl] was dressed in the Roman fashion, in a broad wrap of linen, and she seemed to me very beautful in that outfit, fair and tall; but because she was rather too covered up, I couldn't see her as I would have liked. It happens that yesterday I went to visit the said Monsignor Orsini [the cardinal] . . . and after I had made the requisite avowals in your name, his sister entered with the girl, who this time was wearing a close-fitting skirt without the wrap. We spent quite a while conversing and I really studied the girl, who is, as I've said, of an attractive height and fairness, and she has a sweet manner — not however so fine as ours [our daughters]; but she's all modesty and could soon be led to assume our ways. She's not a blonde, because you don't find that in these parts. Her hair tends toward the reddish, and there's a lot of it. The face itself is a bit round but I don't disapprove; her throat is nicely slender, though it strikes me as a bit thin or, rather, on the delicate side. Her bosom we couldn't see because the custom here is to go around all bundled up there, but the promise is good. She walks with her head not up proudly, like ours, but bent somewhat forward [down], and I believe this comes from shyness. She really is very bashful. Her hands are long and slender. So, all told, we consider that the girl is definitely much above the average, but not to be compared with Maria, Lucrezia, and Bianca [her own daughters]. Lorenzo himself has seen her, and if he's satisfied, you'll be able to tell. I feel that whatever you and he decide will be well done, and I will agree to it. It's in God's hands. The girl is the daughter of the lord Jacopo Orsini of Monte Ritondo and her mother is the cardinal's sister. She has two brothers, one bred to arms and serving with the well-esteemed lord Orso, the other a priest and subdeacon to the Pope. They have half of Monte Ritondo; the other half belongs to their uncle, who has two sons and three daughters. In addition to half of Monte Ritondo, they have three other castles belonging to her brothers, and I gather that they are well settled there and are better off every day because, apart from being maternal nephews of the Cardinal, of the Archbishop Napoleone, and of the knight, they are also related as cousins via their father, for he [the girl's father] is a second cousin to the aforesaid lords, who love them greatly [implying: and so they'll do a lot for the girl and her brothers].

In a second letter of the same day, Lucrezia added:

As I said to you by letter in Giovanni's hand, we've had a close look at the girl. There was no fuss; and if the thing [the prospect of a marriage] doesn't work out, you'll have lost nothing, because nothing at all was said about it. The girl has two good features: she is tall and fair-skinned, and though she doesn't have a beautiful face, neither is it a peasant's, and she does have a handsome presence. Find out if Lorenzo likes what he saw, as there are so many other things in her favour, that if he is satisfied, we also could be. [Then, almost as an afterthought:] Her name is Crarice [Clarice].

For all of Lucrezia's religious poetry, these were the letters of a knowing, practical, worldly woman. But then religion and worldliness were often joined in Renaissance Italy. Though leaning in favour of the girl, Lucrezia is detached. A week later, finding that Piero, her husband, had accused her of being cold about Clarice, she defended her neutrality. The moment it became clear that Piero and Lorenzo approved of the Orsini girl, Lucrezia was delighted and roundly declared, 'I don't think that Rome at present [among the great families] has a more beautiful girl to offer in marriage.'

To add to the resonance and import of Lucrezia's letters, we must think of them in the context of conversations already held in the family, touching every aspect of Orsini connections in Rome and the wider world. This is why she was at pains to pick out certain kinship ties. The Orsini were a family with servitors, agents, and friends all over the peninsula. Lorenzo and his house were getting set to take a calculated leap that would put a remarkable barrier between themselves and all other families in Florence. Yet Lucrezia's take on Clarice Orsini squared with the Florentine way of sizing up girls for marriage. In this respect, she was no different from a hundred other patrician women in the Florence of her day. Revealingly, it is true, she made no mention of a dowry, a fundamental Florentine concern. Cash, jewels, and land were not what the Medici seemed to be looking for when they cast out for a match to the mighty Roman nobility. Clarice would arrive in Florence with wealth of some sort, plus her blood and Roman connections, and this would suffice, though in the end, in fact, she came with an enormous dowry of 6000 florins.

Lucrezia's older contemporary and acquaintance, Alessandra Macinghi Strozzi (1408–71), also knew how to cast a cold eye on girls and dowries. But she, instead, daughter, wife, and mother to hands-on bankers and merchants, always nosed out dowries and counted florins, as though downgrading politics and place. Yet when it came to the politics of social climbing, her own father, Filippo Macinghi, had shown a talent for it. First he married a girl from one of the city's biggest political and banking families, the Alberti. Widowed, he then married a woman from the Ricasoli lineage – ancient Florentine nobility. Finally, with a strikingly handsome dowry of 1600 florins, his own daughter Alessandra had been married up into the Strozzi clan, one of Florence's foremost political lineages. But Alessandra herself, striving to hold on to capital for her exiled sons, paid out smaller dowries for her daughters and married them respectably but down: that is, under their own social degree or station, a matter determined more by the father's line.

In the 1460s, when looking around for suitable matches to please her sons (and herself), Alessandra was hobbled by the fact that they were exiles down in Naples, victims of the damning charge that their father Matteo had joined the enemies of Cosimo de' Medici during the palace revolutions of 1433–34. Thirty years later, none of the leading Florentine families was yet ready to offer a daughter to Matteo Strozzi's sons, because the stigma of political disgrace was inherited. When the boys came of age (eleven), they too had been compelled to go into exile, although a later political emergency forced Lorenzo de' Medici's father to relent and to have the Strozzi ban of exile removed.

In a letter of 20 April 1465, addressed to her eldest son Filippo, Alessandra writes:

> About the matter of a wife, it seems to me . . . that if Francesco Tanagli would let us have his daughter, this would count at all times as an excellent family connection, and of all the prospects that have been brought to my attention, this one has the most to recommend it. I liked the idea of the girl of the [counts] Vernia, but they [her people] have an awkward air about them and smack of the country.

. . . Francesco has a good reputation; he has political standing, even if not at the top level, and is in the circuit of [public] office. And if you asked, why would he let her go abroad to marry? The first reason is that there are very few young men around of good family who are also rich and truly capable. The second is the girl's modest dowry — only 1000 florins, I believe, a sum fit for artisans. The Manfredi girl is getting 2000 to go into the Pitti house and she's fifteen years old, whereas the other girl [Francesco's daughter] is seventeen. So you see the way things stand. The third reason I think he'd give her out [to an exile] is that he has a big family and needs help to start them on their way. I suspect that this is the main reason.

Four months later, in a letter of 17 August, Alessandra returned to the subject of the Tanagli girl, who is never named. Family, contacts, and dowry came first, then the girl's physical features and moral qualities. What did her name matter?

About the Della Luna marriage, I hear that there is a dowry of 3000 [florins] and 1500 in jewels, clothing, and linen (donora). If true, he [the Della Luna man] has come down the dowry ladder quite a bit from what was first being said. One can but point an accusing finger at him for having married into a family of priests. And the rumour is that things are going well for them [in business], so maybe they'll manage to turn things around. . . .

Let me tell you that Sunday morning, on going early to first Mass at Santa Liperata [the cathedral], just as I had done on a number of other holiday mornings, in order to see the Adimari girl, who usually goes to that Mass, whom did I find but the Tanagli girl! And not knowing who she was, I put myself right beside her and turned all my attention to this girl, since she seemed to me to have a lovely presence and to be well-proportioned. She's tall like Caterina [Alessandra's own daughter] or even taller; she's got good skin, not one of your fair ones, but she looks strong. She has a long face and not very delicate features, but neither are they at all coarse; and it seemed to me, judging by her walk and the look of her eye, that there is nothing slow-witted about her. Indeed, I think that if we like the other parts, she would not be a bad buy (*non è da sconciare mercato*) and she would make for an honourable match. I went out of the church behind her, till I realised that she was the Tanagli girl, so that I now know a little more about her. I've never been able to find the Adimari girl, which seems to me remarkable, because I've gone to the expected places so often, but she never comes out as is her custom.

Alessandra went on to consult other informed people about the Tanagli girl, and all agreed, as she reported in a letter two weeks later, that 'whoever gets her will certainly be content, as she's bound to work out very well . . . I wasn't able to look at her face much [two weeks ago] because I think she sensed that I was watching her, and from that moment on she never looked my way again, and [at the end of Mass] went off like the wind.'

In the end, Alessandra's son, Filippo Strozzi, dragged the matter out for too long, and Francesco Tanagli used the delay to withdraw politely from the negotiations, having meanwhile been advised by a close supporter of the Medici not to forge an alliance with a family of political exiles. Filippo instead, in 1467, the year after his return to Florence from exile, was in fact to marry the Adimari girl, Fiammetta, who came from one of the city's oldest houses, harking back to feudal nobility, like the Ricasoli, Pazzi, and Buondelmonti. However, the Tanagli proceedings reveal a characteristic way of reasoning about upper-class marriage in Florence, and the procedure may be more interestingly traced in the letters of Alessandra's son-in-law, the ambitious and well-educated Marco Parenti. He served her and her sons with exceptional tenacity, both in their marriage negotiations and by working for years to get the Medici circle to remove the political ban against the Strozzi.

A long passage from a letter of 27 July 1465, written to his brother-in-law Filippo, down in Naples, may serve as our single example. Marco writes:

All things considered, I now give in [to your mother] and encourage you to make the decision to marry. We have surveyed all Florence and have reckoned things up two ways: the one supposing you were here [and not an exile in Naples], the other just as you are. If you were here and we could go to the top [socially and politically], there would be four possibilities, two of them in the Pitti and Pandolfini families, and of this sort there are no others. . . . The other two are [in the families of] G. Canigiani and messer Piero de' Pazzi, but they [the girls] are rather ordinary. There are many others of good family, but again they are ordinary or coarse-featured (*rustiche*) and [they'd come] with ordinary dowries from run-of-the-mill men. . . . Your turn [to marry] has come at a time of dearth, so you must be patient, and inasmuch as you have to do it, well, make the best job of it.

The other way of reckoning takes you as you really are. Let's see about the type [of girl] we must exclude and the type that remains. First of all, we must give up all those of the sort mentioned above [obviously we can't have them]; secondly [pass up] all big dowries from people of a coarse, demeaning, and lower-class sort (*gran dote rustiche e ignobile*). This leaves us with the small dowries of nobly-born and beautiful girls, if there were any; but since there are none, we are left with those who look less like peasants, though they are not beautiful, and there are so few even of these that you would be amazed. There's one girl in the Rucellai family who doesn't much appeal to us, and by us I mean your mother and sisters and in-laws. Domenico Borghini has one and we like her even less. There may be some others of this sort or farther down the [social] scale unknown to us, but the ones we do know about we disapprove of even more, hence I don't count them. We are much drawn to two daughters of the late Donato . . . Adimali [Adimari] and of a mother from the [noble] Vernia lineage, now married in Bologna; but we are told that each has 1500 florins of dowry and they have no brothers, so we think that they won't try to come down on this amount [that is, because of having no brothers who would seek to whittle down their dowries]. . . . There remains only a daughter of Francesco . . . Tanagli. He wants to spend not too much, and we can have the girl, I'm sure, but we worry that the [small] dowry may spoil things. And I promise you, with all that we're trying to cobble together to fit your circumstances, that if we pass up these two [possibilities], we wouldn't know where to turn. [Even so,] the big dowry of the one, we fear, may ruin our chances [as others too will be attracted], and we don't even know if you would be acceptable to them [the guardians of the Adimari sisters], and we fear that the small dowry of the other may block that route for us, though we know that you would be to their liking. . . . The Adimari are nobler than the Tanagli, but they [the sisters] have no close relatives, no father, no brothers — lots of uncles and cousins, yes, though they are men of no account (*omacci*), with relations all of the same type. Still, this drawback has an advantage, that you wouldn't have to bother with them. The other [the Tanagli option] is the exact opposite: though they are not a great family, yet they are old and of good stock and this branch descends from knights. The father of the girl is my age [forty-five], a man of superior value, well-mannered, a good speaker, affable, and with lots of grace. He has some standing in public life; has a good number of relatives, all men of esteem; and his sister is married to Antonio . . . Alessandri [an eminent family]. His own wife hails from the Guidetti, well-known men of substance; his wife's sister is married to messer Antonio Ridolfi [a key figure in the Medicean oligarchy: the man who later advised Francesco Tanagli against a Strozzi marriage]; and he has many other honourable and esteemed kinsmen. His brother married Francesco Vettori's daughter, etc. He has twelve children, six boys and six girls. . . . And when I wanted to get down to the business of the dowry, he refused, preferring rather to ask if the other matters fully content us and indicating, about the dowry, that he wants to rely on my own judgment and discretion. This, then, is where things stand. Now it's for you to weigh matters up and let us know what you think. The girl is tall like our Catherine but more shapely; she has good flesh and skin; her face is not . . . [a great beauty's], but neither has it anything in the least off-putting. She holds herself well and has a nice air about her. . . . If you like this prospect, tell us how far you would be willing to come down on the dowry.

What to say about this letter, which speaks so well, if pedantically, for itself? The Strozzi exile down in Naples had obviously put in a request for a good-looking girl. The author of the letter, Parenti, had reliable contacts up and down the scale of Florentine society, but he was also relying on informed middlemen (*sensali*). He is attentive to social fine points. New men and new money are contemptuously rejected.

Money matters, to be sure, but it needs to have been around for a while. The desired essential qualities reside in reputations, first-class political connections, and family antiquity. These, in turn, call for the added support of the girl's fine presence, her looks, of course, and a respectable dowry. However, for a political exile just then, given the state of the marriage market, a link with Francesco Tanagli comes through as the most attractive prospect, owing to his valuable political ties. And while once upon a time the important political families looked around for marriage alliances in their surrounding urban localities, now the entire city is their neighourhood.

'Social Climbers' I have called this chapter. But what climbing could there be for families such as the Medici and Pazzi, when they already occupied the summit of the social hierarchy? In fact, security was never certain, even there, and the top place could be an illusion. Even in Venice, where the highest office-holders of old vintage had been turned into a closed noble class, there were strong, invidious, bitter, and shifting distinctions within that class.

Marriage in urban Italy was the defining moment for the family group and individual, at all events among the middle and upper ranks. This was the moment when men and women knew who they were, as they performed an on-the-spot assessing of their forebears, background, present expectations, and future hopes. By choosing marriage with x rather than y, or by being so chosen, the parties in question made a curt statement of identity regarding the chooser and the chosen. Marriage was the potential moment of the transfer of name and property between generations. It fixed person and family in an animated system of hierarchy, degree, and rich social relations; and what you were, identity, congealed at the point where the fixing took place. Everything else dissolved into lesser particulars.

Like Alessandra Strozzi and Lorenzo de' Medici's mother, Marco Parenti knew all this by conditioned instinct. His family began their ascent around 1400. But in the letter, he takes the assessing, impressionistic way of the two women and turns it into a calculus. All the possibilities are posted up and then peeled away, as he moves toward a practical core, never losing sight of Filippo Strozzi's needs and realistic prospects, in a Florence that was as tough as nails when it came to bargaining over marriage. All illusions were now sheared away, and people were made to see who and what they were.

Which is not to say that social climbing was impossible. Indeed, it went on all the time. Political and material fortunes rose and fell. Old families lost wealth, place, and marriage prospects. Too many daughters and dowries could ruin a house. In the absence of primogeniture, which gave all real property (or at least the lion's share) to the eldest son, as, say, in England, too many surviving sons also ate away at family wealth through the workings of partible inheritance. Being split up, the patrimony was soon dispersed, unless some of the sons could make up for the fragmentation through the profits of trade or banking. Despite Marco Parenti's snobberies, therefore, new wealth married massively into old lineages and soon began to pull on its political ties. A family without sons could not hold public office, and so lost political name and place. A generation of foolish men could undo themselves in politics. And it was always the case that political status counted, and counted tremendously, because high office in Florence was an honour to conjure with. It intimidated; it attracted marriage feelers; it endowed men with real power.

Much has been made here of old families and new wealth. What was old, and what new?

Marked by a prestigious name and history, Florence's most distinguished bloodlines claimed feudal origins and went back to the eleventh and twelfth centuries. Such, for example, were the Uberti, Guidi, Tornaquinci, Ricasoli, Pazzi, Buondelmonti, and Adimari. In time, some of these families associated themselves with trade and banking. Certain business families could point to their beginnings in the late twelfth and early thirteenth centuries. But the most illustrious 'bourgeois' lineages, such as the Strozzi, Albizzi, and Medici, got their real start in the late thirteenth century, when they began to appear in the forefront of government by election to the new office of the Lord Priors of the Guilds, the Signoria. Now they were able to combine commercial wealth with political authority, and from this time on, a place at the summit of the social scale was always a union of wealth and high public office. Neither sufficed by itself to assure a place in the upper class; and Florentines who attained office and money after the onslaught of the Black Plague

(1348) would be seen as 'new men' by their 'betters' in the fifteenth century, particularly if they had risen from the ranks of guildsmen whose work dirtied their hands.

In the course of their political climb, the Pazzi did not fail to play the marriage card. Andrea, the maker of the family wealth, married the daughter of a prominent political figure, Jacopo di Alamanno Salviati. His three sons – Messer Jacopo, Antonio, and Messer Piero – married into the Serristori, Alessandri, and Giugni families. The Alessandri and Giugni were regularly found in high office, and the Serristori ranked at the time with the richest dozen or so houses in the city. Later, three granddaughters would be married into frontline political families – Martelli, Niccolini, and cousins to the mainline Medici. Andrea's grandson Guglielmo took Bianca de' Medici as his wife, thereby becoming Lorenzo the Magnificent's brother-in-law. But 1478 ended this brilliant social flight.

By the time Piero de' Medici turned to the Roman nobility for his son Lorenzo's marriage partner, he had certainly taken counsel. He had heard from his own father, the consummate politician Cosimo; from the Milanese ambassador to Florence, Nicodemo Tranchedini; and from his own brother-in-law and chief of the Roman branch of the Medici Bank, Giovanni Tornabuoni, who had made the discreet initial inquiries. Florence's principal family was looking for an alliance with an equivalent family in Rome, hence negotiations could not but be realistic; and yet the Medici were climbing. Cosimo had seen to it in 1444 that Piero himself married into old Florentine stock, the Tornabuoni, merchants and bankers yes, but an offshoot of the ancient Tornaquinci patriline; and Lucrezia Tornabuoni went to Piero with a mere 'tradesman's' dowry (in Alessandra Strozzi's terms) of 1009 florins. In selecting Lucrezia for Piero, Cosimo had opted for a strong and reliable political bond; the richest man in Florence did not have to count florins.

Piero, however, was to be the last Medici male in his patriline to marry into 'trade' and a native Florentine house. Henceforth, seeking to enhance or elevate social identities in marriage, Medici men would marry outside the city into princely lines. Or they would become cardinals and popes.

Bankers

IN THEIR ASCENT from obscurity, the early career of the Medici was much like that of other Florentine families. Originating in the city's thickly-settled hinterland, they migrated to flourishing Florence in the twelfth century, where they took up money-changing and money-lending. Very likely, too, they also edged their way into the speculative land market, which in that period was extraordinarily lucrative. By 1300, having also multiplied in household numbers, they had made a name for themselves as aggressive 'commoners' (*popolani*) and were affiliated with the more conservative Blacks against the Whites, in the struggle between the city's dominant factions. Almost too much at home in a world of political tumult and mass exile, they built up a reputation for lawlessness and were pursued by this reputation until the end of the fourteenth century. In 1400, the Medici were put under a political ban for twenty years, except for only one of their households, the one headed by the up-and-coming banker, Giovanni di Averardo, known as Giovanni di Bicci.

By then, too, the family had got its name on to the political record with an impressive number of appearances in the highest office of state, the nine-man Council of Lord Priors. Only eight to ten other houses managed a better record of this sort in the fourteenth century, among them the Strozzi and the Albizzi. And yet, revealingly, Florentine heads of state seem rarely to have called upon the Medici to offer reasoned political counsel, nor were they summoned to conduct foreign embassies. Based in part on their crimes of violence, a name for strong-arm methods undermined their possible political influence. But Florence then was a more lawless and blustering place than in the time of Lorenzo, and his fourteenth-century forebears were able to get marriage ties with the Cavalcanti, Donati, and Falconieri – houses more ancient and honourable than themselves. The patina of *gentilezza* would come in due course.

Energy, political ambition, and commerce in cash underpinned much of the Medici past and would clinch their future. In probing a scatter of their last wills, the historian of their early career, Gene Brucker, found that they often fought off guilt and fear for their souls by making special religious and charitable settlements. They were making restitution of their 'ill-got' gains, and confessing, in effect, to loan-shark practices of the sort that threatened the immortal soul, according to contemporary religious beliefs.

The banker Giovanni di Bicci (1360–1429), who launched the family's fortunes, was Lorenzo the Magnificent's great grandfather. Starting out as an apprentice in the firm of a fourth cousin, Vieri di Cambiozzo ('Big Change') de' Medici, who had one of the biggest banking houses of the age, Giovanni worked his way up to a small partnership and prospered along with Vieri. In 1393 he struck out on his own, took on a junior partner, and in 1397 moved his headquarters to Rome. Shunning centre-stage politics and keeping a low profile for years, he opened branch offices in Florence, Venice, and Naples, and quietly accumulated a vast fortune, mainly by collecting papal revenue from distant points, by clever exchange operations, and by advancing ready cash to popes for immediate expenditure. In the closing years of the Great (papal) Schism, and the scandal of three contending popes, he made himself banker to an old friend, Pope John XXIII (1410–15); but after John's deposition to the status of anti-pope, Giovanni seems to have lost nothing, went on flourishing, and finally opened an office in Geneva, at that moment the financial heart of banking north of the Alps.

With a genius for making friends abroad and attracting webs of eager supporters at home, the Medici made riches the base and bedrock of their hold on Florentine government. Already counted among the city's first fifty taxpayers in 1402, by 1427 Giovanni di Bicci's efforts had carried him to the top of the scale of wealth in Florence, which, in those years, ranking as the financial capital of Western Europe, was the home of more than seventy international bankers. The top place in the city belonged, officially, to the great landowner Palla di Nofri Strozzi – amateur scholar, knight, and banker too, with net assets of 101,422 florins. But if we combine the wealth of two brothers, merchant bankers and the sons of Bartolomeo Panciatichi, a famous 'usurer' from Pistoia, then the first place belonged to them, with their net capital of 127,000 florins. Years later, however, Lorenzo reported that the true value of Giovanni di Bicci's estate in the 1420s was in the range of 180,000 florins; and the modern historian of the Medici Bank, De Roover, accepted this claim as entirely plausible. Indeed, in August 1432, the Florentine government owed the Medici Bank 155,887 florins for money lent to it over the previous twenty months, though it is likely that some part of this capital belonged to the bank's depositors.

Political faction was more or less endemic in Florence. In the late 1420s, when the city was engulfed by a clash between factions, Palla Strozzi threw in his lot with the anti-Medici bloc, and in 1434, following the triumph of the Medicean party, was banished from the city forever. Nor was this all. Drawing on well-known tactics, the new regime used targeted taxation, penalties, and the sequestering of property to try to strip him of his wealth. The destruction of the Panciatichi brothers was accomplished even more effectively. Looked upon as 'outsiders', having no true political standing in Florence, linked by marriage to too many of the political losers, and already subject to confiscatory taxation, they and their heirs were so hounded by property and wealth taxes that they were driven into debt, and ended by fleeing from Florence and its tax levies, or skulking as guests in the houses of others, sometimes locked into their own homes (legal asylums against arrest for debt), and even steeped in poverty and squalor.

As Lorenzo was to observe, to be rich in Florence, and to be without office and political authority, was to run the risk of financial and social annihilation: a lesson never to be lost on the Medici.

On the death of Giovanni di Bicci in 1429, his son Cosimo de' Medici (1389–1464) faced staggering challenges. Upper-class Florence was locked into a grim tooth-and-nail struggle at the summit of politics. War, heavy taxes, and the presence of 'new men' in high office had divided the political class. In his later years, even Giovanni di Bicci had been prised from his low profile – forced to take a more open and leading part in politics. But for Cosimo, in 1429, care of the family's imperial wealth and banking business had to come first.

He was schooled in the devious arts of Renaissance banking, in which profit was cunningly held to come not so much from the taking of interest ('usury' in doctrinal terms), but rather from exchange operations, particularly in the transfer of money from one place to another or between persons. Interest, in other words, was often concealed as payment for 'risk' in the real or alleged movement of cash. And Cosimo, like his father, proved to be a genius at this. He carried the fortunes of the Medici Bank to their peak. To the larger branches he added offices in Ancona (1436), Bruges (1439), Pisa (1442), London (1446), Avignon (1446), and finally Milan (1452/53). By extending the scope of the Bank's operations, these new offices multiplied the possibilities for authentic exchange transactions and for profits. Earnings from the Roman branch fell by half, but this drop was more than offset by the gains in Venice, Geneva, and the earnings from the new branches. Owing to gaps in the record after about 1435, the Bank's overall profits under Cosimo remain something of a mystery, but it is clear that down to about 1450 he piled more wealth on to his princely inheritance. His tax returns, much like his father's, are unreliable guides to his assets. In 1458, for example, though he had 13,500 florins of capital in the Milanese branch of the Bank, the sum shows up as a mere 3000 florins in his tax returns of that year.

Cosimo certainly felt that he was right to submit false information. When dealing with tax officials, this was standard practice in Florence. But in addition, international banking was in flux, and the big Florentine houses were losing out. Numbering seventy-two in the 1420s, by 1470 only thirty-three remained, some seven or eight of them having failed in the mid 1460s. Even Cosimo had made questionable moves along the way, which must have worried and nagged at him, in view of his knowing ways and instincts. Troubles quickly surfaced after his death. The London and Venice branches were on the brink of collapse; Milan was danger-ously over-stretched; and Lorenzo's father, the sickly Piero, on taking over the direction of the Bank in 1464, was forced to tighten credit or to alienate clients and supporters abroad. Cosimo's old friend, Francesco Sforza, Duke of Milan, died in 1466, two years after the banker, and left a debt to the Medici house of 115,000 ducats, only partly pledged against pawned jewels and a limited run of the future tax on Milan's salt sales. Before the end of 1467, this debt had risen to 179,000 ducats. The astute banker had been unable to avoid the dangerous game of mixing loans with power politics. He had set up the Ancona and Milan branches in part at least to assist Sforza, in the belief, it seems, that he might at some point be driven to call on the great soldier's mercenaries.

For all Cosimo's talents, in short, his son Piero inherited an ailing giant. And although he had learned accounting as a boy, he possessed few practical skills in the complexities of international banking. Result? As Lorenzo was to do later on, he had no choice but to fall back on wavering policies and on the advice of branch managers, who were themselves toiling to understand the changing money market. Besides, here was an arena in which competition was too often tied to the cash needs of perfidious or irresponsible princes. To top it all, in 1465–66, Piero was confronted by one of the gravest political threats ever to face the Medici. Painfully ill, he had less than four years to live, and his son, Lorenzo, was a mere seventeen years old. Though the Bank's distant branches were in considerable trouble, back in Florence, bolder and louder voices at the forefront of the oligarchy were calling for an end to the tightened political controls that had been clapped on the ruling class during the previous thirty years. How could banking not give way to politics?

A Political Tale

THE STORY BEGINS with the lucrative business of Renaissance mercenaries: war, the most costly of all public undertakings. Costly because the hiring of soldiers brought immediate government debt and flurries of added taxes; angrily divisive too, because heavy taxes raised sharp differences within the governing ranks and led to quarrels about the sort of men who were best qualified, in invidious social terms, to hold public office. Florentine society was shot through with the envies of status and with hunger for the spoils of patronage.

This was Florence in the 1420s, the decade of the first Medicean glissade into power. War with Milan, and a failed attempt to grab the neighbouring little republic of Lucca by force of arms, opened the city to political unrest. Taxes climbed; passions ran high; and in the consequent anxieties, a circle of 'new men' gathered around Giovanni de' Medici and his son Cosimo, whose wealth and know-how behind the scenes also attracted men from the distinguished families. No class lines were easily visible. Yet sensing a grave menace, some of the powerful old families, captained by the prominent Niccolò da Uzzano, Rinaldo degli Albizzi, and Ridolfo Peruzzi, now pulled together to try to draw the city under the stricter rule of the old houses. In a word, Medici money, much of it made in banking abroad, was shattering the political balance of the city's principal families.

In the spring of 1433, just after Florence concluded a peace with Lucca, and Cosimo was being seen as a war-loan hero, he sensed the coming crisis. Proceeding quietly, he moved a large sum of money at the end of May, putting nearly 9000 florins into the custody of certain monks and friars, men whom he had previously favoured. He transferred another 15,000 florins from Florence to his bank branch in Venice; and he sold 10,000 florins of his shares in the Florentine government debt to the Medici branch in Rome. He was now ready for a political storm, and it broke in September, when a new group of Lord Priors took office.

On the pretext of desiring his advice, they summoned him to the government palace and suddenly arrested him. Fearing that they would have him poisoned, he was himself ready to deal out violence and prayed that his friends and allies would spring a military *coup*. But the Priors, acting against the wishes of his chief enemies, elected moderation and instead exiled him for ten years, along with several other family members, first to Padua and soon after to Venice. Revealingly, two other men, not members of the family, were also banished, signalling the social sweep of the Medicean party: a knight from the illustrious Acciaiuoli family, and Puccio Pucci, an energetic new man.

A year later, Cosimo's top enemies would no doubt sigh, 'if only we *had* killed him!' But they lacked the organisation and ruthless realism of the Medicean crowd. Every set of Lord Priors took office for a term of two months and was then followed by a new governing council. Continuity was provided by two advisory bodies of twelve and sixteen men, plus the practice of continual consultation with leading citizens. Surprisingly, however, after banishing Cosimo, the 'aristocrats' failed to rig the elections of the succeeding groups of Priors. And a year later, on 1 September 1434, a pro-Medici Signory was sworn into office, having been drawn 'by lot' from the non-rigged electoral purses. Several of the aristocratic leaders made pleas for armed resistance, took up arms for a day, but then lost heart, withdrew, and were overwhelmed. Cosimo and his brother returned victoriously to Florence on 6 October, and the Eight, the high office charged with the city's political security, now began to deal out the expected reprisals.

Soon, 106 men were exiled from the city, and more than eighty others were deprived of the right to hold public office, that all-important signifier of social station. The entire anti-Medicean leadership was removed from the political slate, along with their most active supporters, in a wave of expulsion that continued until 1439, and by that year another twenty exiles had been added. When allowed to remain at home, lesser folk in the attainted circle fell silent. Of the more than 200 men eliminated from public life, many were also fined, and all would be drawn into the sights of targeted taxation. Benedetto Dei, a contemporary, noted that if the families of the exiles were also counted, about 500 people left the city in 1434–35 alone. The penalties of exile and loss of political rights were then renewed every ten years, but so effectively, as the Strozzi family discovered, that thirty years later the descendants of the original exiles were still finding stiff opposition in their efforts to negotiate the desired Florentine marriages.

Over the next twenty years, the victorious party of the Medici introduced a series of electoral devices and strategies that ended by concentrating power in too few hands. They went too far; resentment swelled and came to a head in 1458, when the name of Luca Pitti suddenly springs into prominence in local political jottings and chronicles.

The original builder of a grand house on a conspicuous rise, afterward the famous Pitti Palace, Luca came from an old political family, alike in vintage to the Medici, and was for years one of Cosimo's most loyal assistants. In the early spring of 1458, tenacious resistance in the legislative councils convinced party bosses that the opposition had got out of hand, that most ordinary members of the political class wanted an end to the system of electoral controls. They wanted the circuit of important offices opened up to more citizens like themselves, and feeling had become so sharp that the Medicean junta considered a *coup d'état*, but decided instead to wait for a more favourable Signory. This turn finally came at the end of June, when Luca Pitti was drawn from the electoral purse for the top post, Gonfalonier of Justice, head of the next group of Lord Priors.

They took office on 1 July and Luca went right to work. On the 2nd, holding a major consultation with more than 200 of the most eminent citizens, he was prepared to subvert the traditional legislative bodies with a scheme for a new council with extraordinary powers, the One Hundred. The plan had been secretly under discussion for months among the leaders. Sensing, however, a hostile current of opinion, he and the Priors backed away from the scheme and came up, instead, with a bill to anticipate the revision of all the citizens eligible for office. Since a more traditional mode of election had been partly brought back in the mid 1450s, Luca Pitti and company now proposed to reintroduce the restrictions that would again verge on hand-picking the succeeding groups of Lord Priors. In the last week of July, however, this bill was defeated repeatedly in the Council of the People, and it was at this point, to the fury of the Mediceans, that the Archbishop of Florence issued a threat of excommunication against those who violated the constitution by offering open rather than secret ballots.

The moment for the mailed fist had come. On 1 August, in sustained discussion with the Lord Priors, certain of the regime's key figures made a secret call for a *Parlamento*, a demogogic assembly of citizens. Although carefully absent from the crucial consultation in the government palace, the cagey Cosimo de' Medici was represented by his son Giovanni, who made a mild and disarming statement. Yet that very day, informing the Milanese ambassador that he was ready for a show of arms, Cosimo transmitted a request to his old friend and heavy debtor, Francesco Sforza, lord of Milan, for a dispatch of troops to Florence. On 2 August the government chose the identical course of action: arms and a big (but thoroughly controlled) assembly of citizens. On the 3rd they arrested the foremost leader of the opposition, the well-known jurist, Girolamo Machiavelli. On the 4th two more men were arrested and, after being tortured for days, all three were banished. Some days later, another fifteen citizens at least were exiled for ten or more years. Meanwhile, about 150 other citizens were peremptorily dispatched to their villas, with orders not to come back to Florence without the permission of the Lord Priors. By the 9th of August foreign infantry and cavalry had entered the city. A day later the call went out for citizens to assemble on the 11th in the main government piazza. And on this day, as men arrived for the *Parlamento*, they found the square and all the streets leading into it patrolled by soldiers and armed citizens. In no time at all, Luca Pitti and the Lord Priors got the throng's approval to appoint a dictatorial council (a *Balìa*) of 351 men and to return the eligible-name purses to the strict control of the Medicean ruling circle. The assembly of citizens was then dismissed. The office of the Eight got back its sweeping powers to strike out at political dissidents. And before the end of the year, the new 'scrutineers' – keepers of the names eligible for office – disqualified some 1500 men from the right to hold office.

Lorenzo de' Medici that summer, the future poet and politician, was only ten years old, but some echo of the troubles surely reached him in stray or direct conversation. He was being groomed to inherit a magnificent (if risky) political legacy, and by the age of twelve was already receiving requests for favours and sending out letters of patronage. Even at ten he must have been too precocious to be kept away from hearing talk about politics, and of this there was more of the unpleasant sort two years later.

In 1460, Girolamo Machiavelli, who had been banished to Avignon for twenty-five years, was arrested in the Lunigiana mountains not far from Florence, questioned again under continued torture, accused of stirring up a conspiracy among Florentine exiles, and died a week or two later, at the age of forty-five, almost certainly from the effects of the ropes, irons, and perhaps fire. His confessed deeds resulted in the exile of another twenty-five citizens.

Lorenzo was to go on seeing flurries of political anxiety, increasingly so now that the electoral-purse fixers and other top officials often convened in the new Medici Palace. His grandfather Cosimo was over seventy and ailing; his own father Piero was occasionally disabled by gout; and worse still, the most powerful citizens around Cosimo were ambitious men who did not underestimate their own importance – Agnolo Acciaiuoli, Dietisalvi Neroni, Luca Pitti, and a few others, all holding the prestigious dignity of knighthood, with its entitlement to social precedence.

The scene bristled with ironies. In literature, irony gives a voice to reversals and contrasts; it forces us to wonder. In life, it alerts us to the unpredictable, and Florentine politics had this in bitter measures. For the ascent of the Medici would have been absolutely impossible without the aid of men from the distinguished old families. They colluded. Medicean politicians such as Acciaiuoli, Pitti, Soderini, and the parvenu

Neroni would have had less authority without the Medici and the tightened system of manipulation in the business of electoral purses and eligible names. Yet ambitions grew on each side. In 1434 and again in 1458, the leading opponents of the Medicean ruling group were removed from the scene at a stroke, and the victors looked suddenly invincible. But as long as republican institutions remained – legislative councils, active name lists, back-up offices, circulation through office, and the occasional need to consult lesser citizens – the Medicean party, including Luca Pitti, had to continue leaning on citizens whom they sometimes looked down upon with a dash of contempt. And now the political tale took another twist.

In 1463, the year before Cosimo's death, the Milanese ambassador in Florence realised that at least two of Cosimo's most loyal lieutenants, Agnolo Acciaiuoli and Dietisalvi Neroni, had turned against him and his son Piero. They were waiting for the old banker to die and had no intention of taking orders from the younger, sickly man – they, men of more mature years and far more political experience. By the autumn of 1465 the unity of the old Medicean leadership had crumbled, and the Medicean party suffered crushing defeats in the legislative councils. Members of the circle were responding to rank-and-file pressures inside the wider oligarchy, as once again there was a growing call to expand the pool of political eligibles and to replace the fiddling in the top purses with a true drawing of the Signory by lot. These desires were strongly evident even in the most Medicean of the larger councils, the new *Cento* (the One Hundred), which had been created only seven years earlier, after the *coup* of 1458. Quietly known as *Poggeschi*, the reformers wanted nothing less than to restore the eligibility of all citizens who had been politically purged over the course of the previous twenty to thirty years.

From this point on, until the crisis burst into the Piazza of the Lord Priors in September 1466, Lorenzo's father Piero, natural leader of the anti-reformist faction (the *Piano*), was caught up in a mortal struggle. But it was fought behind the scenes, in private conversation and secret dealing, quite as much as by the votes in councils, where Piero and his circle of backers were increasingly defeated, although he seldom attended discussions in the governing bodies, and his name was never frankly associated with particular proposals. Nevertheless, the two factions understood each other only too well, for the opposition was now captained mainly by former top collaborators of the Medici.

The remarkable breadth of the opposition to the government of the Medicean patronage system fully surfaced in late May 1466, when about 400 citizens from the highest levels of eligibility, including numerous prominent office-holders, were bold enough to sign a public oath in frank support of the older and more democratic system of government. Even Piero's first cousin and rich business partner, Pierfrancesco de' Medici, appeared among the signatories. But there would also have been many other citizens who, while favouring the oath, were too cautious to sign it, despite the fact that the endorsers included men such as Luca Pitti, Agnolo Acciaiuoli, and Manno Temperani. By July, at any rate, the current of new feeling had carried the reformers to the point where they seemed ready to abolish the Council of One Hundred.

Seeing the writing on the wall, Piero pulled strings – it was rumoured – to have the purses for the Signory opened up and tampered with, so as to get a drawing of Lord Priors committed to his cause. He required no more than six favourable names of the Signoria's nine. Although he was the only man in Florence powerful enough to get away with such a daring ruse, no evidence of it has ever come to light. Yet strong suspicions remain, particularly because such action was perfectly consistent with his political ruthlessness; he was ready to spare no expense; able politicians know how to cover their tracks; and the fact is that on 28 August 1466 a pro-Medicean Signory was pulled from the purses, slated to take office four days later. That day too, the 28th, in an act of desperation and straining to overcome their own differences, the Lord Priors summoned the leaders of the two factions, Luca Pitti and Piero de' Medici, to the government palace. Rinuccini informs us that Luca presented himself 'unarmed', but that Piero, claiming illness, sent his sons, Lorenzo and Giuliano. A patriotic witness, Benedetto Dei, reported that 'the city was up in arms' and convulsed with anxiety.

Both sides were seized by the fear of armed conflict and many deaths. Luca Pitti had confided to a cohort on the 12th of August that fresh companies of Milanese soldiers had been spotted at Imola, in readiness for the march to Florence in support of Piero, who in his turn accused the opposition of having secretly solicited help and soldiers from the Marquess of Ferrara, Borso d'Este. The relevant correspondence speaks, indeed, of the movement of different bodies of troops destined for the Florence region. At the last minute, however, the republican opposition backed away from an armed clash, but not the ill Piero, all the less so when a *coup de théatre* came to his aid. For on the 29th, Luca Pitti had a private meeting with him, proposed a family marriage alliance involving one of Piero's daughters, and swung completely over to his side, to the shock and disarray of the reformers, his recent companions. On the 30th, speaking as an advisor to the outgoing government, the frightened Agnolo Acciaiuoli made a plea for peace between the two parties, for Luca and Piero to remain at home, and for the Eight to move forcefully against all armed foreigners in the city. He refrained from referring openly to Piero's soldiers. That day too Piero spent a tense morning in talks with the Archbishops of Florence (Giovanni Neroni) and Pisa (Filippo de' Medici). Locked away in his study at the Medici Palace, the three men must have ended in strong words, shouts, and threats, for the Medici prelate, Piero's distant cousin, offered 1500 armed men in his defence, while the city's Archbishop, brother to one of the top anti-Medicean leaders (Dietisalvi Neroni), threw in his lot with the reformist faction. Cursed and reviled, the Florentine primate was soon forced to withdraw from the city in exile.

On 1 September, Luca Pitti had another tête-à-tête with Piero, this time declaring that he was ready 'to live or die with him'. The proof came the next morning, in a consultation held by the new government in – of all places – the Medici Palace. Luca was the first speaker to get up and call for 'a *Parlamento* this very day'.

Looking back now, we may elect to see Luca's *volte face* as craven comedy; but for Agnolo Acciaiuoli, Niccolò Soderini, and Dietisalvi Neroni, his erstwhile partners, it was the unfolding of a tragedy. Acciaiuoli's sharp complaint against armed foreigners on 30 August had been a shaft aimed at Piero.

The city teemed indeed with Piero's hired soldiers, and having been convoked at his 'home' on the Via Larga, all the citizens present at the 2 September consultation voted to a man, by voice first and then by

Fig. 3 Palazzo Vecchio.

signature, in favour of the *Parlamento*, 'a very large number [however] doing so against their will and against the good of the city', as noted by a contemporary witness, Carlo Gondi. The thirty-five signatures reveal that the group belonged to the core of the Medicean oligarchy and included many members of the recent but now suddenly vanished opposition. Word of their decision was communicated directly to the government palace (Figure 3), some 600 metres away, where the new Lord Priors nervously awaited their Yes vote. Favouring Piero but also fearful of his soldiers, they now ordered the tolling of the bells for a *Parlamento* to be held early that evening.

Piero had ordered about 3000 mercenaries into the city, so that as citizens walked into the government square for the *Parlamento*, they found themselves facing ranks of soldiers. Another 4000 or 5000 mercenaries were being held back in reserve, in the vicinity of Florence, not counting the Milanese troops farther away. At this point too the seventeen-year-old Lorenzo made his first dramatic appearance on the political stage, fully armed, on horseback – he was an excellent rider – and moving about among the soldiers in the Piazza of the *Signori*. He then dismounted and joined the Lord Priors, as they faced 'the Florentine people'. His father, the 'sick' Piero, was back at home on the Via Larga.

Now that the republican opposition had faded away, the outcome in the piazza was altogether predictable. Piero de' Medici's Lord Priors got a dictatorship in council (a *Balìa*); they brought back 'hands-on-purse' controls for twenty years, meaning that the new Medicean leadership would again hand-pick succeeding governments; and they renewed the broad, arbitrary powers of the feared police council, the Eight. But this time around there was no mass exiling of citizens. Only the top leaders of the opposition, along with a few small fry, were forced to abandon the city, the lot as ruined men. The Eight and the *Balìa* could not banish the 400 citizens who had signed the republican oath of the previous May; nor could they void the political eligibility of all those suspected of having held back from signing merely out of fear or caution. Since expulsion from Florence also meant banishing the sons of the banished, once they were eleven years of age or older, the ensuing wave of exiles would have removed too large a part of the most active members of the political class. Reprisals on this scale were dangerously excessive and daunting. Besides, Piero possessed literally the deciding cash and foreign troops, and he also now had the enemy – cowering and compliant – fully in his camp, already doing his bidding. Was this the sickly, inexperienced, 'gouty' Piero? Did any Florentine then remember the strains of the Italian poet writing in about 1300, 'Hurray for him who wins, for I am on his side!'? Not that fear itself could be cynical, but it became so when the defeated passed over with such alarming speed to offer public help and encouragement to the enemy as winners; and too soon there was a measure of this, as in the example of Luca Pitti, who afterwards was to be greatly despised.

As for the young Lorenzo – armed and mounted in a moment of choking anxiety for the city's ruling class – his bold entry into politics, staged in the most significant of all public squares, was a swaggering reminder of the Medici family's ultimate basis of authority in Florence, the money that could buy military power.

Contrary to popular belief, the genius of Renaissance Italy was not all spent in art and literature. Quite as much went into politics, never more so than among the heavyweight politicians of Medicean Florence. Hence any desire to understand the Florentine bloodbath of April 1478 imposes the need to single out this genius too.

In their campaign to cling to power, once their 1434 victory had been secured, the leaders of the Medici party resorted to a selection of stratagems. The result was all statecraft, for they went about the business by appearing to respect the constitutional norms, and all the while subverted a constitution that allowed for the representative input of different groups and voices. Here is a brief of their ways and means:

I. Eligible names. The right to hold public office was the most prestigious and effective degree of citizenship in Florence, but it was conferred by 'scrutiny' commissions. Poring over the names of citizens in secret, they approved some and rejected others. There was no legal appeal. The final list of the select, privileged citizens was the pool of possible office-holders. Now some or many of the approved names, entered on billets or labels, went into purses from which they would be drawn by lot for office. But, select the scrutiny commission and you selected the selectors. With these checks, unwanted individuals were far less likely to qualify for the elite circuit of public office. A republican oligarchy and with a population of under 45,000 people, Florence was a small-town ('eye-to-eye') society in which the 'scrutineers' knew the acceptable men, or certainly knew others who knew them.

2. The Council of Lord Priors (the *Signoria* or Signory). Eight Priors and the Gonfalonier of Justice made up the government of Florence. A two-thirds majority vote, the so-called 'power of the six beans', was decisive. So, control six of the nine votes and you controlled the government. The Lord Priors normally ran the day-to-day business of government, initiated all legislation, led and controlled discussion, hammered away (or not) at the legislative councils, could initiate the

holding of 'scrutinies', and summoned *parlamenti*.

3. General assemblies (*parlamenti*). In emergency conditions – more often a fiction than a reality – the Lord Priors (six of them) had the right to summon a *Parlamento*, a general assembly of the citizenry. Once gathered in the main government square, the assembled citizens would then be invited to call out Yes or No to the question of whether or not they wanted an all-powerful council (*Balìa*). In an atmosphere of duress and surrounded by armed men on all sides, the Lord Priors inevitably got what they wanted. The Mediceans used this call to 'the people' in 1434, 1458, and 1466.

4. The all-powerful council (*Balìa*). Numbering anywhere from about 235 to 350 men, a *Balìa* could suspend the constitution, claim 'the authority and power of all the Florentine people', and override the written laws, all while acting under the direction of the Lord Priors. Such a council was utilised to strike at internal enemies, to snuff out political opposition, to make way for a revision of all names eligible for office, and to impose unpopular legislation or new taxes.

5. Purse 'fixers' or managers (*Accoppiatori*). This commission of ten men – five after 1466 – controlled the name billets that went into the purses for the top offices: the Gonfalonier of Justice, the Lord Priors, the war-office Ten, the Eight, and the *Monte* Officials. In an election for the Priors, names were drawn from the appropriate set of purses by lot, and the first eight to be clear of any legal impediments became the next group of Lord Priors. This was standard procedure in Florence. But the fixing itself was in a transparent game, and no one played it better than the Mediceans,. Having the authority to reduce the number of names in the relevant purses down to seventy and then fifty, where once there had been two thousand (!), the fixers all but hand-picked the successive Lord Priors, that is, one government after another. Need it be said that the purse fixers were among the closest collaborators of the Medici?

6. Exposed beans (*fave scoperte*). Voting in republican councils was done with Yes (black) and No (white) beans. In the act of voting, councillors were meant by law to tender their beans secretly, with the colour fully concealed, so that no one around could see how a man was voting. This law was often broken with the hectoring encouragement of the

Medicean Lord Priors, adding a note of brute intimidation to the proceedings. Now the nay-sayers must dare to reveal themselves, and no man could vote with a fair conscience. Angered by this practice and sharply denouncing it in July 1458, the Archbishop of Florence, the fearless Antoninus, put it under a ban of threatened excommunication. His warning was posted on the doors of the cathedral.

7. The psychological setting. This obviously was not a stratagem but rather a resource that came with the possession of power and the expanding political control over men's lives. Florentines were pressed for years to follow the lead of the Medicean oligarchs, not only by means of the exposed bean in council, or the thronged government square surrounded by soldiers, but also by the citizen's own desire to win political favour, to be assigned lower tax levies, to succeed in getting the right marriages for sons and daughters, and to encounter friendly judges in the law courts: in short, by the yearning for a place in the circle of privileged political citizens. The fear of losing favour made for a long-term climate of devious intimidation.

This was the panoply of blunt and roundabout controls imposed on the Medicean republic. Yet the amazing thing is that the ruling party continued to worry about the independence and civic energies of citizens, particularly as displayed by bouts of stubborn resistance in the legislative councils. But how put an end to these? The republican constitution could not be bent enough to guarantee complete Medicean control. Time and again, when given the opportunity to voice their true desires, the supposed friends of the Medici – all those approved of and found eligible for office – turned out to be unreliable. If allowed to vote in strict secrecy, too many of them were ready to vote against powerful councils, restrictive scrutinies, new tax levies, new commissions, and a tight fixing of the purses for high office.

CHAPTER THREE

Profile: Manetti

P OLITICS IS LIFE itself. This startling claim could have been raised aloft as the practical motto for all ambitious men of the Florentine upper classes, because office of the higher sort in Florence was all about being honoured, feared, and flattered. It offered men a more solid identity and was all but palpably real. Lorenzo de' Medici's younger contemporary, Guicciardini, once said that never to have been a member of the Lord Priors was, for a Florentine, almost not to have been a man. He was talking about the city's propertied citizens, and he meant that a life without that high honour was the life of someone who had failed to obtain his full share of being and doing.

During his two-month term of office in the Signoria, a Prior rarely if ever left the government palace, where he also slept, took all his meals, and was attended by a personal servant. He and the other seven Priors wielded an authority that could be awesome; and if the experience failed to change him, it would none the less change the way his neighbours regarded him. He would come to know everyone of any importance in the city, while also getting a view of Florence, of its innards, of the world, and of foreigners, which he would then have in common with a select circle. And if he sat in the Signoria two or three times in the course of his life, as was usual for chosen members of the leading families, then his was the uppermost circle.

Politics came close to being a destiny, like the distinguishing clothes worn by Florentines, indicating their place on the social ladder: notary, artisan, scholar, knight, labourer, physician, merchant, widow, maiden, bedecked prostitute, or face-marked convict. If they were in politics, most men came to it by being born into one of the privileged families; hence it was wholly natural for them to seek public office and to do all the things required to attain it. But if a man had a right to it and somehow failed to be picked for the right offices, despite effort and merit, then he would bitterly resent the barriers, the opposition, 'the enemy', or the dark work of *fortuna*.

Oligarchy and faction had been fixtures in Florence's political life for nearly three centuries. Now and then, as we have seen, families and even entire lineages fell into disfavour or were pushed out of politics and driven into exile, as one bloc of houses gained the upper hand over another. But after 1434 and the spreading, tentacular influence of the Medici under Cosimo, the large cluster of leading families had to confront decisive changes in the distribution of power. The Medici were simply too rich, and too much covert authority was tilting toward Cosimo. They were also gifted political fighters – organised, resourceful, hard, and with a talent for buying or attracting clients and supporters. Working through a network of these associates, they orchestrated their moves in the different political councils.

These claims take on flesh and colour in the particulars of a few profiles: three men and their contrasting lights, three foils for Lorenzo de' Medici and the Pazzi family. They edge us into a shadowy region of individual resentment and passion. Giannozzo Manetti, the first of the profiles, serves to reveal the background of strains that prepared the way for the April Plot. The other profiles, in Chapters Five and Twelve, probe deeper into this shadowy region.

Giannozzo Manetti (1396–1459)

MERCHANT AND BANKER, scholar, statesman, writer and translator, Giannozzo Manetti was one of the more considerable personalities of the age. Although steeped in banking and the luxury cloth trade, he also mastered classical Greek, Latin and Hebrew; produced orations, commentaries, treatises, polemics, short biographies and erudite translations; and became one of the outstanding Florentine diplomats of the day. Being also a brilliant *ex tempore* Latin orator, with the ability to cast other humanists into the shadows, he contributed to Florence's fame as a city of learning and quick minds. But he also proved to be too independent for political bosses and a bad example for others, with the result that Cosimo de' Medici's closest collaborators set out to bring about his ruin in the characteristic way of Medicean oligarchy – by targeting him with crushing taxes.

Domiciled on the far side of the Arno, in the Santo Spirito quarter of the city, Giannozzo's family began their social climb in the early fourteenth century, as indicated by a series of well-connected marriages. His paternal grandfather, a banker and moneylender, was the first member of the house to have a term in the Lord Priors (1358). But in the next generation, his father Bernardo, an extraordinary banker, traded political place for money by so surrendering himself to the amassing of a great fortune, much of it made in Naples, Spain and Portugal, that he had too little time for politics and held only minor public offices up to the year of his death (1429). By then, however, he had amassed such wealth that he came to be seen as one of the richest men in the city, in the very years when Florence counted as Europe's financial capital. His son Giannozzo, accordingly, inherited a fortune that made him the social equal, so far as money went, of the richest Medici, Pazzi and Strozzi.

In about 1421, at the age of twenty-five and rather against his father's will, Giannozzo turned to a life of austere study, and for the next nine years, working with clerics and private tutors, he studied Latin, classical Greek, and then Hebrew. His studies took him through some of the Latin poets, Cicero, and certain philosophers, Aristotle especially. It was said that he came close to memorising St Augustine's *City of God;* and with a live-in preceptor, he perfected his Hebrew, until he was able to read through the Old Testament with ease. A dedicated Christian and a 'fervent controversialist', he used his knowledge of Hebrew to produce writings aimed at converting the Jews by seeking to prove them wrong.

Around 1429, he finally emerged from his studies into the marketplace and began to frequent the two famous meeting points of Florentine literati and intellectuals: a site known as the 'Roof of the Pisans' on the western side of the main government square, and the Street of the Book Sellers, the main sales area of the stationers, located behind and just to the north of the Lord Priors' palace. Here he soon made a name for himself as one of the city's most impressive debaters.

Giannozzo stepped into the public arena in the year of his father's death, as Florence found itself in the middle of a harrowing fiscal crisis and with all the wealthy families carrying alarming tax loads. His emergence was almost certainly a consequence of this anxious time, 1429, when he also made his first major appearance in office as one of the Lord Priors' Twelve Advisors, the *Dodici Buonomini*, who met regularly with the heads of government. In view of his wealth and eloquence, and with a grandfather who had been a Prior, he seemed destined for a career in politics. But just as the clash between Florence's two factions climaxed in the thick of the tax crisis, Giannozzo disappeared from the political scene, not to surface in office again until 1435; and for the next eighteen years he was rarely out of the public eye. He would hold almost every kind of office: governorships in Florentine Tuscany, six different terms in the Priors' two advisory bodies, varieties of high commissions, the feared police-council of Eight (twice), the city's University trustees, and a series of major embassies. On the face of it, therefore, he looked very much like a member of the Medicean oligarchy and seemed to enjoy its favour. The record reveals, however, an interesting lack: he was never a Prior. Elected to offices of the first and second rank, he was not selected for the supreme dignities. And yet banking on his patriotism, and prepared to lean on his diplomatic and oratorical skills, the oligarchy trusted him with major embassies to Siena, Genoa, Naples, Rome, Milan, and Venice, in the years 1445–53.

Although politics often went to the financial rescue of families at the core of the oligarchy, Florence's partisan tax officials cut relentlessly into Giannozzo's wealth. Nevertheless, he continued to serve in office, fulfilling his civic obligations, perhaps in part because he hoped to find enough fairness in the men at the top to turn his tax fortunes around. But it was not to be, and in the early 1450s, the government even refused to pay his expenses for a long and costly embassy to Rome, which had required a train of sixteen horses and a requisite number of grooms and servants. Whereupon it happened that finding himself with Cosimo de' Medici one evening, he broke down and gave voice to his smouldering resentment. In taxes and in support of this city, he threw out:

> I have disbursed more than any man in Florence, including you, Cosimo, for up to the present day, I have personally paid out more than 135,000

florins, and the fact that I have done this is known to you and to all
Florence. . . . Never, whether in [government] councils or in secret,
as everyone knows, have I acted against the state. . . . The way I have
conducted myself in office, both in and outside the city, is known to
everyone of you. . . . What I have had in return as payment is also
known to you and to all the men of the regime.

Seeking to reply with gracious words, Cosimo had to admit that all this
was true. And well he might, for in the most important tax census of
the 1450s, the old banker successfully 'filed a return which grossly under-
stated the magnitude of Medici business investments' by something like
65 to 75 per cent of their real value.

Even if we halved Giannozzo's reported sum of 135,000 florins –
and there is no reason to – the amount would be staggering. The full
figure added up to an average of 5400 florins per year, over a period of
twenty-five years, and much of the money must have been raised by
selling, or paying with, government bonds (assets in the Monte). Since
a well-paid law professor of the period earned about 350 florins per
annum, Giannozzo's average of yearly taxes was equal to the annual
salaries of not fewer than fifteen jurists at the University of Bologna,
the centre of European legal studies. The sums in question put the
humanist's household into the class of victimised families such as
the Castellani, Guasconi, Panciatichi, Peruzzi, Serragli, and some of the
Strozzi, all of whom saw most of their wealth vanish in taxes and fines
in the decades after 1434, mainly for obscure reasons of personal and
political vendetta.

Giannozzo's friend and biographer, Vespasiano da Bisticci, idealises
the man, and we do well to take his picture of the humanist's preternatural honesty, selflessness, and patriotism with a pinch of salt. But
wherever reported facts can be checked, as on the number and business
of his embassies, Vespasiano's *Commentary* is reliable.

What exactly had Giannozzo done to turn the leaders of the
Medicean oligarchy against him? The evidence indicates that he was luke-
warm about Cosimo's powerful support for Francesco Sforza's takeover
of Milan in 1450, and that he sought closer ties with the Republic of
Venice. In 1449, on a three-man embassy to Venice, which also included

Neri Capponi and Cosimo's son Piero, he was prepared to spurn the great banker's highhanded interference from afar, which aimed at a sudden break in diplomatic relations with the Venetians. He said so to Capponi, who at once shot back, 'I don't want to wrestle with a lion [Cosimo]. If you want to, you go ahead. I don't want to be chased out of Florence.' Giannozzo gave way.

But his strains with the ruling group actually went back to the 1430s, long before any differences emerged over Florentine foreign policy, so the problem must also be sought elsewhere. Again and again Vespasiano asserts that Giannozzo's enemies were moved by envy of his virtue, patriotism, intellectual gifts, and (by implication) his wealth. This claim may be more sensibly and differently put. Something about the humanist troubled the inner circle of oligarchs: he was not respectful enough; he tended to speak his mind; his diplomatic poise was daunting; he possessed the wealth to be his own man; and since he was not sufficiently caught up in a patronage web, he did not frequent power brokers and so was not 'political' enough. Hence his suspect independence.

In the years when his fame for eloquence and learning, like his celebrity as a diplomat, was spreading through Italy, his troubles with some of the top members of the oligarchy peaked, as disclosed by his outburst to Cosimo. Vespasiano notes that Luca Pitti, one of Cosimo's leading henchmen, 'was the man who undid him with tax levies'. So we have the immediate culprit. But the oligarchy was a team, not a one-man show; and targeted taxes, like the denial of just reimbursement to ambassadors, required collective action. Nor could such targeting have gone on for so long and so effectively without the collusion of the team captain, Cosimo.

Recent efforts to rescue the Medici from blame in the hounding of Giannozzo are subject to challenge. In 1453, when in despair the humanist abandoned Florence and moved to Rome, believing that to stay on at home would end in his complete financial ruin, he astonished the ruling group. Feeling suddenly accused, the Lord Priors sent him an ultimatum, giving him ten days to present himself in Florence and trumpeting a threatened ban of exile in the great government square, in the Old Market, and outside the door of his Florentine house. His neighbours and many members of the political class were no doubt amazed. The government even failed to post a safe-conduct to him, thereby letting him know that he was subject to arrest from the moment he set foot on Florentine territory. The only charge against him really – though it failed to hold water – was that he had cooperated with one of Florence's chief enemies, King Alfonso of Naples, by dedicating a work to him, his treatise *On the Excellence and Dignity of Man*. (In fact, Florentine relations with Alfonso blew hot and cold.) Presenting himself to the Priors a day before the ten-day deadline, and going down on his knees as he arrived before them, Giannozzo's self-defence, according to Vespasiano, soon had them in tears. Shortly thereafter, surprisingly, he was elected to an office at the head of government, the war-office Ten, a magistracy more powerful in wartime than even the Lord Priors. But knowing his Florence and its envious patronage webs, Giannozzo served in the Ten for a short time only, and then, obtaining the required leave, wisely got out of the city again, secure in the feeling that he could count on the patronage both of King Alfonso and Pope Nicholas V, a scholar and once a modest cleric whom he had known in Florence years before.

Had Giannozzo been disloyal to his republic in honouring the monarch Alfonso? His was not 'an age of ideology', as the next century was to be. Italy had states under princely and republican rule. And if a man got his living from a prince, he was obliged to praise him and the ideal of monarchy, even if he hailed from a republic. This was the way of Renaissance men of letters and even of statesman, as attested to by Castiglione's *The Courtier*. There was nothing of dishonour or 'treason' in such action. When Giannozzo finally accepted the idea that *fortuna* had turned against him in Florence, and he had already won King Alfonso's admiration by his conduct as a Florentine ambassador in Naples, he naturally warmed to the king and produced dedications in praise of monarchy as well. But this did not void his republican loyalty to Florence. The expectations of the age allowed praise for one and a citizen's commitment to the other.

Giannozzo's Latin style was so studied and ornate, it has been argued, as to be the sign of a born courtier. He loved grand constructions, and his rotund and balanced sentences could certainly be made to glorify the powerful. Not surprisingly, since, like all humanists, he was especially well trained in the art of eloquence (rhetoric) and knew how to turn that learning to his advantage. But apart from letting it gain major embassies for him in Florence, he refrained from using his golden words to curry favour with the oligarchy's bosses. In Florence itself he was a republican, and he sought that kind of tone and style with his peers.

Written in the 1450s, his several letters to Cosimo de' Medici's son, Giovanni, express his readiness to do favours for the Medici abroad. In fifteenth-century terms, however, contrary to recent readings, the letters are not warm, not truly friendly, and not in the least flattering, though flattery is what the Medici had come to expect as their due. Giannozzo, in short, maintained his dignity, holding on to the sense that he was somehow their equal in moral terms, whatever their different weights in the political arena.

In view of Cosimo's capital powers in Florence, it would have been mad for Giannozzo, when in Rome or Naples, to refuse to offer his help, if it was called upon by political leaders back home. He had a constellation of friends and family in Florence; in time, one of his sons would serve as a Lord Prior; and he continued to hold Florentine properties. In the mores of the day, unless conflict was openly acknowledged by the differing parties, appearances in letters, and even a note of flattery, were always preserved. This was as true in private exchange as in diplomatic correspondence.

The trouble with the white-haired Giannozzo (white since the age of thirty) was that he would not play the game, not bend the knee, and not be one of the boys. If this demonstrated a certain moral integrity, it also showed the oligarchy a proud and uncompromising personality; and in Florence at least, in Medicean high politics, this might suffice to carry the man to his financial ruin. The Pazzi family played the game and bent the knee – partly – till about 1470 and the decade of the tragic generation, but they drew the line with the Magnificent Lorenzo.

CHAPTER FOUR

The Pazzi Family

R EADERS WHO SKIM the financial parts of this chapter should know that Florentine men of the propertied classes were sticklers about keeping accounts; that their everyday life was largely about trade, money, investment, profitability, tax dodging, and the passions of politics. If there was such a thing as a Florentine worldview, then these concerns occupied the centre of it, and did so in a strained alliance with a belief in God and the afterlife. A patriarchal vision of the family also held a place in this mélange of thinking and feeling.

Origins

W HEN THE CHRISTIAN warriors of the First Crusade scaled the walls of Jerusalem in 1088, Pazzo Pazzi, a fighter from Florence, was the first man over the top. The reward for his bravery, given into his eager hands, was three small stones, supposedly from the Holy Sepulchre. Nearly two centuries later, another Pazzi, again in the company of French knights and also for combat in the Holy Land, received a shield from the king of France.

In proof of their heroic origins, the Pazzi had only to point to the yearly celebration of Easter in Florence, where 'sacred fire', then distributed to the faithful for their Easter candles on Holy Saturday, was struck from the stones that the Pazzi first-crusader had brought back to the city. The cart bearing the fire was drawn by oxen and driven to San Giovanni, the baptistery facing the cathedral, by members of the family, who then drove it back to their houses, to make a ceremonial stop. Their coat of arms, derived from those of a French ducal family, depicted crescents, battlemented towers, and distinctive twin dolphins on a blue field with nine crosses. Hence their insignia were about war for the Christian faith; and dolphins, in the folklore of the age, signified generosity and freedom. The windows and courtyard columns of the elegant Pazzi Palace (Figure 4, p. 76), built in the late 1460s and early 1470s, would be fretted with symbolic devices, such as lanterns or vases giving off sacred fire, and billowing sails both to signify Pazzi contacts with the Angevin prince, René of Anjou, and involvement in overseas commerce.

The Pazzi were happy to trade on this tale of their family origins. They no doubt believed it, as did many others in Florence, although the legend about the stones did not get started until the fourteenth century. Moving along a shadowy trail, the claim stemmed from their long association with the Easter cart. Some of their early ancestors had almost certainly gone out to the Holy Land in the train of French lords. By the middle of the twelfth century they were an outstanding political house, and in the thirteenth century, having broken with the Pazzi feudal lords of the Valdarno, their banners were already prominent on Easter Saturday. Antiquity lent them a certain air. Not surprisingly, therefore, they passed into local anecdote, and Dante, utilising celebrity in the *Divine Comedy*, has two of their members in hell, suffering for their sins of violence and treachery. In fact, in the decades around 1300 – Dante's time – the deadly political clash between the Blacks and Whites in Florence saw the Pazzi in action among the leaders of the Blacks, the more aristocratic of the two dominant factions. And during much of the fourteenth century, they were closely associated with the right wing of the oligarchy, the so-called Guelf Party. A mob set fire to their houses during the workers' revolt of 1378.

Since the Pazzi could boast a long tradition of knighthood among their numbers, having had at least one knight on their rosters in almost every generation, let's note that Florence detached the title of knight from mounted combat in the late thirteenth century, made it largely honorary, and began awarding it to men of obscure origins, a calculated 'in-your-face' gesture against the old nobility. But it was always a rank of maximum respect, attained in a ceremony of dubbing by a prince or lesser lord, and in Florence by action of the Lord Priors and the intervention of a local knight. Prominent ambassadors, rich bankers, political leaders, and men with lofty connections were the chief candidates for knighthood. The laws governing dress entitled knights and their ladies to wear fancier clothing, and they enjoyed pride of place on all public occasions. Affecting simplicity, the Medici in Cosimo's line avoided the dignity (Lorenzo was never *Messer* Lorenzo), whereas the Pazzi, true to their traditions, coveted the honour; and in the fifteenth century, though brought up to be hardnosed bankers and merchants, three members of the family were knighted: Messer Andrea di Guglielmino and his two sons, Messer Piero and Messer Jacopo, the conspirator hanged in 1478.

Looking back to their early history, the Pazzi must have felt that pride in their origins had helped to sustain them at the end of the thirteenth century, when the expanding 'bourgeois' Commune classified them legally as 'grandees' (*magnati*), thereby strictly excluding them from the city's ruling councils, along with dozens of other 'magnate' houses. These were the powerful clans and families whose arrogant conduct in the streets, often combined with lawlessness, had made them the political enemies of 'the people'. Not until the 1430s, and the generation of Andrea di Guglielmino, would the Pazzi be readmitted to the city's top offices.

Despite their feudal past and the aura given them by the profession of arms, the Pazzi were already engaged in banking by the middle of the thirteenth century, when (I conjecture) younger sons, breaking the old mould, were able to strike out on their own, having first been apprenticed to small merchant bankers, possibly relatives by marriage on the female side. By 1300 they were also inscribed in the Florentine guild of international wool merchants. Most of the city's big banking houses had merchant origins.

At the beginning of the fifteenth century, the Pazzi family ranked nowhere near Florence's top taxpayers. Even if some of them spent much time in the country, as was still the case with certain old families, any considerable urban wealth of theirs would not have been missed by the city's sharp-eyed tax officials. At that moment, the richest of the Pazzi, the heirs of a certain Poldo, held the eightieth place on the taxrolls in their quarter of the city, San Giovanni.

But Andrea di Guglielmino de' Pazzi (1371–1445), apprenticed as a boy in the 1380s, had already set out on his trek to build an immense fortune. Based in Barcelona by 1399, this entrepreneur was heavily engaged in banking and the cloth trade. Later, returning to settle in Florence and electing to become a 'commoner' (*popolano*), so as to open the way to public office for his sons, he disavowed his 'grandee' legal status in a private legislative bill. Here he confirmed that he had been engaged in trade since his boyhood, but for the sake of his good standing in business, he requested the right to retain his family name and coat of arms, contrary to law on the disavowal of magnate status, which required that these also be changed. The request was granted. By 1427, this founder of the family's famous branch had raised his household up to the sixth place among the taxpayers of the city's richest quarter (San Giovanni), with tax returns disclosing a net capital of 31,000 florins – more than enough to fund an international bank.

His contacts were to be equally remarkable. In September 1442, King René of Anjou, pretender to the Neapolitan throne, was for some time a guest in Andrea's house. The French magnate used the occasion to knight him and to give his own name in baptism to Renato, Andrea's newborn grandson. In January 1443, Messer Andrea, the new knight, entertained Pope Eugene IV to a lunch in the convent and church of Santa Croce, receiving him in his private quarters, located above the future Pazzi Chapel, where the work of construction had recently commenced. At that point too, as it happened, the Pope had a large deposit of 4000 florins in the Pazzi Bank.

Business and Banking

To appreciate the ways and means used to destroy the Pazzi in 1478–80, we need to glance at the scope of their developing business interests.

Andrea's wealth, as reported in 1427, was in land, farms, houses, shares in the government debt (the Monte), and business capital. Of the grand total, about 16 per cent was officially held in real property; all the rest was in commercial assets. In reality, in keeping with Florentine business practice of the day, the mobile part of his capital was likely to have been very much larger. A mere four years later, the government owed his Florence Bank 58,524 florins in war loans, though the top banking firm in this line of lending was Cosimo de' Medici's company, with outstanding war loans of 155,887 florins.

The first surviving record of Andrea's net assets (1427) charts the doings of a brilliant merchant banker. He had different business partners in a medley of companies, each of them ranking as a discrete corporate entity. Registered under a variety of names, but assigned chiefly to him as the prime investor, his seven partnership companies were headquartered in Florence, Pisa, Rome, Barcelona, Avignon, Montpellier, and Paris. And while banking was his primary business, he was also engaged in the luxury cloth trade, overseas shipping, insurance, and traffic in the French salt tax (*gabelle*). A prime investor in four galleys, recently damaged and then disposed of, he had long been in the business of buying parts of the royal salt monopoly in France by putting a percentage of the due cash up front and then marketing the salt in smaller units.

In Florence, Andrea held a major share in a silk company, registered in the name of Ormanno degli Albizzi, whose father, the powerful politician Messer Rinaldo, was soon to be Cosimo de' Medici's enemy number one; and Ormanno, like his father, would end his life in exile. But this Albizzi partnership, though necessarily based on a modicum of friendship, did not keep Andrea from business contact and cooperation with the Medici. Listed among the deposits in his Florence Bank were nearly 5000 florins credited to Cosimo's Bank. This indicated that Andrea was reinvesting Medici funds at a higher rate of interest, a point which alone throws passing light on his contacts and confidence, and that he would have a continuing relation with the Medici. The money market in special loans to the Florentine government was shared by the leading local bankers. In 1427, Florence's 'Bank Officers' (hence the city) already owed Andrea 6864 florins, and over the course of the next few years, standing head and shoulders above all the city's leading creditors, he and Cosimo would often work together as members of this commission.

The Barcelona and Pisa companies traded in the wholesale of silk cloth, and while the first was registered in the name of Andrea's fifteen-year-old son (Antonio) and their co-citizen Francesco Tosinghi, the Pisa company was in his own name. Since the Tosinghi family descended from the Visdomini lineage and hence from feudal nobility, like the Pazzi, it is likely that the two houses had ties of kinship. More interestingly, the two companies were also banks: they lent and invested funds. Renewed every two years, but not necessarily under the same names, the current Barcelona firm went back to 1417, when Andrea first set it up with a Florentine partner from a strong political family, Girolamo Guasconi.

In Rome, Andrea's operations hinged on a bank listed in the name of Francesco Boscoli, another *fiorentino*. Boscoli both managed and held a one-third share in this partnership, which was almost certainly in the business of transferring north European Church monies to the papal court, in addition to doing local banking.

The Montpellier and Paris partnerships were somewhat shadowy and link Andrea with two of his cousins. Set up as small banks, they were also possible bidders, like the Avignon company, for parts of the salt *gabelle*, one of the most lucrative of French taxes. All told, therefore, Pazzi business ventures in France were considerable; Andrea was acquainted with King Charles VII; and his affairs there are testimony to the family's continuing ties with the French.

But his varied activities call for a larger setting and framework. In the early fifteenth century, although Florence was the chief home of European bankers, the heyday of the Florentine economy lay in the past, in the period before the catastrophic Black Plague of 1348–49. More than ever, accordingly, banking in Florence had to be based on technical skills, as well as on foreign business, such as at Rome, Barcelona, Bruges, Avignon, and Geneva. The jewel of the old Florentine economy, the cloth trade, especially in the more competitive silk industry, also required new and more aggressive enterprise. The lustre of the commercial successes of the Medici, Pazzi, Strozzi, and other Florentines thus stands out all the more.

In the absence of Pazzi account books, however, it is impossible to pin down the details of banking and trade profits. Florentine tax returns seldom list interest on loans and bank deposits. They are also silent, for the most part, about one of the standard activities of the big banking houses – the periodic shipment of bullion from one part of Europe to the other. The Pazzi companies used both mule trains and Florence's Flanders galleys to move gold and especially silver. In September 1429, a Florentine galley called in at Port-de-Bouc, a port near Marseilles, to pick up four loads of silver belonging to Andrea de' Pazzi's home banking firm and intended for shipment either to England or Flanders. As owner or chief merchant, Andrea himself commanded one of the galleys in 1440; and at about the same time, serving as an officer on another galley, his eldest son Antonio sailed to Barcelona, Valencia, and Southampton. Antonio sailed again in 1442, and in this year too Andrea's youngest son Jacopo, the future conspirator, made a voyage to Southampton, probably also as one of the men in charge of the vessel. In the 1460s, again, Jacopo seems to have hired galleys on various occasions. His nephew Giovanni commanded a Florentine galley in 1473, sailing to Port-de-Bouc, Barcelona, Valencia, and then back to Porto Pisano. That year too, as the chronicler Dei reported, the Medici, Pazzi, and Capponi companies of Florence received shipments of 150,000 florins from Lyons and Avignon.

Over the course of three generations, the Pazzi were more or less continuously involved in the large-scale, international shipment of goods and bullion: the two lines of trade and banking that earned the highest profits. Venetian estimates of the period held that long-distance trade brought in 'annual incomes [on the average] of 40 per cent of the invested capital'. At the more modest end of the business scale, however, in daily local activity, a Florentine banker would sit at his 'table' in the Mercato Nuovo, accepting deposits and paying out money on orders from clients. Interest of about 8 per cent on 'time accounts' – deposits locked in for specified periods – tended to be a standard rate. Higher rates were very much harder to come by. But banks themselves were more likely to lend at rates of 12 to 30 per cent or a good deal more. In 1455–59, the Cambini Bank in Rome – a much smaller operation than the Medici or Pazzi firms – earned average yearly profits of 30 per cent of the investment capital; whereas in Florence, the Cambini realised average profits of 62 per cent in the 1460s, and 42 per cent in the 1470s. In those years, profits on the transportation of bullion were bound to have been higher. Wherever there was a perfect balance of trade (a utopian occurrence), there was no need to ship gold and silver; but since the need recurred, international banks like those of the Medici and

Pazzi were in the best position to profit from the shipment of coin and bullion by sea or over land.

The ordinary way to transact business over distances was by use of the so-called 'bill of exchange', a kind of promissory note that was chiefly handled by the big banking firms and their distant correspondents. Issued by a bank and payer, say in Florence, a bill of exchange would authorise payment in the currency of the destination, say Bruges, and stipulate a sum of money and a lapse of time, such as ninety days: that is, x amount to be paid to a named individual in exactly ninety days and negotiated through a specified firm in Bruges. Taking a fee for the transaction, and skimming profit from the currency exchange, the banker nearly always gained. But currency values fluctuated; the time lapse in the exchange operation carried an element of risk; the possible charge of usury was squelched in the supposed risk; and hence the bankers involved, or their agents, had to be money-market experts.

In trawling through Andrea's business activity, I have called attention to the different names of his companies, each with its own 'corpus' of investment capital, because years later, in the aftermath of the April Conspiracy, investigators would single out the practice, in order to get around it. The seizure of *all* Pazzi assets would be presented as fair punishment for their April 'treason', and the legal curse laid on them was taken right back to Andrea as founder of the treacherous line. Yet his emphasis on the names of the various partnerships indicated a conscious policy of striving to limit liability: each company was a different *ragione*, 'a separate legal entity'. If one of the Pazzi companies capsized into bankruptcy, then those partners alone would be liable. The family bank in Avignon, for example, was contracted and therefore registered in the names of two of Andrea's sons, the illegitimate Guglielmo (aged thirteen) and Piero (eleven); and there is no way to explain such apportioning, except as an attempt to divide and spread the liabilities. Indeed, the aim of this policy was highlighted by the fact that Andrea legally emancipated his sons in 1429, before the age of majority (eighteen in Florence), again in the effort to endow them with a separate legal and property status, distinct from himself, although at the time the youngest of them, Jacopo, was only seven or eight years old.

The Medici Bank was organised along the same lines: in legal terms, each of its major branches operated as an independent enterprise. The question, then, of how exactly creditors moved against a bankrupt company turned into a legal tangle, usually in Florence's Court of the Merchants (*Tribunale di Mercanzia*), where political name and stature were likely to carry considerable weight, as men angled to profit or to protect themselves amidst the uncertain structures of a nascent commercial law. Inevitably, therefore, in hitting back at the Pazzi in 1478, the ruling group around Lorenzo would seek to publicise the claim that the different Pazzi companies were legal fictions, almost fraudulently so, behind which the brothers and cousins moved, so to speak, as one body and soul, so that the manifest guilt of two of them (Francesco and Messer Jacopo) necessarily involved the wealth (and somehow the brute intention) of all the others. In short, contrary to the design of business contracts seeking to restrict liability and to protect individual households, the separate partnerships of the Pazzi were lumped together and treated as one, the better to despoil and strike them down.

Andrea's tax returns show that one Pazzi firm might carry another in its accounts as a bad debtor, one to be written off, such as the partnership with the Guasconi link. This was because the debtor company was either running in the red or had shut down for business. Here was the practice of separate liability. Yet it is also clear that Andrea's companies were in part connected by a pattern of criss-cross investment. The Avignon partnership had over 1000 florins deposited in Andrea's Florence Bank. This bank in turn had more than 9000 florins invested in the Barcelona silk company. And the bank in Rome, listed in the name of Boscoli, had a deposit of about 2800 florins in the Florence firm.

Andrea protected his loans and investments by diversifying. Acting through his Florence Bank, he had lodged more than 3000 florins with the big Borromei (Florentine) Bank in Bruges; and he had lent substantial sums of money to a variety of silk, wool, and even used-clothes partnerships of the up-market sort in Florence. But his biggest debtor *c.* 1430 was the city itself, the likely holder of his most lucrative investments. For as his rival and collaborator Cosimo de' Medici also knew, the annual interest on war loans to Florence in the years 1429–32 was never less than

15 per cent, and the take was far more likely to go up to 60 and even 100 per cent. With their gigantic loans to the city – Medici 156,000 florins, Pazzi 58,500 florins – we begin to see one of the great sources of wealth of the two families, during those years at any rate.

The location of Andrea's houses in Florence enhanced the glow of his wealth. They stood in the heart of the prestigious old city (see Map I), close to the target points of the April Conspiracy: beside a turn known as 'the Street-Corner of the Pazzi', a ninety-second walk from the cathedral, lying to the north-west, and less than two minutes away from the 'castle' of the Lord Priors to the south-west. Here was Andrea's principal residence, situated between the two little parish churches of San Procolo and Santa Maria in Campo. His other properties here – a rich cluster of Pazzi houses and 'the Pazzi courtyard'– stretched south but mainly east, between the old Borgo di San Pier Maggiore (aka Borgo degli Albizzi) and the present day Via de' Pandolfini. The Pazzi had resided in this area, first on the north side of the Borgo (till the 1390s), and then to the south, for more than two centuries. Understandably then, they had a main chapel in the church of San Pier Maggiore, where, however, the mighty Albizzi family, with their three chapels, ranked as the major patrons: reason enough for Andrea to seek a final resting place farther east and south, in the most monumental of all Franciscan churches in Italy, Santa Croce. Franciscan mendicants often appealed to rich bankers and merchants. They did the best job of helping to drain off any nagging guilt associated with the sin of usury.

Like all Florentine men of substance, Andrea owned farms and houses in the neighbouring countryside. His tax returns itemise no fewer than thirteen family farms, nearly one hundred separate land parcels, three mills, and more than a dozen houses, most of these for working peasant families. Yet when assessed in straight market terms, all this property amounted to little more than 5000 florins: a sum which flags the striking disparity between the scale of rural and commercial values. The wealth of the city of Florence overwhelmed its rural hinterland. Held to a bare subsistence level by local relations, labour among the peasantry – it may be rightly asserted – was dirt cheap. And it is easy to see why the urban upper classes had bought up most of rural Tuscany. During the political emergencies of 1466 and 1478, there was every reason to say – and it would be said — that the Medici, relying on the allegiance and hired support of large numbers of peasants, had called them into Florence.

Moving toward 1478

THE MATERIAL FORTUNES of the Pazzi over the next half century may now be quickly traced, as they passed from Andrea to his sons, and then to the tragic generation of 1478.

In tax returns completed on 31 May 1433, Andrea listed more or less the same rural properties as before, but the possession of family shares in the government debt had now jumped to 28,000 florins in titular values, not including any part of the war loans still outstanding. As in the case of the Medici reports to the tax office, these loans are passed over in silence, as though lying outside the purview of the city's tax juris-diction. At a glance, his declared banking and business assets were distrib-uted as follows:

4250 florins   The start-up capital of his Florence Bank

2000   His share in a Banchi–Capponi silk business

2180   Share in woollen-cloth partnership with two Capponi brothers

2000   Start-up capital of his son Jacopo's woollen-cloth firm

1800   His share in the start-up capital of his Pisa Bank

—   Unspecified share in Albizzi silk firm, accounts incomplete

—   Share in a previous Pisa company, accts incomplete

—   Share, galleys-to-Flanders voyage, accts incomplete

—   Share, Rome bank, with Francesco Boscoli, accts incom-plete

—   Share, Barcelona partnership with son Antonio & with Francesco Tosinghi, firm dissolved, accts incomplete

—   Share, Avignon partnership with sons Guglielmo and Piero

—   Share, Montpellier & Paris partnerships, too many bad debtors

—   Share, Provence bank, with Niccolò Cambini, accts incomplete

—   Share, partnership with son Piero & Poldo Pazzi, losing money

Andrea listed one major debt. He owed 8628 florins to his own Florence Bank: funds that he had used mainly for investment purposes, not for the small sums dribbled out to goldsmiths, employees, and servants, or to labourers and artisans for building works at his residential properties in town and country.

But the most striking feature of the report is in its blanks, the unspecified sums. Out of anxiety over threatened penalties and heavier taxes, most rich Florentines would not have dared to submit such incomplete returns. Andrea, instead, claiming that he had lacked the time to work through his accounts, admits to drawing his statement up in haste, while also trusting that the tax inspectors will accept it as true and allow him to supply the missing particulars at a later time. Afterwards, he would negotiate an agreement with them. But it says a great deal for his contacts that he was willing to take risks with a tax organisation that could be notoriously brutal.

In the 1440s, the Pazzi Bank in Rome occupied a very strong position. Andrea and his partners were almost alone, ironically, in having the benefit of unlimited credit from the Medici. This meant that they were then able to turn around and lend or invest at higher rates of profit. Like the Medici, moreover, the Pazzi enjoyed direct papal employment for years. They took in varied funds for the Roman Curia from different parts of Europe, and from 1451 to 1478, under five different popes, were continuously active in the receipt and transfer of papal revenue from Germany. All the profit here derived from the movement of monies and the business of exchange transactions; and Andrea's sons would also be engaged in this activity, to be succeeded in turn, during the 1460s and 1470s, by the banking firms of two grandsons.

The old patriarch Andrea died in October 1445, leaving three sons well schooled in the mysteries of banking and trade, each of them committed to the quest for public office. All served terms as Lord Priors (see pp. 94–5), and two of them, Piero and Jacopo, would hold the top post, Gonfalonier of Justice. Serving Pazzi interests through the common practice of endogamy and marriage alliance, two daughters, Lena (Elena) and Albiera, had been married into the rich business lines of the Lamberteschi and Bardi houses.

The death of Messer Andrea did not issue in the sudden break-up of an extended family, in which all members were takers of 'one bread and one wine'. Already emancipated legally, the married elder brothers, Antonio and Piero, were living in separate establishments by 1441, in houses adjoining the Pazzi enclave. And it now emerged that sharp strains divided sons and father, who kept a record of their financial debts to him, accused all three sons of spendthrift ways, and even threatened to disinherit them. At that point, at all events, they were not being the careful business stewards that he had brought them up to be. Nevertheless, in March 1446, dismissing the disinheritance threat as a spur intended to change their ways, arbitrators made a tripartite division of the estate. For the major tax census of 1447, accordingly, the three brothers drew up separate returns, although Antonio and Piero had already done so for an earlier round of levies in 1442.

Taxes and so-called 'forced loans' in Florence were based, generally speaking, on assets of several sorts: real estate, commercial capital, shares in the public debt, and cash. When actually occupied by the owner, a citizen's residence alone was exempted from taxes.

Messer Andrea obtained a small tax grace shortly before he died, the details of which reveal that he had paid nearly 40,000 florins in taxes in the ten years between 1435 and 1445: still a far cry from Giannozzo Manetti's mammoth disbursements, but indicative, all the same, in view of Andrea's favourable standing with the Medicean regime, of his enormous banking and business profits. In the new run of documents (1447), glancing back to this time, the eldest brother, Antonio, seizes on the recent death of their father to lament the closing of their banks in Florence and Avignon (they would reopen), the loss of clients, the constraints of debt, and the continuing toll of heavy taxes, still as high, he complains, as in the prosperous years of the late Messer Andrea.

Piero and Jacopo allow Antonio to speak for them about the family business affairs, despite Antonio's claim that each brother 'now administers his own things for himself'. But apart from lodging a general complaint, Antonio provides no picture of their current business deal-

ings, and nor do the others. Instead, they record their real-estate holdings and shares in the government debt, and this account shows that the
solid fortunes of the family had been reinforced. Their assets in government shares now totalled more than 63,000 florins, for a possible income,
at 5 per cent, of 3150 florins per year; and when the Commune failed to
make interest payments, the credited sums accrued. Each of the three
households held a portion of the shares:

Antonio	12,000 florins
Piero	15,500
Jacopo	20,000

An additional credit of 16,000 florins would later be divided among the
three brothers, but in 1447 it was still listed in the name of their father,
because income on these shares was reserved for payment of the continuing work in the Pazzi Chapel.

The family's wealth in farmland had also risen sharply:

Antonio	8 farms and many land parcels
Piero	12 farms " "
Jacopo	10 farms " "
(unassigned)	3 farms and about 100 land parcels

The farmland of the final entry had once belonged to their sister
Lena's husband, Lamberto Lamberteschi, now an exile and a political
outcast on the run. It is likely that these properties were being held as
security for Lena's dowry.

All married, the brothers went on living piously in the old family
neighbourhood, their houses standing cheek by jowl around the 'Corner
of the Pazzi' and stretching both east and south. But Jacopo, the youngest
of them, was the one who had inherited their father's house and would,
by expansion and rebuilding around 1470, convert the old pile into the
handsome Pazzi Palace (Figure 4). Much the most enterprising of the
three brothers, he had also ended in possession of the Montughi properties and villa just north of Florence. Here, in April 1478, he was to
hold his fateful talks regarding the assassination of the Medici brothers.

Fig. 4 The Pazzi Palace.

The Tragic Generation

A HAZY PICTURE OF Pazzi business interests reappears in the family tax returns of 1458. The eldest brother Antonio had died in 1451. Piero, student of the classics, orator, splendid ambassador, and known prodigal, was to die a few years later, his contemporary Alessandra Strozzi alleging that he was killed by an excess of pleasure and misused wealth!

Soon enough, therefore, the fame and direction of the family would be in the hands of Jacopo and the 'star-crossed' generation, his nephews.

The new reports list more farms and land parcels, offering yet another glimpse of expanding Pazzi wealth in the Tuscan countryside. In little more than ten years, the capital value of their shares in the Florentine government debt had risen from 63,000 to 90,400 florins – Jacopo now holding the lion's share, with more than 51,000 florins of the total in his name. But it should be noted that the bulk of this increase came very likely from the payment of interest-bearing forced loans and accruing credits. Suffice it to add that when affluent Florentines paid certain obligatory 'loans' or taxes in full, policy turned these into negotiable, interest-bearing shares in the public debt; whereas payment of the same levies at a much lower level, namely at one-third the sum, converted them into outright tax payments.

In reporting on their business interests, the brothers and nephews again show as little as possible to the tax inspectors. Rich Florentines were usually edgy about tax returns. In many cases, citizens even with-held notice of deductible debts ('I owe so much to x'), because these would then have turned into taxable assets for their creditors, a breach of contract if they had bound themselves by verbal agreements to be silent about such transactions. Still, the Pazzi had to put some of their cards on the table for the simple reason that, like the Medici, they and their affairs were too well known. These were the cards:

(1) Jacopo had a silk-cloth company in Geneva, 'Jacopo de' Pazzi and Co.', which was managed by the Florentine, Francesco di Lutozzo Nasi, holder (with his son) of a one-fourth share. Investment capital: 4000 florins.

(2) Piero and Jacopo had a bank in Rome, managed by their Florentine partner, Jacopo de' Mozzi: 'our father [Andrea] set it up [the bank] for the convenience of having cash from men at the papal court.'

(3) There seems to have been a bank in Avignon, where Piero was the key figure, and in fact he was there when the returns were drafted in 1458. But since he had failed to forward the necessary particulars, his sons beg to be allowed to provide this information on his return from France.

(4) A woollen-cloth firm in Florence, run in the name of Jacopo 'and partners,' had been shut down some two years before. Proft-and-loss accounts were incomplete.

(5) Jacopo had a Florence partnership in the silk trade, managed largely by his associate, Giuliano di Francesco Corsellini. Investment: 1500 florins.

Having studied the three sets of returns, tax officials estimated the net wealth of the different Pazzi households as follows:

Antonio's heirs	10,238 florins
Piero	9505
Jacopo	16,775
Total	36,518 florins

Of the total, half was accounted for by the actual market value of Pazzi government shares (20 per cent of 90,400 florins), while the other half included about 9000 florins in real estate and 9000 in business capital.

A more accurate idea of Pazzi business activity may be gleaned from the rough balance sheets in Piero's returns. The debit-and-credit columns of the Geneva silk firm put the transactions of the business in the range of 17,000 florins, including the value of current cloth stock. In Rome, the Pazzi Bank was dealing in sums that added up to just over 36,000 florins. Among the major debtors of the bank (borrowers obviously) were some of the top men in the Curia: Pope Calixtus III himself, Cardinal Orsini, the cardinals of Messina, San Marco (Venice), Fermo, and San Sisto (Juan Torquemada), as well as numerous other prelates, some of them from as far away as Poland, Germany, Catalonia, and Rhodes. The Genevan and Florentine Pazzi firms were also, interestingly, major debtors. On the other hand, the leading creditors of the bank included the cardinals of Rouen, Portugal, Cologne, Bologna, and Zamora, in addition to the Prefect of Rome and, indeed, 'Messer Andrea's heirs', the Pazzi brothers and nephews.

The scale of Pazzi operations was even larger than the above record suggests. Jacopo's statement discloses that one of the partnerships still had silk cloth in Barcelona, valued at 2700 florins (more than half the worth of Andrea's lands and houses in 1427): so something was going on there. Elsewhere (unspecified) the Pazzi were claiming 2226 florins for many bolts of cloth. Filippo Strozzi's company down in Naples owed them 2726 florins, again for cloth. Jacopo had been a recent partner in yet another silk business, 'Lorenzo Dietisalvi and Company'. And just a few years later (1466), the great turncoat and power broker, Luca Pitti, in that most dangerous of times for him, had 750 florins on deposit with the Florence bank of 'Jacopo de' Pazzi and partners', earning a likely interest of 8 per cent, unless, as a *gran maestro*, he was rewarded with a little more.

Although the Pazzi are known chiefly as bankers, they were also heavily engaged in the manufacture and sale of luxury cloth, the old mainstay of Florentine industry.

In 1469, Messer Jacopo and his nephews presented officials with their last property and business statements before the catastrophe. Their assets had dwindled:

Messer Piero's seven sons	7500 florins
Antonio's three sons (Guglielmo and Francesco included)	8518 florins
Messer Jacopo	10,800 florins

The details disclose a general rise in landed property and the hint of a search for investments of a more stable sort. The family had also got rid of blocks of shares in the public debt, possibly, in Jacopo's case, to help raise cash for more profitable ventures. But Antonio's sons retained the bulk of their Monte shares. Florence owed them 5659 florins in back interest on these holdings.

Let's look at a comparison. If the net assets of the three households are lumped together, the resulting rough sum of 26,800 florins falls short of the 31,000 florins recorded for Andrea in 1427. So that over a period of about forty years, the overall fortunes of the family seem to have declined, indeed dramatically so, considering that three separate households, with many more 'mouths' (a tax term), now possessed less wealth, when combined, than Andrea's one. In 1478, therefore, would Lorenzo de' Medici be facing a rival family already undermined by financial loss, and hence increasingly desperate? Not likely, especially as any partial decline in their fortunes was offset psychologically, if socially transposed, by the number of Pazzi males. When taken together, moreover, the three households still held the second place on the Florentine taxrolls, second only to the Medici.

More tellingly, the three sets of 1469 returns all but entirely withhold banking and business capital from the tax inspectors. Messer Jacopo, now the patriarchal head of the line, did not bother to itemise a single investment in trade or finance, confident that his report would even thus pass muster. Speaking for Antonio's heirs, Guglielmo (Lorenzo de' Medici's brother-in-law) listed banking firms in Rome and Lyons, but credits these with no assets, because of a debt of 5000 florins to Renato de' Pazzi's company in Florence, and indeed it appears in Renato's report. This company in turn, which is said to have no investment capital, is described as being a kind of storage space and correspondence headquarters (*fondaco*). Renato also lists his brother's firm, 'Andrea de' Pazzi and Co.', in an entry showing that this partnership was in the business of producing fine woollen cloth strictly for the Pazzi Bank in Rome, where it was sold to local merchants and to men at the papal court. Yet Renato and his brothers were credited with net capital assets of a mere 1500 florins 'in trade and cash'.

In the early 1460s, Guglielmo de' Pazzi and a partner, Francesco Nasi, owned one of the most important banking firms in Geneva, which was then transferred to Lyons in about 1465, where it continued to flourish down to at least 1473. Florentine bankers used this French city as a kind of international clearing house

The Pazzi had companies in Rome, Florence, Lyons, Avignon, Marseilles, Bruges, and Valencia. In 1472, for example, their bank in Bruges 'had a staff of eight members', while the Marseilles company had only four. Bruges was to become a major outlet for Pazzi banking a few years later, when the angry Pope Sixtus took the papal alum monopoly away from the Medici Bank and transferred it to the Pazzi in June 1476. Based in the middle of the richest cloth-producing region in northern Europe, the Bruges operation had to find local markets for the dyeproducing alum. But little more than a distant echo of these varied business interests gets into the Pazzi returns of 1469: silence is what speaks there. The obvious suppression of information, Jacopo's effrontery, and the quiet connivance of tax inspectors underline the strong standing of the Pazzi in government circles, a position clinched ten years before by Guglielmo's marriage to Bianca de' Medici. Brothers and uncle understood that no exacting eyes would be fixed on their tax returns.

In 1474, when Pope Sixtus IV dismissed the Medici as his principal bankers and substituted the competing Florentine house, he put a large volume of new business into the hands of the Pazzi in Rome. Though this was at once news for gossip, there was no reason officially to record the change in Florence, nor did it get into the fiscal records, because the 1470s failed to bring another round of required tax returns; and by the time the next one came, in 1480, the names of Andrea de' Pazzi's descendants had been cleanly expunged from the taxrolls. As far as the government of Florence was concerned, Pazzi survivors of the April Plot no longer possessed any real property or other assets of their own; and if they did, they were holding on to such wealth – it had been ruled – illegally.

If we look back from the 1470s to Andrea's wealth in the 1430s, it appears that his heirs went into a business slowdown for a decade or so from about 1445. But from the later 1450s, the 'cursed' generation began to make a strong financial comeback. Renato, Francesco (the conspirator), the young Andrea, and one or two others promised to be enterprising merchants and bankers. In December 1478, eight months after the April Plot and in the company probably of an older agent, the fourteen-year old Antonio, Guglielmo's son, was already in Bruges, toiling to hold on to the family assets there against the international reach of Florentine diplomacy. He had the support of the King of Naples.

Because of linking brothers and cousins, the business partnerships of the Pazzi have given the impression that they were ruled by harmony and family solidarity. Yet the patriarch Andrea's two elder sons, Antonio and Piero, had left the family home for their own houses by 1441, and when they filed individual tax returns the year after, the city's tax officials refused to recognise their separation, presumably because of their business partnerships, but also, it seems, because such fragmentation, coming so soon, may have struck them as unusual in so rich a family.

After Andrea's death, as we have seen, his three sons quickly staked out their individual claims on the patrimony, in accord with the judgment of the arbitrators, and all continued to live apart. As the most business-like of the three brothers, Jacopo seems to have been closest to his father, with the result that he got the main properties; but his notorious passion for gambling could not have had the approval of the family. At the same time, his brother Piero's grand style and likely neglect of business would inevitably have provoked quarrels. And yet the brothers continued to co-operate in partnerships, drawing in their nephews as well. Was this done on the principle that the devil you know is better than the ones you don't know? A wise proverb, surely, in a city that appeared to teem with cunning men, even as attested to in the best Florentine tales of the age, which sometimes verge on turning trickery and craft into an icon.

The next generation saw a similar distancing among brothers and cousins. When Renato went out to his villa at Trebbio on the day before the April Plot was sprung, was he hinting that he had picked up the scent of some terrifying matter, and so chose to be far from the scene? If he left the city because of a hunch or mere suspicion, and otherwise really knew nothing about the plot, how – knowing so little – could he have gone to Lorenzo to denounce his uncle Jacopo and cousin Francesco? For all their internal lesions, whether serious or superficial, uncle and nephews comprised a meaningful bloodline; they were still collectively identified; all would share in the family's lasting honour or infamy; and the consequences would also touch Renato's far-away brother, the Bishop of Sarno, an agent of the King of Naples.

Living in Rome, where he ran the Pazzi Bank and was the familiar of cardinals, princes, of the Pope himself and of sword-brandishing noblemen, the proud and choleric Francesco, as we shall see, allowed this rather lawless world to go to his head. Back in Florence, meanwhile, his brother Guglielmo, husband to Bianca de' Medici, was compelled to orbit somewhat closer to the Medici, despite the fact that he too had been elbowed out of public life by Lorenzo.

CHAPTER FIVE

Profile: Soderini

Tommaso Soderini (1403–85)

A S LORENZO DE' Medici's father Piero lay dying at the end of November 1469, Tommaso Soderini, politician and merchant, made his way about a small circle of Medicean patricians, talking up support for the Medici house and the young Lorenzo, who would not have his twenty-first birthday for another five weeks. This group passed the word around, and on the very day of Piero's death (2 December), in the evening, 700 citizens met in the church of St Antonio, where Soderini and several others addressed them. The next day a company of politicians arrived at the Medici Palace to reassure the young man and, in effect, to hand him the weight of Medici power in Florence. By the action of this inner oligarchy, Lorenzo now became the regime's top man, or rather, in an expression of the period, a *gran maestro*.

Already a bedrock political realist, Lorenzo had not just waited around for the self-appointed group to come to him. He had perhaps even asked himself the question, how many of the 700 citizens who collected at St Antonio's were really diehard Mediceans? Knowing that Florence nourished a muted political opposition, he had acted. In the days leading up to his father's death, both by letter and talks with Milan's ambassador to Florence, he had been in urgent contact with the Duke of Milan, Galeazzo Maria Sforza, seeking guarantees of support and the promise of Milanese troops, in case they should be needed. 'All my hope', says a letter of 2 December, 'is in you alone, whom I pray will give thought to my state and safety, which can only come from Your Excellence.' And two days later, emphasising his devotion to the Duke, he commits 'my soul, my body, and everything I have' to him – not in vain, for by 6 December the Duke had promised to send 1000 soldiers to Florence in a show of support for Lorenzo, and Sforza also wrote to the Lord Priors, strongly recommending his protégé. If necessary, in short, cold steel would speak for the young love poet in the realm of politics (he had been writing verse since about the age of fifteen). But thanks to Tommaso Soderini and a few others, armed violence and even open dispute were avoided. Who was this man who had negotiated things so coolly?

Resident on the far side of the Arno, like the Pitti and the Manetti, the Soderini were one of the city's most honoured political families – more distinguished than the Medici themselves, at least down to Cosimo's time. Tommaso's branch of the family – a bastard line, as it happens – broke from the main lineage about 1400, a few years before his father, the illegitimate son of a prominent Soderini and a French woman, was executed in Florence for forging and flaunting documents that sought to establish his legitimacy. It was a case of aggravated fraud. In the late 1420s, when Tommaso's older brother Niccolò was accused of plotting the murder of a powerful anti-Medici politician, the brothers reached out successfully for the help of the Medici. Florence was in the thick of a fierce factional struggle. And in the 1430s, when Cosimo triumphed, Tommaso and Niccolò Soderini began their march toward the front ranks of the new oligarchy. The 'real' or mainline Soderini instead, hurt by their ties with the opposing faction led by the Albizzi, lost their political place and ran into desperate financial troubles, with the result that their creditors, the illegitimate cadet branch, were able to buy up the old family houses, located near the river, by the southern foot of the Carraia Bridge.

Hewing close to the Medici, Tommaso and Niccolò revealed a gift for politics, and in about 1442 Tommaso acted to cement his ties with Cosimo by marrying Dianora Tornabuoni, sister to none other than Lucrezia, who would marry the great banker's son Piero a year later. The Tornabuoni figured among Cosimo's closest political allies, and in the next generation a brother of the two sisters, Giovanni, would run the Roman branch of the Medici Bank. The Soderini brothers worked their way up to the top tier of the oligarchy. Then the unpredictable play of personality intervened. In the late 1440s, Niccolò was beginning now and again to resent the tightening political controls of the Medicean party.

At a certain point in the 1450s, feeling himself misused on a particular embassy, impatient and more daring than his younger brother, Niccolò drew away gradually from the Medicean leadership and turned against the whole system of electoral manipulation that kept them in power. The prudent Tommaso, however, went on to become one of the guiding members of the ruling group, a man who was always prepared to work for the unpopular 'purse' restrictions on access to high office. The two brothers were never to heal their political fracture.

In 1466, when the clash between the two factions, Mediceans and anti-Mediceans, edged Florence to the brink of civil war, Niccolò Soderini, one of the defeated 'rebel' leaders, was banished from the city in perpetuity and shorn of his wealth, in a process of vengeance and prosecution that went on for years. He died in exile. Tommaso, instead, always cleaving to the Medici, flourished; and in December 1469, trailing thirty years' experience in public life, he was one of the two or three men in Florence with the stature to seize the leadership, rally the Mediceans, and deliver power to Lorenzo. His loyalty to the Medici cause was a counterweight to his brother's 'treachery'.

Sixty-six years old, the ageing Tommaso now entered into an odd and dicey relationship with the young Medici lord, whom he had just helped to make the unofficial head of state. His informed contemporaries must have wondered about how the wily old politician, married to Lorenzo's aunt Dianora (so his uncle by marriage), would get on with an ambitious, clever, proud, and strong-willed young nephew.

Over the next dozen years, although the two were often to be in strong disagreement, Tommaso turned out to be the one man in Florence who could openly defy Lorenzo in the political arena. They almost seemed at moments to be rivals, but the young man put up with his opponent. He needed a friendly antagonist. It was good policy in republican Florence to show that he could brook some opposition. Besides, the opponent came, as it were, from within the family, and never posed the threat present in the Pazzi, with their riches, numbers, European contacts, and explosive pride.

Tommaso's position in Florence was unusual, to say the least. His debt to Lorenzo's grandfather was incalculable. Cosimo had enabled him to climb to the pinnacle of public life, at the same time as the older, legitimate branch of the Soderini slipped into obscurity. He even rescued Tommaso from a shameful financial collapse, the bankruptcy of his textile firm in the 1450s. But there were also other, continuing pressures on Tommaso, which sometimes made him unreliable. Having inherited a modest fortune, saddled with a large family, and struggling to keep up with his richer political peers, he was driven to use office, like his silk-cloth company, as an essential source of income. The result was that he acquired a reputation for greed. Conforming too easily to a common practice of the age, he accepted bribes happily, the large ones coming mostly from foreign ambassadors and from the states that were ready to pay for his influence in Florence. Once at least, in the 1470s, Lorenzo himself had to kick in money to help win him over to a particular foreign-policy line. Tommaso's political pre-eminence had rewarded him with enviable contacts abroad; he was alleged to possess exceptional cunning and wisdom; he had the sharpest political mind in Florence, the Milanese ambassador believed; he could dicker and deal with all the top men in the city; and he was the chief proponent of the claim that the Medicean system of electoral manipulation and fiddled purses put the 'best' and 'wisest' men into high office. The young Lorenzo, therefore, needed the backing of this old statesman.

Shrewd and thoroughly ambitious, Tommaso did not underestimate himself; nor did he sell his favours cheap. For all his debts to the Medici, he had also served them in politics for thirty years; and though being the key assistant in Lorenzo's step up to power, he could not easily accept playing second fiddle to a green young man. The outcome added up to some ten years of sticky relations, with ups and downs in their collaborative efforts, and with Lorenzo – angling to bring old Soderini into line – relying on the help of others, including foreign ambassadors, as well as on moral pressure, money, and even the occasional private banquet.

The careers of Tommaso and Niccolò – men made by the Medicean system of electoral shenanigans – reveal that Lorenzo and the Medici, wish as they might, were never able to rely on the unswerving loyalty of the old political families. Memory and political routines still held a rich store of republicanism for possible future use. Even as they gave way cautiously to Cosimo, to Piero and to Lorenzo, young patricians were brought up to expect to have a voice in politics; and why should that voice, now and again, not be heard? In some essential way, as 'gut feeling', they wanted to see the Medici as peers. Their traditions called for this; so too did Florence's constitution. No amount of fixing or window-dressing could easily uproot two centuries of republican government from their hearts. This legacy helps to explain both Niccolò's rebellion and Tommaso's predilection for Venice, a liking that even went, at times, against Lorenzo's foreign policy, which always favoured the Sforza and the Milanese Duchy over the Venetian Republic.

CHAPTER SIX

Enter Lorenzo

A Public Education

THE APRIL PLOT drew much of its drive and fears from the tensions among the city's political families, and once it failed, conspirators made at least two more attempts on Lorenzo's life, while secret plans for other efforts came to nothing. But the assault of 1478 was not the first directed against his primacy. In April 1470, less than four months after his father's death, fifteen men, led by the exile Bernardo Nardi, the son of a former Gonfalonier of Justice, were hanged in Florence and neighbouring Prato for incitement to insurrection. The episode, one expert has noted, turned out to be 'part of a vast plot concocted by exiles in Ferrara, Siena, and Rome, and known even to the Pope himself'. The angry Lorenzo suspected the very connivance of leading men in Prato.

Over the span of a mere twenty years, by the mid 1450s, a single Florentine family had made itself the head and heart of a tightening oligarchy. But as the Medici grew in stature and clout, the tides of feeling for and against them also waxed, until Cosimo and his sons were no longer free to step down voluntarily. They and their circle of satellite families had planted too much fear, too much resentment. In any eruption of political conflict, office and property lay on the gaming table, and the losers would also face the despair of exile, far away from friends and family, prey to nostalgia, to fears, suspicions, and hopes, and often nagged by material distress. Unless they themselves rebelled and called for the return of exiles, all the complicit families stood to lose place, honour, and wealth, if the Medici should do the unheard of thing and back away from power. And so Lorenzo was necessarily brought up both to inherit his father's political patrimony and to wield it.

Men born into the city's pre-eminent families were already half way to being public figures. They were recognised in the streets even by people who didn't count, not to mention those who did. But to be one of the principal Medici – or a Pazzi for that matter – was somehow to be altogether public. The space enclosed by the city's towering walls became an amphitheatre, and high public office was centre stage. Here was destiny for a youth like Lorenzo. A contemporary witness noted that he 'stood above the average height, was broad shouldered, robustly built, muscular, remarkably agile, and olive complexioned', but so 'short-sighted that he saw very little from a distance', and had rather a 'flat nose and a harsh voice. Yet his face, though nothing handsome, had great dignity'.

His education for formal entry into public space began in childhood. At five, garbed in French dress and affecting a grave air, he was sent to congratulate the visiting French prince, Jean d'Anjou, who had just been knighted by the city's Lord Priors (May 1454). At ten, performing in the chapel of the new Medici Palace, he and his brother Giuliano recited verse and prose for the Sforza prince, Galeazzo Maria, on the occasion of his first visit to Florence (April 1459). For the same occasion, mounted on a white horse, Lorenzo took up the rear of a parade of thirty musicians and twelve youths from Florence's leading houses, two of whom were Renato and Giovanni de' Pazzi. The twelve were attended by servants in splendid livery, and behind the musicians came Lorenzo's own banner, showing a large falcon caught in a net and throwing off feathers. His addiction to falconry would later issue in one of his most delightful poems, *Hunting Partridges*.

Lorenzo was educated at home by private tutors, chief of whom Gentile Becchi, who had him concentrate on classical Latin and a variety of religious texts. Encouraged to do so by his parents and by Becchi, he began to write letters of patronage at the age of eleven, looking to dole out favour. At twelve he was dispatching formal letters to his father, being the advocate for others (adults) and requesting that '[you] honour me in this'! In due course, his patronage would require that he produce a continuing torrent of letters and spoken commitments. Later still, he was to be the city's great marriage broker, the key fixer of arranged matrimony among the top families. On at least one occasion, indeed, he brokered a princely marriage, linking the Bentivoglio of Bologna to the

Manfredi of Faenza; and, asked to do so by King Louis XI of France, he even tried to arrange a marriage between the heir to the French crown and one of the daughters of King Ferrante of Naples.

In 1463, now fourteen years old and on the premise no doubt that he should get to know Tuscany, he was allowed to travel with young friends to Pistoia, Lucca, and Pisa. At sixteen, in May 1465, he passed formally into public life, in the role of emissary to a princely court. Travelling in the company of Guglielmo de' Pazzi, he was sent out by his father to represent the Medici on a grand occasion: the entry into Milan of the thirteen-year-old prince Federigo, son of the King of Naples, come to collect Ippolita Sforza, daughter of the Duke of Milan, who was being married by proxy to his elder brother, Alfonso of Calabria. Federigo was then to accompany her back to Naples with a retinue of great noblemen. Lorenzo journeyed to Ferrara, Verona, and Venice, where he was received by the Doge, before going on to the Milanese festivities. Here, in the great house given to his grandfather by Duke Francesco Sforza, but now the seat of the Medici Bank in Milan, Lorenzo entertained lavishly, assisted by his Pazzi brother-in-law. And with his well-known prodigious intelligence, which of course would not miss a cue, he was achieving the whole point of his trip: to meet Sforza himself, as well as the ducal family, and to familiarise himself with the ways of princes and statesmen.

Less than a year later, he was overtaken by a dramatic commission. Having started out on a trip to Siena, Rome, Naples, and Ancona at the outset of March, to conduct banking and political business for his father, news of the unexpected death of Francesco Sforza (8 March 1466) reached him in Rome. The communication chilled the Medici: Sforza's military muscle had long been one of the guarantees of the Medicean hold on the Florentine republic. Lorenzo, therefore, had to act fast, and take up the cause of the new Duke of Milan, Galeazzo Maria Sforza, in conversations with the Pope and King Ferrante. With Cosimo dead (1464) and Piero 'the Gouty' already cripplingly ill, the young man was forced to look upon Galeazzo Maria, with his standing army, as his most vital ally abroad. He had several audiences with Pope Paul II, then proceeded down to the Neapolitan kingdom, where he visited Ippolita Sforza, went on hunts with the King, and found the court – to his relief – much in favour of the new Duke. Very likely, too, he had been dispatched to Naples, to warn the court of the swelling republican sentiment back home and to feel out the strength of Neapolitan support for the Medici. Naples, as it happened, had a small community of industrious Florentine exiles.

When Lorenzo got back to Florence in May 1466, he returned to a scene simmering with the desire to abolish Medicean 'purse' controls and to restore office rights to all those who had been despoiled of these over the previous thirty years. Most of the top Medicean collaborators had defected, having turned openly into 'reformers' who were prepared to take power back from the Medici and to share it with a larger stretch of the political class. Piero de' Medici found himself confronted by a revolt at the summit of the upper class. The crisis peaked at the end of August. Invited to appear before the Lord Priors, as already noted, he instead sent his sons Lorenzo and Giuliano to speak for him, and then, a day or two later, followed this insolent gesture with a show of 3000 mercenaries, his own hired men, who had somehow been allowed to enter Florence. Guards at the city gates had been corrupted or threatened with violence. Five days after his meeting with the Priors, Lorenzo armed himself, mounted a horse, and joined his father's soldiers in the main government square. The leaders of the reformers were exiled or bullied into silence and cooperation. Medicean power was reimposed and tightened. Though only seventeen years old, Lorenzo was 'elected' to the all-powerful *Balìa* of that autumn (1466), and in December, in yet another departure from constitutional law, he was voted into the major Council of One Hundred. Thereafter, Piero had occasionally to restrain Lorenzo from asserting himself in state affairs. The youth had views of his own and certainly thought of himself as capable.

The next three years were a little lifetime for Lorenzo. He took the plunge into literature, composing verse and reading widely. But politics remained stubbornly in the wings, and he never forgot it for long. He was to have two souls always, two sides: one for literature and the other for callous action in the world. His love poetry, which he took to be the best of his verse, was utterly detached from the life of Florence – kept artfully away from anything realistic or practical. Idealising, learned, and ultra-refined, it was the verse of a man who was testing and displaying his mastery of the Tuscan idiom of elevated love, in a coruscating play of argument, oppositions, and subtle feeling. The different poems focus narcissistically on the speaker as lover, on his mercurial moods, joys, defeats, and sufferings. Through them he passes a binding filament of remarks on *fortuna*, death, time, and his martyr-like devotion. Love and his beloved are at once his torment (death) and salvation (life), but the values keep shifting:

> I long the most for what I least desire,
> To live the more, I hanker for my end,
> To flee from death I beckon death,
> Looking for peace where no rest ever was.
> . . .
> Seeking ice in fire, scorn in pleasure,
> Life in death and war in peace, I work
> To break from my own coiling ropes.

If the 'noble' or highbrow love poetry of the Italian Renaissance was – as many contemporaries claimed – an elaborate disguise for lechery, then it has to be said that Lorenzo's verse took the charade up to exceptional heights.

On 3 December 1469, the day afer his father's death, when a delegation of self-appointed politicians visited the Medici Palace to offer him the first place in the affairs of state, Lorenzo was no stranger to the use of muted violence in public life. He had been party to it in the government square at the outset of September 1466, and was now in close touch with the Duke of Milan, who had soldiers ready for a hurried march to Florence. Florentine exiles would have to consider this, if they should move to stir up the silent opposition at home, as they had tried to do a year earlier, hoping to block Lorenzo's vault into power.

A report to Borso d'Este, Duke of Modena, from his ambassador in Florence, underlines the fact that opponents of the Medicean regime were again finding their voice – only to be gradually silenced. On the evening of Piero's death, at a rally controlled by the Medicean leadership in the convent of St Antonio, two frontline oligarchs had argued 'that it was necessary to acknowledge a lord and superior . . . who could deal in a consistent manner with all current affairs pertaining to the government of our Signoria [the Lord Priors]'. The ambassador's report concluded:

> It is thus understood that the secret affairs of the Signoria will pass through Lorenzo's hands, as they passed through his father's. This is what his friends will work for . . . [with an eye to giving him] the highest standing, and they will be able to do it because they now have the government in hand and the [office] purses open, just as they want them. Many others [however] with whom I have spoken hold a contrary opinion and maintain that in a few days' time everything [political decision-making] should be taken back to the [government] palace. But if now, at the very beginning, they [Lorenzo's friends] pilot the vessel as they desire, above all in the election of the future Lord Priors and other officials, then I believe that they will reach the port they want.

Borso's ambassador was right. Lorenzo and his friends eased their vessel through uncertain waters for thirteen months and then, in 1471, unfurled a series of operations that rapidly put fewer and more obedient pilots at the helm of state.

'These Pazzi relatives of mine'

L ORENZO NOW CAME up against the problem of the Pazzi, though it was a problem of his own making too, because he had made it clear that he would brook no serious social rivals, and certainly not his Pazzi relatives by marriage — men with magnificent contacts abroad, fabled wealth, large family numbers, old blood, and considerable eminence in the city. Tommaso Soderini was never in this sense a rival. Giuliano himself, Lorenzo's brother, went through a long period of melancholy and fits of anger in the 1470s, persuaded that his brother was keeping him away from politics, away from the proscenium and a princely marriage. And indeed, in view of the political needs of the Medici and their encirclement by a devious opposition, there was something odd about the fact that when Giuliano fell to his assassins at the age of twenty-five, nothing certain had yet been done for him, with an eye to increasing the family's resources, either in the form of a marriage or by the procurement of a major post in the Church. Lorenzo, after all, was married by proxy in December 1468, when not yet twenty years old, and the marriage was consummated the following June.

The budding Florentine lord began to meet the Pazzi at social occasions from at least the age of ten, when he took part, in 1459, in the festivities to celebrate the marriage of his sister Bianca to Guglielmo de' Pazzi, an alliance strongly endorsed by grandfather Cosimo. Thereafter, occasional meetings with his Pazzi kin became part of the routine of family life, such as on hunts in the Tuscan countryside. In 1465, he travelled to Milan and other cities with Guglielmo; and a few years later, Guglielmo accompanied Giuliano and four other men to Rome, to fetch home Lorenzo's spouse, Clarice Orsini. Not surprisingly, therefore, this brother-in-law and other members of the Pazzi family turn up as passing *personaggi* both in Lorenzo's verse and in that of other poets of his circle. By the late 1460s, he must have known as much about the Pazzi – including details of their business secrets – as any man in Florence.

In September 1475, in a letter to the Duke of Milan, he declared that the Pazzi owed their high standing in Florence 'to our house.' He meant that they had risen to political and social prominence because of the favour which had been shown them by the Medicean oligarchy. And if the Pazzi terms of office in the Lord Priors are listed, Lorenzo's point carried weight:

> 1439 Andrea di Guglielmino de' Pazzi (1 March)
> 1443 Antonio di Andrea (1 November)
> 1447 Piero di Andrea (1 May)
> 1450 Antonio di Andrea (1 September)
> 1455 Jacopo di Andrea (1 July)
> 1462 Piero di Andrea (1 May), *Gonfalonier*
> 1463 Jacopo di Andrea (1 July)
> 1466 Guglielmo di Antonio di Andrea (1 March)

1469 Jacopo di Andrea (1 January), *Gonfalonier*
1472 Giovanni di Antonio di Andrea (1 July)

Andrea, the wellspring of the family riches, and his three sons and two grandsons all appeared in the governing magistracy, twice in the post of command, Gonfalonier of Justice. They set a striking record, for the Pazzi had never previously sat in the Signoria, having long been ranked as 'magnates.' The Medici, however, were happy to count on their support, as on that of other grandee houses, because they feared the large numbers of political exiles and were grateful to have an array of prestigious names among their followers. Nevertheless, the question naturally arises: if Lorenzo was going to assign all credit to the Medici for the enviable status of the rival house after 1439, would he also have been ready to credit his family with the financial destruction of the brilliant humanist Giannozzo Manetti, or of the others who were hounded and crushed by the regime?

Years before the April Conspiracy, sensing a menace to himself in the obvious ambitions of the Pazzi brothers and cousins, Lorenzo set out to halt their political advance by working furtively to block their access to high office. He also began to mock them and to run them down, and the Pazzi very likely returned the malice, if indeed they hadn't been the first to sting. Florence was known as a sharp-tongued and rather cruel town.

The problem of the Pazzi to one side, Lorenzo displayed his political talents from the very start. In conversations with him during the autumn of 1469, the Milanese ambassador to Florence was impressed by his ways. The fledgling conducted himself 'like an old [experienced] man', and was even willing to engage in gentle criticisms of his father, the dying Piero, for having too peremptory and arrogant a manner, and for alienating friends. The ambassador himself had observed these qualities in Piero. But Lorenzo, he reported, aimed to hold power like his grandfather Cosimo, 'with as much civility as he could manage', which of course meant vote-rigging and 'handling' (that is, fixing) the purses for high office.

In the winter of 1470, within months of his accession to the 'secret business' of the Signoria, Lorenzo and his immediate collaborators tried but failed to get the election of the Lord Priors into their tighter 'hand' controls. A year later they returned to the fray, now favoured by Priors and a Gonfalonier who was one of the most loyal of Medicean servitors, the knight Agnolo della Stufa. Moving in at once with an oblique but tenacious campaign that peaked in July, they got successive groups of Lord Priors to push the desired controls through the necessary councils. They were seeking mechanisms that would ensure the continuous election of obedient Priors and a subservient first legislative council, the *Cento* or One Hundred.

In January 1471, by the barest margin of two votes, they got the *Cento* to approve a five-year measure, giving the Medicean purse-fixers the virtual right to appoint their successors. The next large step was taken in July. Lorenzo and his friends persuaded the legislative councils to consent to a *Balìa* by leading them to think that this body would have limited authority. Despite blandishments and misinformation, the three different councils had to be repeatedly pressured, and while they finally approved the measure, they did so by bare majorities of eight, one, and two votes! Lorenzo's group then packed the *Balìa* with their own followers and yes-men. Next, they had the structure and voting powers of the *Cento* changed so as to give them decisive control over this key legislative council. They capped their revolution in government by rewarding the *Cento* with exclusive authority over electoral, fiscal (tax), and military affairs, thereby stripping the two old legislative councils of their traditional powers. The new changes were meant to last for five years only, and this was another ploy, for Lorenzo and company succeeded in getting their altered engine of government reconfirmed. His beautifully-orchestrated 'reforms' had been a matter of timing, numbers, disinformation, intimidation, bribery, and electoral machination. This was Renaissance statecraft as art: the paradigm of what it was to rule by 'civil' and 'constitutional' means in Medicean Florence.

Meanwhile, as disclosed by the Milan ambassador's communications to his Sforza lord, the Pazzi were certainly on Lorenzo's mind. The envoy reported that the young Florentine boss had angled to keep Messer Jacopo de' Pazzi out of the 1471 *Balìa* and, in compensation, to substitute his own brother-in-law Guglielmo. Instead of which Jacopo and some of his cronies were voted into the *Balìa*. In other words, the desired structure of electoral fixing remained imperfect. That year too, revealingly, Lorenzo had failed to keep the Florentine (and Medicean) statesman, Otto Niccolini, from agreeing to a marriage between his son Agnolo and Lisa di Piero de' Pazzi.

Yet the curious thing is that in the winter and early spring of 1470, in a drawn-out, heated debate, Jacopo de' Pazzi, member of an important committee (including Lorenzo), had supported Lorenzo's foreign policy by taking a strong position in favour of Milan and the Sforza, while on the contrary two top Mediceans, Antonio Ridolfi and Tommaso Soderini (ambiguously), had plumped for King Ferrante. Lorenzo, however, unafraid of Ridolfi and Soderini, must have known something about Jacopo that made him distrust the man. Having already decided to humble them, Lorenzo was revealing his touchiness about the international contacts and prestige of the Pazzi family. The next sign of this surfaced at the end of 1472, when, despite their élan and six adult males, the Pazzi were found to have obtained only three name-billets or inserts for the purses of high office. Although one Pazzi, Giovanni di Antonio, obtained a seat in the Lord Priors of July–August of that year, the clan soon understood that they were going to be kept away from the levers of power.

The nepotism of Pope Sixtus IV now took matters to the fatal turning point of December 1473, when the Pazzi Bank in Rome lent him most of the purchase price of 40,000 ducats for the Romagnol town of Imola, which Sixtus then conferred on one nephew, Cardinal Pietro Riario, for transfer to another, Count Girolamo Riario. Since the vendor, Duke Galeazzo Maria of Milan, had temporised about selling the town to Florence, rather embarrassing the Florentine leadership by his duplicity, Lorenzo urged his banking rivals to deny the purchase money to the Pope, especially as the Medici Bank had already refused to lend him the needed sum. Whereupon the Pazzi – presumably Messer Jacopo and Francesco – not only made the loan but also told the Pope that Lorenzo had cautioned them not to make it. And who delivered the Imola purchase money at the end of December, then getting the keys to the town in February? None other than the next Archbishop of Pisa and future conspirator, Francesco Salviati. Lorenzo's distant agents were certain to have kept him informed.

A Mystery

THE LOAN TO Sixtus marked one of the most revelatory of all moments in pre-Conspiracy relations between Lorenzo and the Pazzi. Florence's dealings with the Pope, no less than with the Duke of Milan and Romagnol lords, were a matter of foreign policy. Ranking as the unofficial head of state, Lorenzo had his own designs for Florentine diplomacy, and they were distinctly expansionist. If the chance arose, he was eager to pick up more territory for Florence and thereby earn the accolades of a populace that was always ready for a heady dose of aggressive patriotism or, better, 'imperialism'. New territorial acquisitions meant more sources of tax income and – at least in imagination – a stronger Florence. So how could the Pazzi cut into the middle of these affairs to conduct, as it were, their own foreign policy? How dared they defy Lorenzo in such capital matters? Were they casting the die, and throwing in, as well, an argument from profit and morality, by claiming that they after all were bankers, that the Pope was good business, and that they had a financial or even a moral right to go to his aid? Lorenzo's reply would surely have been that they owed something to their native city and also to him as relative and heir to the family that had 'made' them. Well, they might have asked in turn, what loyalties did they owe to Florence while Lorenzo, in an expression of the day, was 'boss of the shop'? Besides, how could strained relations with Pope Sixtus be good for Florence? And not to put a fine point on it, what did they owe a man who was keeping them out of high office and out of their honourable place in the sun?

The Pazzi had decided to stand up to Lorenzo. The defiance of 1473 indicated that a barrier of anger and resentment already stretched between them, even if they all tried to preserve appearances and used Bianca de' Medici's husband Guglielmo as a kind of bridge or buffer. With its 40,000 to 45,000 faces, and its webs of patronage and close personal ties, Renaissance Florence was going to be too small for the likes of Lorenzo and the Pazzi.

That the Pazzi were surpassingly ambitious and rather insensitive can scarcely be doubted. But then Renaissance Florence was not an eighteenth-century drawing room. As late as January 1478, Lorenzo did a good turn for Renato de' Pazzi, intervening by letter with a doctor in Milan, to urge that he come to Florence to attend Renato's sick wife. In the 1470s, again, he sent out letters of patronage for Guglielmo, seeking to help some of his friends and dependents; and in 1473 he supported Messer Antonio de' Pazzi, later Bishop of Sarno, in his quest for Church incomes (two benefices) in Florentine Tuscany. His final show of favour for the Pazzi Bank was made almost against his will, at about the same time as their sensational loan to Pope Sixtus. In December 1473, separate mule trains of precious goods, belonging to the Medici and Pazzi, were seized by Savoyard officials. The goods were being transported from Lyons to Florence, and the Pazzi train, loaded with silver for minting, was stopped in Chambéry, whereas the Medici caravan was halted at Turin. Lorenzo quickly got the Duke of Milan to intervene, and the shipments were soon released, although the Pazzi were forced to pay a hefty 2500 florins in costs. Letters from Medici agents reveal the animosity between the two houses and suggest that the seizure of the Medici mule train had rather forced Lorenzo to act for the Pazzi as well. But from this point on relations would be a semi-courteous war front.

In July 1474, Pope Sixtus removed the Medici as his principal bankers and then, late in the year, ran an audit on their alum accounts. One reason for removing them was that the papal alum monopoly, entrusted to the Medici, had plunged in value, owing to a glut in the market for alum. Lorenzo reacted angrily to the audit, protesting that his family had been papal bankers for more than a hundred years and that such proceedings dishonoured him. Replying through the Duke of Milan, Count Girolamo Riario bluntly asserted that the Pope had every right to check his accounts. The Depositary, the papacy's big financial plum, did not at once pass into the hands of the Pazzi, but they were already being heavily favoured.

Worse was to come. In October of the same year, Sixtus appointed Francesco Salviati to the Archbishopric of Pisa and got the approval of the college of cardinals. Lorenzo was so ill at the time, that no immediate reaction was recorded, but he was certainly appalled, hurt, and outraged, as he was later to reveal. He had not been sounded out on the appointment, nor had the Lord Priors, although consultation with local government was common in such matters. On the western fringes of Florentine territory, Pisa was a likely catapult to the same but richer dignity in Florence. Lorenzo even feared that the Pope was preparing Pisa's Archbishop-elect for a cardinal's hat; and if there was to be a Florentine cardinal, Lorenzo was determined that the chosen should be a man picked from his own circle. What most upset him, however, was his sense that all Florence knew Francesco Salviati to be related to the Pazzi, to have warm ties with them, and to be flourishing under their protection. Messer Jacopo de' Pazzi had very likely bankrolled his education, and Salviati's career now lay in the protective shadow of the Pope, whose nephews had also struck up close personal relations with him and with the banker, Francesco de' Pazzi. More specifically, in matters of kinship, Messer Jacopo's mother was one of Salviati's aunts, apart from which Salviati and one of the young Pazzi (Giovanni di Antonio) were also related through their links with the rich Borromei family. Lorenzo, therefore, rightly assumed – and deeply resented – Salviati's readiness to be at the beck and call of the Pazzi. Yet how was Lorenzo, nominally a mere citizen, to stand up to the power of papal appointment? Though confided to someone else, the dangers were implicit in the Pope's dark threat of the following year (1475): 'We may have to use our irons, so as to help him [Lorenzo] see that he is a citizen and we are the pope, because thus has it pleased God.' Thereafter, still making a point, he would refer to Lorenzo as 'a simple merchant'.

When Florence refused obstinately to have Salviati as Pisa's new archbishop, and denied him the right of entry into that subject city, Sixtus replied menacingly, raising the threat of excommunication and an interdict. Lorenzo now turned for help to his closest ally, Duke Galeazzo Maria Sforza of Milan. On the subject of the hated Salviati, his letters to the Duke ripple with emotion:

> I beg you to get the Reverend Bishop of Como, your ambassador [in Rome], to give the impression – which I know to be true – that I am both loved and esteemed by your Illustrious Lordship, and that you see my affairs as your own, which they truly are. . . . An outright injustice and wrong are being done to me . . . nor can His Holiness [Sixtus] hold himself offended, unless it be because Messer Francesco Salviati is being kept from taking possession of [the high dignity of] Pisa. Over this offence, if it be one, which is being committed by our

entire city, he wants to revenge himself on me alone. It is true that by the grace of God and the favour and warm support of Your Excellency, I would think that I could bring about [Salviati's] possession of the Archbishopric, but I do not think that I should consent to such a public shame for my own sake, for this city does not deserve the like from me. . . . The hard thing in this case is that one of our citizens, Messer Francesco, although having deceived Florence and acting against the will of our Signoria, is more loved by the Pope than is the honour of this whole city. And what terribly matters to me and to our entire government is that there are certain citizens here [i.e., the Pazzi above all] who claim that it [the disputed dignity] is their business and who have given His Holiness to understand that they will do all they can, whether I like it or not, to see that Messer Francesco obtains possession. So Your Excellency can imagine how little I could think of using my influence to help satisfy His Holiness in this matter, not to mention actually doing so.

Lorenzo again notes that the contested see is the true reason for the Pope's anger, and closes the letter by imploring the Duke to intervene forcefully, 'in order that this injustice be not done to me, inasmuch as it injures both my honour and my material interests, so much so that if Your Excellency can get me out of this, it shall stand among my greatest obligations'.

This and the preceding entreaties all concerned Lorenzo's *figura*, his public image. Throughout his years as behind-the-scenes *capo* of Florentine government, he was chronically concerned about his 'honour' and the figure he cut in public. The source of this touchiness lay in the dangers and ambiguity of his position in Florence, where he was neither prince nor simple citizen, neither lord nor ordinary office-holder, and always vulnerable to the shadowy schemes of political exiles in their efforts to recruit military support abroad, no less than to the underground current of resentment against the Medici. Day after day, therefore, in politics and in the world at large, he had to appear strong, on top of things, in control. And this imposed the requirement — for his own sense of security too — that he receive (and that he be seen to receive) generous amounts of respect and honour.

The elites of Italian cities long had such close relations with neighbouring princes, noblemen, grand clerics, and vestigial feudal lords, that they had absorbed the trappings of a code of honour, and were able to turn it into a working value for themselves. Lorenzo knew all about the importance of good faith and honesty in merchants, but as the Florentine head of state, married to an Orsini, and at the centre of a vast web of patronage, he also made much of another ideal, his public image, and this was all about 'honour'.

Little more than a week after his last letter to him (23 December 1474), Lorenzo returned to his painful subject in another letter to the Duke. He denied that his current troubles with Pope Sixtus stemmed, as alleged by Count Girolamo Riario, from his support for the mercenary captain and anti-papal rebel, Niccolò Vitelli, who aimed to storm the papal stronghold of Città di Castello. Instead, the real bone of contention was Pisa. Therefore if, as reported,

> [Pope Sixtus] has received letters from many citizens here in favour of [Francesco] Salviati, this seems to me the main reason why he should be kept from taking possession [of the Pisan dignity]. For if the Signoria and the [leading] men in public life are not disposed to have him, then those who want him [the Pazzi and others] and who have written letters in his favour must be men who do not get on well with those who rule [Florence], making it all the stranger that in a difficult city such as Pisa, someone who is not acceptable to the men in government should be acceptable to them. Just imagine how easily Your Excellency would put up with a man who tried to enter Pavia say, or another of your cities, with the help or favour of men suspect to Your Excellency. Some people claim that Salviati is well born, that he has a circle of well-connected relatives and is [even] related to me. These things are all true, but his ways and habits, in the present case especially, render all this forgettable.

Lorenzo added that he had tried to make various deals with Salviati, offering him one of three other sees – Arezzo, Pistoia, and Volterra – if he renounced Pisa; but none of these would do him. Speaking, for example, of the Aretine post, Salviati's reply claimed that its income was too small for his needs and that he would have to have an additional clutch of Florentine benefices. The rest of Lorenzo's letter rebounds from the papal audit of Medici banking accounts and the removal of certain loan guarantees. A first audit had in fact been done less than a year before, and the accounts had fully squared. But since the new audit was being indecorously noised about, Lorenzo noted that it could not fail to raise suspicions about Medici honesty. 'And you know, Your Excellency, how very important are the credit and good faith of a merchant.'

The Salviati case was drawn out for nearly another year, with increasing rancour on each side, as the Archbishop remained barred from Pisa, and with the brunt of the Pope's anger rightly borne by Lorenzo, the key figure in the campaign against Salviati's 'possession'. The Florentine *gran maestro*, however, was also responding to the wide influence of the Pazzi. He saw their billowing importance as papal bankers and the effects of their *éminence-grise* behind Salviati's rising star in Rome. He also saw little things, though they had more than a touch of maddening symbolic resonance, such as the incident of late December 1474, when the Duke of Urbino refused to lend him a particular jousting horse, because 'I sent it to Renato de' Pazzi, who requested it from me.'

Did the Pazzi have friends and contacts everywhere? Well, yes they did, and Lorenzo met the next sign of this in August 1475, when the King of Naples invited Pope Sixtus to confer the Bishopric of Sarno, one of his favourite hunting grounds, about eighteen miles east of Naples, on one of Messer Jacopo de' Pazzi's nephews, Antonio di Piero, who held a doctorate in canon law. The Pope at once complied. Informed of the appointment, Antonio and the Pazzi family back in Florence immediately accepted his elevation; but contrary to propriety and custom, news of the action was not routed through the Lord Priors or Lorenzo, to give them the opportunity to approve or disapprove. The gesture was readable as a slap in the face.

The truth was that King Ferrante saw Lorenzo as an obstacle to his interventionist ambitions in central Italy and was pleased to favour his opponents. When news of the Sarno appointment reached Florence, the Milanese ambassador noted the fact that it 'provoked much talk and gossip', and showed 'little regard for Lorenzo or his political establishment'. By 'stirring up discussion of the sort intended to condemn his regime as unfree and against liberty, indeed as princely and overbearing', men intent on loose talk about the Sarno affair ended by 'exhorting all those concerned to take up [republican] freedom again . . . and some people, I find, are being dishonest, so that unless something is done, they will cause trouble.'

Lorenzo was naturally stung by the news of this latest affront, coming, as it did, on top of reports that Ferrante and the Duke of Urbino were yearning to break his hold on Florence. He was even warned by the Duke of Milan to be on guard about his own person and Giuliano's. But having the Lord Priors and the Eight 'in his hands', said Milan's ambassador, Lorenzo responded by saying that he felt secure about his position in the city and did not at this point need the support of foreign troops. His unique litany, as voiced to Duke Galeazzo Maria Sforza, was candidly this: that he Lorenzo owed everything he was to him; that he held Florence for him, that is, for the sake of Milan's foreign-policy interests; and that if the Duke would make a show everywhere of the fact that he loved Lorenzo, and hence would always go to his aid, then all would be well for the Medicean regime both in Florence and abroad.

Two days later, 7 September 1475, in another missive to the Duke, Lorenzo turned directly to his Pazzi anxieties, pinning these both to Salviati and to the see of Pisa. He had learnt, probably from the Duke's ambassador, that all the murmuring against him in Florence issued from the Pazzi:

> They are the source, I mean these Pazzi relatives of mine. Thanks to their ill nature and because they have been puffed up by His Majesty the King [Ferrante] and the Duke of Urbino, they are seeking to harm me as much as they can, and doing so against all right, since, as Your Excellency may know, the standing they enjoy in our city they owe entirely to our house [the Medici], to whom they are most ungrateful. I shall do what is needed to prevent them from hurting me and I'll keep my eyes on them; nor do I think much of their fantasies [regarding their own deserts and ambitions], because they enjoy little credit here and are criticised by all men of understanding. . . . As you know, the new Archbishop of Pisa is very much the creature of the Pazzi, being connected to them both by family ties and bonds of friendship. In

Rome I am pressed more than ever to work for the granting [to him] of the Pisa possession, which I believe would result in great reputation for the Pazzi and for me the opposite, a point I cannot ignore, since they are the ones who have bad-mouthed me in Florence. I beg Your Excellency to exert pressure on Count Girolamo [Riario], to make him understand that you wish to spare me this shame and that you consider that it would be almost yours as well, because of my being so very much your servitor. . . . Thus [perhaps] will Rome understand that I am truly loved by Your Excellency.

But the Duke of Milan was dealing with a most determined pope. Besides, Count Girolamo Riario, recently married to the Duke's bastard daughter Caterina, was his son-in-law, so Sforza had obligations there too. In the end, Lorenzo was forced to climb down. Late in October 1475, Florence bent the knee and accepted Francesco Salviati as Archbishop of Pisa, but not before Pope Sixtus himself had reluctantly made two concessions. He authorised Florence to collect a yearly tax of 6000 florins from the Florentine clergy, to be used exclusively for its annual University expenses; and he accepted the Signoria's right to confirm episcopal appointments in the lands under Florentine rule. Speaking to the Milanese ambassador at this point, Lorenzo took another shot at the Pazzi. He vowed, the diplomat reported, that if those 'Pazzi relatives of his go on making trouble for him . . . thinking that they got the better of him in this affair, then he would make them regret it . . . and if they refuse to live in peace, he would see to it that they recognise themselves in their mistakes.'

The parties had struck a compromise, but the war was not over. They were all too hellishly proud – Pope Sixtus, Lorenzo, the Pazzi, Francesco Salviati, and Count Girolamo. For all of them, too, name and place and riches were on the line, and for the Florentines, life as well. For Lorenzo, there was Florence itself, the Medici house, and the hundreds of Florentine clients who would lose out if he lost. The ambitious Salviati had his own soaring career in sight. Sixtus looked to his pontifical authority and the success of his nepotism. The Pazzi were holding out for their honour and position in the city, the adhesives which held their identity, while also relying on their great banking and commercial contacts abroad. Somewhere too, in the Pazzi cause, however self-serving (though their contemporary Alamanno Rinuccini denied this), there was the republican argument: the demand for a more honest and open polity in Florence. For Count Girolamo, finally, the struggle with Lorenzo was all about the resources needed to expand and hold his upstart principality in Romagna. In view of the quantities of pride in play, none of the sides in question was to forget the humiliations suffered along the way.

Yet all the while the upper-class mores of the age required that appearances be kept up, producing in this case some exemplary letters of a well-turned hypocrisy. Lorenzo, Count Girolamo, and the Pope all got round to saying that they loved each other, or that they saw their close relations according to the metaphor of fathers and sons. Up to the moment of the April Conspiracy itself, Lorenzo had cordial relations, ostensibly, with the Archbishop of Pisa and members of the Pazzi family, not only with Guglielmo, but also with Renato, Messer Jacopo, and some of the others. Since their paths frequently crossed in the main streets and major squares of that small city (see Map 1), their arena was a school for the factitious. They were, after all, capable of lunching together down to their fatal Sunday.

Meanwhile, Lorenzo and the Pazzi tasted at least two other moments of gall. In June 1476, the expiration of a contract ended the Medici Bank's control of the papal alum monopoly, and the franchise now went to the Roman company of Guglielmo and Giovanni de' Pazzi. Papal bankers normally used the monopoly of this cloth-dying mineral to help secure loans to the Holy Father. Nine months later, in March 1477, Lorenzo struck back. Despite the opposition of men in his own immediate circle, he got a bill through Florence's legislative councils, depriving daughters of major inheritances if they had no brothers and were flanked by one or more male cousins. Enacted with the Pazzi specifically in mind, this measure disinherited Giovanni de' Pazzi's wife, Beatrice Borromei, who had expected to inherit her father's large fortune, and the legacy passed out of the family altogether. Seeing that Lorenzo was set on doing egregious harm to the rival house, Giuliano himself was repelled by his brother's role in the passage of this law. The Pazzi loss of the Borromei legacy, however, could touch neither their reputation for hospitality nor the wide reach of their allies, banks, and textile companies. The scene was set for more dire action.

Of the several mysteries remaining, one at least calls for a provisional solution here. Recent study has shown that life in Italian Renaissance cities could be profoundly conformist, even cruelly so, from local neighbourhoods all the way up to 'city hall'. How was it then that the Pazzi, or at least some of them, found the courage to defy Lorenzo? Messer Jacopo, Francesco, and perhaps Renato de' Pazzi all knew, by 1474, that they could count on the support of Pope Sixtus, King Ferrante, the Duke of Urbino, and Count Girolamo. In his confrontation with the Florentine chieftain, Archbishop Salviati was carried impetuously by the knowledge of having the Pope's unwavering support. Residing mostly in Rome, Francesco de' Pazzi was losing touch with the Florentine scene; and being rushed on by his anger and rashness, he overestimated what could be accomplished in Florence. Messer Jacopo, however, was at home, fully in touch with the ebb and flow of Florentine feeling, despite having been edged out of the councils of state. And he, after all, knew everyone, enjoyed an outstanding reputation, and frequently entertained foreign ambassadors – spies for their lords back home. Yet the wealth of the Pazzi, even when joined to their brilliant connections abroad, could not save them from the destructive power of the forty or so men (the inner oligarchy) around Lorenzo.

I suspect that the Pazzi had long nourished a secret modicum of envy, reaching back to the father of its recent fortunes, Andrea di Guglielmino, who worked with Cosimo among the city's Bank Officers and probably ran a Medici enterprise early in the century. Later on, again, he was often to have business dealings with the Medici house, and during his few years in public life was perhaps the only banker in Florence who could call on unlimited credit from the Medici Bank. But of course he was no political godfather à la Cosimo; nor did he build a great, eye-catching palace, treating the city to the visual statement of a princely attitude. Here, in the Medici Palace in 1459, the young visiting prince, Galeazzo Maria Sforza, found every convenience and comfort. Andrea de' Pazzi, *par contre*, though he was never to see it finished, built a chapel of austere geometric harmonies and seems to have worried about his soul. Not that Cosimo neglected his, not at all: he frankly negotiated a papal bull to help atone for his sins of usury, and spent large sums of money on the renovation and décor of several churches and convents. In the end, however, the grandeur of the new Medici Palace was to be his most visible legacy.

If a mild and then increasingly critical view of the Medici went back to Andrea, an astute and perhaps grasping personality, the feeling was cautiously and even secretly passed on to his three sons – Antonio, Piero, and Jacopo: a generation that went on to be talented in its own right, if also, it appears, too proud and eager for eminence in public life. Some of his descendants were drawn to the classics, the educational programme of the humanists, Piero especially so. The young thinker Marsilio Ficino knew them well, because Piero, with his addiction to classical letters, helped to give him a start in life by hiring the youth as a private tutor for his large family in about 1450, when Ficino was 17 or 18 years old. But private criticism of the Medici inside the Pazzi households did not keep them from forging an alliance with the leading house, as attested to by Guglielmo's marriage to Lorenzo's elder sister in 1459. Florentine common sense all but demanded such a union: it was both good business and necessary politics, and the Pazzi, like the Medici, were hard-nosed business folk. Indeed, there seems to have been a previous bond between the rival families. Piero de' Pazzi, reportedly, went out of his way to befriend Lorenzo de' Medici's father; and a well-known personality of the day, the stationer Vespasiano da Bisticci, insists that the two became good friends. Guglielmo, as it happens, was Piero's eldest son.

All the same, as early as 1462, Alessandra Macinghi Strozzi, a keen observer of the Florentine scene, with a ready ear for political rumour and business gossip, noted that a shiver of silent but fierce rivalry ran between the two houses. Such a condition in tiny Florence meant that there was the more reason for them, for the Pazzi especially, to maintain cordial relations, and to put up bridges, such as when the younger men went out hunting together. Alessandra was entering her observations in a letter to one of her sons, then resident in Bruges. On recently meeting Piero de' Pazzi for the first time, he had been greatly impressed and was inclined to do business with him, but Alessandra was seeking to throw cold water on his enthusiasm. Having told him of Piero's 'triumphant' return to Florence from an embassy to France, where he had been knighted by King Louis XI, she proceeded to lodge a warning: 'Remember this, that according to what I hear, those who are with the Medici have always done well, and if with the Pazzi, the opposite, since they are always destroyed. So be advised.'

What on earth was she talking about? Piero seems to have had a good friendship with Lorenzo's father, as claimed by Vespasiano, and the families were linked by a marriage. Moreover, the political record indicated just then not only that the Pazzi were having extraordinary success, but also that they were squarely in the Medici camp. So we must assume that Alessandra was picking up insiders' rumours about hidden matters – gossip issuing from the intimate Medici enclave, from men who knew all about the current strains and jealousies. She was suggesting that in private or offstage wheeling and dealing, men favoured by the Pazzi were less likely to meet with success than those who were doggedly loyal and tied to the Medici. But if this was so, then even the supposed friendship between Piero de' Pazzi and Piero de' Medici was little more than a prodigious masquerade, daily cover for a strong undercurrent of tension between the two houses.

Yet Alessandra's son-in-law Marco Parenti, another cool observer, was greatly drawn to the Pazzi, especially to the two knights, Messer Jacopo and Messer Piero. The latter seems to have been a most attractive and engaging man, and generous to a fault. Marco continued to seek them out, sending on news of their doings to the far-away Strozzi brothers. Describing Piero's grand return to Florence in the early spring of 1462, he noted that all the city's knights, doctors of law, and leading citizens, along with foreign ambassadors and several visiting princes, went out of the city gates to meet him. Piero entered Florence on horseback and proceeded to the government square, where the Lord Priors gave him the flags 'of the People' and 'the Guelf Party', thus acknowledging and confirming his knighthood. Afterwards, a great concourse of citizens went to his house, and so many were allowed to enter, that Piero himself, once inside, could scarcely turn around.

It was after this colourful and popular 'triumph' (her word) that Alessandra, the gossipy recipient of whispers and murmurings, returned three times in a single letter to the menace that hung over the Pazzi. She

told her son that although Piero had entered Florence 'with more magnif-
icence than has been seen for a long time in the entry of a knight, I
wouldn't base a great deal on this, because in Florence appearances are
sometimes one thing and the facts another.' She then capped this half
aphorism with her warning about the Medici as winners and the Pazzi
as losers, returning once again, toward the end of the letter, to a caveat:
Piero 'does not enjoy the reputation you think he does . . . because [in
certain matters] he opposes those who have more power than he does.
He lost more than he gained by this recent trip of his. Let's leave it at
that.'

Six weeks later, on 1 May 1462, the knight Messer Piero de' Pazzi
began his term of office in Florence's highest dignity, Gonfalonier of
Justice, head of the Lord Priors. Alessandra's tell-tale informers could
only have come from the Medici enclave.

CHAPTER SEVEN

April Blood

My Most Illustrious Lords: My brother Giuliano has just been
killed and my government is in the greatest danger. Now is the
time, my lords, to help your servant Lorenzo. Send all the troops
you can with all speed, so that they may be the shield and safety
of my state, just as they have always been. Your servitor, Lorenzo
de' Medici

[Letter to the Lords of Milan, 26 April 1478]

The Setting

THAT YEAR 26 APRIL was the fifth Sunday after Easter, yet something religious lingered in the air. To look around, at any rate,
Florence was a city given to religious observances, home to more than
sixty parish churches, to a host of friaries and convents, and to scores
of pious confraternities. Some of these companies, to punish sin and in
memory of Christ, still came together to engage in a ritual of self-flag-
ellation, and certain prayers honoured the virtues of self-inflicted pain.

Sliced in two by the Arno River, but fully enclosed by gigantic walls
and twelve great gates, Florence had a population of about 42,000 souls,
so that there was at least one parish church for every 680 inhabitants,
not counting all the other places of worship. It was one of the largest
cities in Europe and in those years, no doubt, the most remarkable. On
that Sunday Botticelli was there. Three celebrated Florentines – Dante,
Petrarch, and Boccaccio – had died in the previous century. But here was
Machiavelli, barely nine years old, hard at work on his study of Latin.
Who else was in the city that morning? A legion of obscure Florentines,

to be sure, but also the humanist Poliziano, the twenty-six-year-old Leonardo da Vinci, and one of the scientific thinkers behind Columbus's journey to the New World, Paolo Toscanelli.

The floating dome of the cathedral, imparting an air of serenity, was the first imposing sight spotted by travellers. Next, most likely, they would espy the government palace's soaring belfry, machicolated and poking up like a warning finger. Once in the city, and set on examining the famous Baptistery or the cathedral of Santa Maria del Fiore (St Mary of the Flower), the discerning eye would have picked out a dozen new private palaces, all of them displaying elegant stonework. None however was so big and splendid as Lorenzo de' Medici's (Figure 5), stretching along a wide street, only a minute or two away from the cathedral. Although erected by his grandfather Cosimo, it had been completed less than twenty years before. But an informed pilgrim, knowing that many of the city's sights were indoors and in churches, might have chosen to take an eight-minute walk from the cathedral to the Franciscan church and convent of Santa Croce, to visit the adjoining Pazzi Chapel, a sanctuary of striking geometric harmonies, designed by Brunelleschi and built for one of the richest bankers of the fifteenth century, Andrea di Guglielmino de' Pazzi, a family name that would haunt the year 1478.

For that Sunday in the early morning, in a Florence expecting no such thing, scores of secretly-armed men were preparing to overthrow the nine-man council at the head of its republican government, seen by many, however, as already on its way to being a Renaissance tyranny. They expected to snatch real power away from the hands of the Medici. But first they had to kill Lorenzo, a supremely talented politician, and his handsome younger brother Giuliano. The conspirators had lodged that night, both in town and country, with members of two Florentine families, many of the visitors passing as attendants in the entourage of the young Cardinal of San Giorgio and of the Archbishop of Pisa. A few other participants in the plot may have been on their own in several Florentine inns, such as the Inn of the Bell or the Hotel at the Crown, which were located in the neighbourhood of the city's brothels, a few minutes' walk from the cathedral in one direction and the fortress-like government palace in the other. These two points, great church and palace, were the target sites of the action. A papal mercenary, the Count of

Fig. 5 The Medici Palace.

Montesecco, had also arrived in the city that morning, at the head of 'thirty mounted crossbowmen and fifty foot soldiers, all as beautifully attired and handsome as any company that had ever been seen, claiming that they had come from Imola to accompany Pope Sixtus's nephew [the Cardinal of San Giorgio] back to Rome'. If suspicion possessed any man in Florence that morning, one like so many other Sunday mornings, the perception never came to light.

Lorenzo had not made an Easter trip to Rome, as he had been expected to, or the attempted assassination would have taken place in the Holy City. His enemies had been planning the assault for months and had eagerly waited for him, hoping that he would journey to Rome and seek to heal his sharp differences with Pope Sixtus IV. Driven by the fear of discovery and with time running out, they next fixed the action for 19 April. The expected site? Lorenzo's own villa in the low hills just north of Florence, though in the diocese of Fiesole, where he was to offer a luncheon banquet for the Pope's nephew: a perfect arrangement for his enemies, because La Loggia, the main Pazzi villa at Montughi, lay in the same hills. But when Giuliano, feeling ill, failed to turn up for the lunch, the conspirators had suddenly to abort their proceedings. If one of the brothers survived the assault, the Mediceans would close ranks around him and have the staying power to foil the attempted *coup*. A double murder was the only way. So in the course of that Fiesolan afternoon, it dawned on the Archbishop of Pisa, and one or two banker friends, that on the next day they must send a messenger to Lorenzo, informing him that the Cardinal longed to visit the Medici Palace in Florence, to see the family's *objets d'art*. Proud of the *palazzo* and the collection, Lorenzo at once invited them all to lunch there on the following Sunday, along with the ambassadors from Naples, Milan, Ferrara, and some of the city's most honoured knights. His relations with the Pope were fearfully strained; the young Cardinal was a papal blood relation with the credentials of an ambassador; high hospitality was diplomacy; and Lorenzo, in matters of courtesy, was a match for any man.

Everything, then, was set for 26 April. The parties agreed to meet in the cathedral, Santa Maria del Fiore, just before High Mass, after which all would go on together to the Medici Palace for a banquet, along with a company of Florentine knights and other dignitaries; and once again it was expected that Giuliano would honour the Cardinal by his presence.

On the appointed morning, however, having come into the city from La Loggia, the Pazzi villa, the Cardinal and his retainers went directly to Lorenzo's house, where he changed from his riding clothes into his high clerical robes. Some commanding figure in his train, one with a military eye (the Count of Montesecco?), had clearly chosen to begin the action with a swift inspection of the palace. Already waiting for the Cardinal in the cathedral, Lorenzo was informed of his surprising arrival and he at once doubled back to the house, soon running into his guest near the palace's great entrance. Host and guest then returned to the cathedral – Mass had been delayed for them – moving by now amidst a numerous company and crowding the Via de' Martelli (aka Via Larga) as they proceeded. The Archbishop of Pisa, the Cardinal's brother, the Count of Montesecco, and certain members of the Pazzi and Salviati families were also present, and all were flanked by servants and other companions.

At some point the plotters again discovered that Giuliano would not be lunching with them, and a dramatic change of plans, now far more urgent, was again forced on them. They feared that an additional company of crossbowmen might already be approaching Florence and that news of this would streak through the city. Time had run out. The double murder must take place in the cathedral, which entailed a further complication, for the Count of Montesecco, the designated assassin, refused to spill blood in that sacred ground. Whereupon two priests, already alerted and armed, and clearly less scrupulous than the hit man, were pressed in as replacements. Knowing everything, the Archbishop and Messer Jacopo de' Pazzi also knew, therefore, that their presence at High Mass would have to be cut short.

When the entire party finally entered the cathedral, they broke up into separate groups. Mass commenced at last. And now, in one major but possibly fanciful account (Machiavelli's), discovering that Giuliano was nowhere to be seen, Francesco de' Pazzi and Bernardo Baroncelli went back to the Medici Palace, where, finding him indisposed, they talked him into walking up the street to Mass with them. Jesting and touching him on their return to the cathedral, one of them hugged him playfully, but really so as to find out whether or not he was wearing a hidden breastplate. Soon enough the appointed moment would reveal that he was wearing no leather or armour under his linen that morning.

The Assault

THE SIGNAL FOR the deed came at a moment in High Mass, possibly the elevation of the Host, though some said the priest's communion, while others fixed on the words, *Ite missa est*. Memories varied. Witnesses claimed that the first bloody thrust, backed by the exclamation, 'Here, traitor!', was delivered by Bernardo Bandini Baroncelli, a man from an old banking family allied to the Pazzi. Giuliano de' Medici staggered back a few paces, his chest punctured, as a second assailant, Francesco de' Pazzi, went at him with a fury of dagger blows. When the tottering man collapsed in that part of the church, not far from the door nearest to the Via de' Servi, he was in no condition to catch sight of his brother, Lorenzo the Magnificent, who was some twenty to thirty yards away. Giuliano's lifeless body was to show a dozen to nineteen wounds. Again, memories clashed but were curiously precise.

Cries, shouts, and the slap of racing feet erupted in that cavernous space, as seasoned politicians, ambassadors, servants, citizens, women, priests, and children ran about, bolted from the church, rushed into neighbouring houses or wherever their panic led them. Was it an earthquake? Some worshippers feared that Brunelleschi's dome was about to come crashing down, while a few bold and curious spirits pressed in closer to the melée, nearer to those brandishing knives and swords, trying to see what was happening.

Minutes before, two priests had edged their way up behind Lorenzo, who was still moving about on the southern side, by the old sacristy, chatting with friends. The two carried concealed weapons. When the signal came, one of them lunged at Lorenzo from behind, grabbing him by a shoulder, either to steady himself or to turn him round for the stabbing. Instead of which, receiving only a slight wound on the neck, just under the right ear, Lorenzo bounded forward, drawing his mantle up to his left arm and shoulder, then spun around, short sword in hand. He parried another thrust or two, before his retreat was covered by friends and defenders, as he jumped over a low wooden rail into the octagonal choir and crossed in front of the high altar, to seek the protection of the north sacristy. Francesco Nori – one of the top managers of the Medici Bank and a close friend – stepped in to help defend his employer, but he was mortally wounded when Baroncelli's long knife got him in the pit of the stomach. Giuliano's angry assassins had gone after Lorenzo too, despite the fact that the banker, Pazzi, was already limping, having been stabbed in the thigh either by one of his own servants or by himself, in the frenzy to kill Giuliano. The other priest, wielding a sword and small buckler, was fought off by a Medici servant, but in the fight a young man from the Cavalcanti family, one of Lorenzo de' Medici's companions, was badly wounded in one arm. The bleeding Francesco Nori, quickly dragged into the north sacristy, died a few minutes later.

In all that din, witnesses noticed two other strange occurrences. Guglielmo de' Pazzi had been talking to Lorenzo de' Medici, when all at once he began to scramble about crazily, terrified and screaming out his innocence, vowing that he was no traitor, that he was sorry, and that he knew nothing about the exploding events. Raffaele Sansoni Riario, the Cardinal of San Giorgio (Genoa), a seventeen-year-old law student at the University of Pisa, also cringed in terror near the high altar and went on kneeling, praying perhaps even more fervently, until he was protectively surrounded by the cathedral canons and drawn over to the old sacristy. Surprise and pandemonium colluded with the assassins. Baroncelli, Francesco de' Pazzi, and the two priests, along with more than a score of servants and others, all managed to flee from the scene and rush through the city streets – even Francesco, with his pierced leg shedding blood along the way. The Pazzi houses were less than two minutes away from the cathedral's southern doors.

Once Lorenzo and his companions were safely in the north (new) sacristy, they locked its massive bronze doors, letting no one in. There they waited in terror, we must assume, instinctively whispering or straining to catch the sounds outside, as the vast nave was quickly deserted. Even as silence enveloped them, they made no move to emerge from their vestry, afraid of what might be waiting silently on the other side of the doors. When it occurred to them that the wound on Lorenzo's neck had been possibly touched by poison, the young Antonio Ridolfi bravely sucked at it to draw out the fluids. Confused and verging on hysteria, Lorenzo kept asking about his brother Giuliano. He had not seen the stabbing. But no one had an answer for him, or none was willing to offer it. Did they mark the flight of minutes? Was it an hour?

Unknown people began to pound on the bronze doors, claiming to be friends. One of Lorenzo's companions, the glamorous Sigismondo della Stufa, climbed the spiral staircase to the organ gallery to spy out the scene. Looking down, he saw the unmoving Giuliano, sprawled in blood, though from where he stood it must have seemed a shadow. He considered the men beating on the sacristy doors, and seeing the anxious faces of friends and relatives – Tornabuoni, Martelli, and others – gave the signal for them to be opened. The newcomers pressed in, armed to the teeth; and now, greatly enlarged, the company hurried out of the cathedral to the Medici Palace, not more than 165 metres away, to find temporary safety and a great cache of additional weapons. Rushing through the nave, they went around the southern side of the choir to the west and then swung north, to exit at the first side door, in order to avoid any chance of Lorenzo's getting a glimpse of his brother's body. The classical scholar, Lorenzo's protégé Poliziano, moving on the fringes of the hurrying group as they emerged from the north sacristy, caught sight of something so appalling, Giuliano (Figure 6) sprawled in profuse gore, that he hurried on. He could not bear to stop and cover the remains of his friend and informal student, the darling of the young Mediceans.

Others at Mass that morning had noticed that the well-known Florentine knight and banker, Messer Jacopo de' Pazzi, accompanied by a group of attendants, was also present and looking to see that the young Cardinal Sansoni Riario was being well attended. Most of the servants and aides who stood around, some of them with weapons at their sides and in the shorter dress of the princely courts, seemed to belong to the Cardinal's train. Another dignitary, the Archbishop of Pisa, was also briefly in evidence, but being a noted Florentine and having just arrived in the city, he let it be known that he had to hurry off to pay a visit to his ailing mother. And for the time being, at least, no one thought

Fig. 6 Bust of Giuliano de' Medici, by Andrea del Verrocchio.

anything more about his brief appearance, although he was a prime actor in the encircling drama, as he made his way to the government palace, little more than a three-minute walk to the south of the cathedral, flanked by a company of about thirty armed men, many of them strangers, exiles from Perugia, especially hired for the occasion.

In view of his rank and raiment, the Archbishop had little trouble entering the great battlemented structure. Some of his men remained below, where they expected to overwhelm the guardsmen, with a view to seizing control of that level and the floor above, as the prelate and most of his other attendants went up the grand staircase. He sent word to the current head of Florentine government, the Gonfalonier of Justice, Cesare Petrucci, to say that he had a messsage for him from the Pope. Once upstairs, the churchman proceeded alone to a meeting with Petrucci, and he began with a story about how the Pope had promised to favour his son in Rome. He was playing for time, but began to run out of words and to stammer badly, becoming uneasy and darting repeated, nervous glances at the entrance door. They were on the top main floor. Quickly sensing that something was very wrong, the Gonfalonier called out for guardsmen, and the Archbishop made an embarrassed retreat. Petrucci followed him, only to be taken by surprise at the unexpected sight of Jacopo Bracciolini, a well-known writer and classical scholar, one of Salviati's group, who was wildly out of place there just then and must have unsheathed a weapon, because the Gonfalonier caught him by the hair and threw him to the floor, to the custody of an arriving guard. No other armed followers now turned up to assist and protect the Archbishop, his main group of attendants having been trapped on the same floor, in the chancery chamber at the northern end. Here, the room's massive doors, fitted with self-locking devices or springbolts, had mysteriously locked them in when they were swung shut. The government palace was a honeycomb of rooms and corridors, and when the many doors were locked, groups of strangers could be easily divided and isolated.

There was a rising commotion all around. About fifty servants, guardsmen, and aides moved about in the palace that day. But once the Archbishop and the humanist had been taken prisoner, and the rest of their company were trapped between doors or down below, the Gonfalonier and the Lord Priors picked up whatever arms they could lay their hands on, including kitchen spits, ordered the alarm bells to be rung and, locking doors behind them, hurried up to the fortified gallery of the high tower to defend themselves and the government of Florence. A peaceful city was suddenly up in arms.

When the great government bells were hammered at about noon, sounding the alarm, and word of the attempt to kill the Medici raced through Florence, the outcome remained uncertain for several hours. The first voices reported that Lorenzo and Giuliano had been killed, with the result that 'everyone held back, not quite knowing what to do', and with the likely intent of throwing their lot in with the winning side. Having witnessed the scene in the cathedral, one eminent citizen, the knight Piero Vespucci, believing that the Medici were finished, sided briefly with the conspirators and helped one of their friends to escape – Napoleone Franzesi, who was also, as it happens, one of Vespucci's dearest friends and a long-time familiar in the household of Guglielmo de' Pazzi.

Now the most public part of the plot unfolded, involving scores of men. A former head of Florentine government, the chief of the Pazzi clan, Messer Jacopo, led a troop of fifty to one hundred mercenaries into the government square and the adjoining streets, aiming to occupy the Lord Priors' palace and to incite citizens to mutiny against the Medici. He would at once have been recognised by his co-citizens, as he yelled out 'People and Liberty!' – the traditional cry for a revolt against a dictatorial party or faction. But since Archbishop Salviati had failed to take the palace, there was a stand-off around the entrance, where the hired insurgents tried to break in, to occupy it and to release the other conspirators trapped inside. They were held off by a rain of missiles, cast down on them by the guardsmen and Lord Priors high up in the machicolation, just under the belfry. Archbishop Salviati, a band of Perugian exiles, and the humanist Bracciolini were already their prisoners in the chambers below.

Few contemporaries seem to have noted the flow of time. In the tumult and gathering fear, the men engaged had their minds fixed on the action. Others later on, relying on hearsay, drew fickle or partisan memory into their accounts, with the result that considerable disagreement ensued over the details of numbers, times, actions, and places. But the whole event was so entirely seen through the spectacles of party and passion, that the dominant view – Medicean from the start – must always be held as suspect, especially because winners, in controlling the official record, also tend to have the final say.

During the first two or three hours of the attempted *coup*, there seem to have been no armed devotees of the Medicean establishment out in the streets, standing up to the insurgents or trying to block their way.

Why not, in a city so allegedly fond of Lorenzo and the Medici? Once the alarm was sounded, to be heard throughout the city and neighbouring countryside, the chief police magistrate and judge, the Podestà, should have ridden into the government square with a troop of thirty men, as his office required. But we have no reports of an engagement there with Messer Jacopo's armed followers; and with the Priors and palace guardsmen raining great stones down from above into that wide space, it is more likely that the Podestà and his men kept well away from the area, or waited wisely for reinforcements, while also keeping a sharp eye out for the outcome of the attempted *coup*. They were not in any case Florentines, but rather outsiders, as was customary: foreigners serving in Florence on a six-month appointment.

One of the diarists of the day, a Medicean named Giusto Giusti, was in the cathedral at the moment of the planned *coup*. He reacted by rushing to the Medici Palace and hanging about there to help defend it, as did Lorenzo's other armed supporters during the first hours:

> I was in Santa Liperata [the cathedral] just then, and when I saw
> Giuliano de' Medici dead, I ran to Lorenzo de' Medici's house to help
> as much as I could, and I went up to the room for storing arms . . .
> here too came many of his partisans to take arms. I helped to arm
> quite a few of them, and I also armed myself with a cuirass, helmet,
> shield, and a sword, and I stood on guard at the second street exit,
> along with some of Lorenzo's other supporters. . . . There I stayed
> on an empty stomach till 21 hours [about 5:00pm]. Then I disarmed
> beside the room of the kitchen maid, leaving [the arms] . . . with her,
> and she gave me back my cloak, hood, and gown, and I went home
> to eat.

The diarist's colourless turns of phrase here mute the alarm in the city, and his hunger overcomes any pressing worry about reported cries and terror in and around the government square. Perhaps he knew that matters were now utterly out of his hands, though it has to be said that standing outside the Medici Palace, in a borrowed helmet, he and the other citizens would have been no intimidating threat to a band of professional soldiers.

When Jacopo de' Pazzi and his men shouted 'People and Liberty!', how long was it before pedestrians or people at windows began to return the shout, 'Palle, Palle!', in reference to the Medici escutcheon and meaning 'I am for the Medici!'? No source tells us. And Jacopo must have waited anxiously, then despairingly, for a twist of fortune — for the expected arrival in Florence of papal troops, captained by Giovan Francesco da Tolentino from the east and Lorenzo Giustini from the south, two other participants in the plot. But having somehow got wind of the failure of the *coup*, they turned back, unwilling to risk their soldiers.

Francesco de' Pazzi was meant to join his uncle Jacopo in the ride around the government square and connecting streets, calling for a revolt against the Medici. Less than a minute's ride from the square, their houses had adjoining stables. But he was back at home instead, nursing his horribly wounded thigh, as Jacopo, in the course of his fatal ride and repelled from the government palace, was suddenly accosted by his brother-in-law, Giovanni Serristori, and urged to flee. Losing all hope and stricken with fear, amidst the hammering sound of the city's emergency bells, Jacopo now got out of Florence with his men, fleeing by way of the eastern La Croce Gate, which had been seized by the insurgents.

How it happened exactly that the two captains, Tolentino and Giustini, seemed to get word of the failed plot, and therefore slowed their march to Florence, or were actually repulsed by armed bands of peasants, is a question that has never been addressed. It is clear, however, that the answer had everything to do with the city's security arrangements. Once the alarm had been sounded in Florence, that urgent sound also passed into the Florentine countryside, where local residents identified it and passed it on by means of their church and village bells, to be transmitted again to ever more distant hamlets, market towns, and fortified sites. So that within two or three hours most of Florentine Tuscany had been alerted, and local men, scuttering to lookout points, began to scan the horizons for rushing horsemen and suspicious movement. Unless there was a large invading army, peasants would gather to offer resistance. But the alarm bells were also a signal for the two captains: a sign that the plot had failed and that the government, probably still in control, would be able to deal with the small number of conspirators inside the city. Wisely, they delayed their advance and finally turned away.

Early in the afternoon, Lorenzo de' Medici got an urgent letter off to the Sforza lords of Milan, imploring military assistance and expressing his fear and uncertainty. The Lord Priors were soon in touch with Lorenzo, and later that day, zeroing in on the Pazzi family and already determined to strike at them in every possible way, they dispatched a curt letter to Alberto Villani, a Florentine captain on the high seas, somewhere off the coast of Tuscany. Having learned that his vessel was loaded with a cargo of Pazzi goods, they ordered him, on pain of dire penalties, to make for the Port of Pisa, where the cargo would be sequestrated and put under Florentine seal, and Villani would be rewarded. Was this because the Pazzi were known to have major commercial debts to pay off, or was it rather that the family had already been tried, judged, and sentenced?

By now the defenders of the Medici began to seek vengeance and reprisal, and the cavalcading events moved swiftly on to the next stage, taking in a new set of names, details, numbers, and passions. The sacrilegious assault at High Mass, ending in the murder of two men, had triggered amazement and terror, in a rush of feeling then relayed into the streets by the hammering sound of the alarm bell and the sight of mounted mercenaries. Over the course of the next three or four hours, support for Lorenzo slowly swelled, partly because of the Florentine fear of outsiders (*forenses*). All that foreign garb and all those unknown faces: they looked as though they were about to take over the city, even if under the banner of Messer Jacopo de' Pazzi and with the strange intervention of the Archbishop of Pisa, a man well-known in Florence and from the distinguished Salviati lineage.

Retribution

THE BACKLASH OF retaliation on that bloody Sunday began in the late afternoon. Informed of Giuliano's death and the murder of Francesco Nori, the Lord Priors called in the Eight, the much-feared office for rooting out and prosecuting political crime. They questioned the prisoners: Archbishop Salviati, the humanist Jacopo Bracciolini, and then the wounded Francesco de' Pazzi, 'small in body but great in spirit', who was seized naked inside the Pazzi Palace and rushed to the Priors' presence. Legal niceties were brushed aside. Emergency lifted the power of the Priors and the Eight above the ordinary rule of law. Statutes were suspended. A swift show of justice had to be made.

When the chancery doors were finally opened, the Perugians trapped inside were immediately killed or briefly held, and then all were thrown from the high windows, crashing down into the grand square below. The bodies were stripped of their clothes and hacked apart by a gathering crowd. A halter around his neck, Bracciolini, the son of a famous Florentine man of letters, was thrown from a top window overlooking the Piazza della Signoria and left to hang there. An hour or two later, the bleeding Francesco, who in his nakedness had proudly refused to utter a confessing word, despite threats and violence, was hanged. His gibbet, also on the main top floor, was the third window from the Loggia de' Lanzi. It was the turn next of the Archbishop of Pisa, who reportedly made a complete confession, although no record of it has come down. He too was put out to dangle, in a brute ceremony of degradation, made all the worse by his exalted clerical rank. His brother Jacopo Salviati was then hanged from the second window, and behind him the executioners also strung out an important (though unidentified) cleric. The mullions of the first window were to hold five hanging men, one of them a priest. And from a window on the northern façade, another Salviati, one of the Archbishop's cousins, was hanged. The Signoria and the Eight were determined to show every one of them in a posture criminal and vile. To point up the horrendous nature of the plot, as well as to offer an immediate display of justice, they converted the heart of the city into the official place of execution, ignoring the appointed gallows near the Gate of Justice, just outside Florence's great eastern walls.

In his account of the conspiracy, never calling him anything but the Pisan 'director' or 'leader' (*praesul*), Poliziano relates that when Archbishop Salviati was dropped from the window that also held Francesco's naked body, he came to rest alongside it. But he alone goes on to say that the most astonishing thing then happened, which, if true, must soon have been on every Florentine tongue. Whether from rage, desperation, or an act of last communion with a fellow conspirator, the Archbishop suddenly bit so fiercely into Francesco, that even after he had been strangled by the rope, his teeth remained locked on to the breast of his erstwhile companion. A weirdly appropriate act of cannibalism, the deed somehow caught and amplified the violence that had been saved up for the Medici brothers, relatives of the Pazzi by marriage and even distantly related to the Salviati. If the act was nothing more than an involuntary spasm, it would still have sent a shivering resonance into the popular consciousness.

Among the Perugians killed were five brothers, all of them exiles who had been offered the bait of a swift return to Perugia, if the plot succeeded; and now all five went to their death as by a single stroke. Later on that evening, going into the piazza, Poliziano saw a great mass of torn bodies scattered helter-skelter in that decorous space – the result, he asserted, of popular devotion to the Medici and outrage over the blood spilled in the cathedral. The enquiring historian, however, is bound to ask how it happened that there were no guardsmen about that evening to prevent bands of Florentines from trooping around the city, while dragging about the limbs of dismembered men or carrying them aloft on the points of swords and lances? It can only be that the Medicean regime approved of the spectacle. That day alone saw the execution or vengeful slaughter of sixty to eighty captives, many of them hanged from the windows of the Bargello, the neighbouring fortress of the city's chief magistrate and police official.

On Monday, the 27th, eight of Montesecco's foot soldiers and several of his knights were also hanged from government windows. Later that day, their sustaining ropes were cut and the bodies were allowed to fall into the piazza, where they remained all night. The next morning, adding a distinctive Florentine touch to his description, a diarist reported that 'the bodies were fitted into the casements of the shops of notaries at the palace of the Podestà, and there, bare skin and upright, they were left to lean, so that they looked like men depicted or portrayed to look alive, because they were as stiff and naked as the day they were born.'

Guglielmo de' Pazzi, brother to the conspirator Francesco but brother-in-law to Lorenzo de' Medici, the man who had howled out his innocence in the cathedral, saved himself by finding sanctuary in the

Medici Palace, where his wife Bianca seems to have begged for his life. He was quickly banished from Florence. Jacopo Bracciolini's two brothers, one of them a cathedral canon, were also expelled from the city.

When the Cardinal of San Giorgio, Raffaele Sansoni Riario, was able to emerge from the cathedral's southern sacristy, two members of the Eight, together with a number of armed guards, accompanied him to the government palace, although he was taken there in some danger to his life, because a maddened crowd was ready to assault him too. In the event, some of his men were seized, including pages, two priests and one or two boy choristers. They were all murdered, brutally disfigured, and then stripped naked to mark their ignominy. The Cardinal himself was held hostage for nearly six weeks, his life used as a bargaining stake by the Florentines in the effort to soften the reprisals threatened by the foreign supporters of the conspirators.

Over the next four days, all but one of the Pazzi brothers and cousins were arrested. Antonio, Bishop of Sarno and Mileto, and nephew to Messer Jacopo, was condemned in absentia to be confined in his diocese for life; but holding an informal place as a counsellor to the King of Naples, he simply carried on with his life in Rome and the kingdom of Naples, well beyond the reach of Florence and Lorenzo. Renato, however, one of his brothers, was promptly executed. Although no proof of the accusations brought against the whole family, or even against the Bishop, was ever offered, all the Pazzi were accused of having connived in the conspiracy. Guilt could still be seen as tribal, particularly when rulers wished it to be so. And if it be said that Guglielmo de' Pazzi's hysterical cries in the cathedral, proclaiming his innocence, betokened some prior knowledge of things, it could as reasonably be argued that knowing all about the uses of tribal guilt, and knowing also that the hatred between Lorenzo and some of the Pazzi brothers was mutual, his instincts had told him that he too would be held responsible. Whereupon he rushed wisely north to the Medici Palace, rather than south to the Pazzi compound.

Since the Pazzi men were all charged with having known about the plot, their alleged crime was that they had held their tongues: a silence tantamount to treason. Locally imprisoned at first, Bishop Antonio's brothers — Galeotto, Giovanni, Andrea, and Niccolò — were afterwards all dispatched to the fortified tower of the ancient town of Volterra, barely escaping with their lives in the fiercely murderous climate of that week. The young Galeotto was only fifteen or sixteen years old. Lionardo, who was fourteen and intended for holy orders, was banished; and so too was Giovanni's son Raffaele, then a mere seven years of age. Universally considered the wisest and most esteemed of Messer Piero's sons, Renato, the eldest brother, had gone out to his villa in the Mugello, Medici country, on the 25th of April and was therefore absent from Florence on that bloody Sunday. Getting news of the plot, he disguised himself in peasant dress, hoping to flee to safety, but was caught on the 27th. Here, according to Guicciardini, was a man too well-regarded, too well-liked, and too clever to be allowed to live, and so he certainly had to be eliminated, if his patriline was to be erased from the pages of history. He was hanged – mockingly – in his peasant's costume, a skimpy grey gown of coarse wool, but wearing boots and spurs. At the same time, Florentines circulated a story alleging that Renato had privately opposed the conspiracy by arguing that Lorenzo de' Medici was already so mired in shameful debt, that he would soon end in disgrace and ruin. Indeed, it was said, he held that the Pazzi should lend him as much money as he wanted, even if it hurt them, as this would only hasten his destruction.

In the late afternoon or evening of the 26th, men had appeared on the Via Larga, outside Lorenzo's door, dragging a pair of legs, carrying a head on the point of a lance, 'and another part with an arm, borne aloft on a spit' – the remains of an aide to the Archbishop of Pisa, a priest caught in the government square, where he had been beheaded and quartered, and his parts then lifted high to the cry of 'Death to the traitors!' Over the next three or four days, there were 'so many deaths', Machiavelli observed, 'that the streets were filled with the parts of men'. Fond of drama and good stories, the author of *The Prince* was a fabulist himself, but there can be no doubt that for some days the people of Florence were treated to a theatre of hideous sights and sounds.

Captured in flight sometime between 28 April and 1 May, the Count of Montesecco made his soldier's confession on 4 May, and that evening, at the doors of the Bargello, the criminal-court building, he was decapitated, thus being spared the bodily indignities reserved for the government square. The two priests who had agreed to murder Lorenzo, Maffei and Bagnone, had found shelter with the Benedictine monks in the Badia Fiorentina, around the corner from the cathedral itself and across the street from the enclave of Pazzi mansions. They were finally seized on 3 May, and their Benedictine protectors would have been attacked and battered by a crowd, but for the arresting guardsmen and intervention of cooler heads. All the same, on the way to the government palace, the two men were beaten and mutilated: they were turned over, without ears and noses, to the Priors and Eight, to be hanged, like the Archbishop, from a window facing the spacious government piazza.

With one exception, however, there was soon to be a notable change in mood, as the governing elite regained its bearings. The middle and late 1470s were a time of rising food prices and famine. In this setting, the ready spilling of blood, the swelling fury against the conspirators, and the lewd flaunting of torn body parts, must have brought home to the ruling group the sense that the energies of the over-wrought mob, being so unstable, might well take a nasty turn and go against the 'good' sort of upper-class families. After all, there were armed men among the angry demonstrators, and the wild sacking of the Pazzi and certain Salviati houses had only just been prevented. The great wealth of the Pazzi had to be set aside for their likely creditors and the government's coffers, not abandoned to a rabid crowd. Tensions were common in walled-in Florence, roused not so much by differences between the well-fed and the hungry (though these could be exploited), as by the Medicean system of government, with its cleavage between the webs of political privilege on the one side and the many political outcasts on the other.

The destiny of Messer Jacopo de' Pazzi's body was to crown the visual horrors and to make for the exception noted above.

Word of the events of 26 April went out to Florentine lands in every direction, and armed men also fanned out swiftly into the eastern territories, in pursuit of Messer Jacopo, the Count of Montesecco, and their scurrying mercenaries. To confuse pursuers, the fleeing men split up, but on the 27th, after a bloody encounter and some loss of life, Jacopo and his few men were caught by local peasants in a mountain hamlet, Castagno di San Godenzo. Fearing the wrath and disgrace awaiting him in Florence, Jacopo offered his captors seven pieces of gold, says Poliziano, begging them to let him commit suicide. The offer was spurned and he was given a beating. Unable to walk, he was turned over to the guardsmen of the Eight and hauled back to Florence on the 28th, where he reportedly made a confession, again unrecorded, stressing both his belief in the unfailing good luck of Francesco de' Pazzi, who had talked him into the plot, and his bitterness over the family's loss of the rich Borromei legacy. This large inheritance would have gone to the wife of one of his nephews, but, as we saw earlier, Lorenzo de' Medici had stepped in and 'godfathered' a new law, targeting the Pazzi, the legal consequences of which transferred the Borromei estate to other hands.

Consistent with Messer Jacopo's reputation for blasphemy, and promoted by Lorenzo's innermost circle, a rumour was quickly spread, claiming that the 'traitor' had 'commended his soul to the devil' as he was dying. Wearing hose, a short purple gown, and a white leather belt that looked like a handkerchief, he was hanged from the same central window which had held Francesco de' Pazzi and the biting Archbishop two days before. Unlike many others, however, his body was not cut down and allowed to fall into the square, to be fought over by soldiers in their eagerness to lay hands on expensive items of dress, such as doublets and hose. In the week following the aborted plot, men had come to blows, quarrelling over the possession of a fancy pair of men's stockings, displaying, as it happens, a Pazzi family device.

It was afterwards claimed that Jacopo was allowed to confess and receive extreme unction, and so he was buried at Santa Croce, in the family crypt. But his name for impiety was now deliberately broadcast and the charge fanned up, the more to arouse the populace against the Pazzi. Four days of heavy rains had come, and soon men began to pour into Florence from the countryside, arguing that their cereal crop would be damaged and that the rain was a sign of God's displeasure, caused by the fact that an evil and irreligious man had been buried in sacred ground. With a mob threatening to break into Jacopo's tomb, the friars of the convent of Santa Croce, with the authority of the Eight or the Lord Priors, had the body exhumed and carted out for reburial in unconsecrated ground, in a site just inside the city walls, between the Gate at the Cross and the Gate of Justice, the nearest exit point to the gallows. Poliziano claimed that the sun now began to shine again, but even so all was not well. Eerie sounds, it was said, were haunting the new burial site, as if the ground there had turned into a place of demons.

Two afternoons later, a 'great throng of boys' went out to the eastern walls to dig up the corpse again. There can be no doubt that knowing busybodies and agitators moved about among the 'boys'. The Eight in Florence, like the Ten in Venice, employed spies and informers, and more nervously so after the bloodbath of 26 April and the days following. The affairs of Messer Jacopo's body now passed from the concerns of peasants to the hands and contempt of city boys. They knew where to go and what they could get away with, and so worked themselves up that they threatened to stone to death anyone who got in their way. With a nod to the classics, Poliziano says, poetically, that they seemed driven by the fires of the Furies.

Jacopo had been buried with the fatal noose still around his neck; hence no one, it seems, had been allowed to prepare or dress the body. (So had he, in fact, been allowed to confess and to have the last rites?) Catching hold of the corpse by the rope, the boys – outraged in the name of the Medici? – dragged it about all over the city, to the accompaniment of insults and shouts of mockery. It was a dance of death. Now and then a few of them would run up ahead, playing the role of guardsmen, demanding that the streets be cleared for the arrival of a great and distinguished knight. Some aimed sticks and blows at the cadaver, unmindful of the stink. 'And it [the macabre farce] was thought most extraordinary,' adds a contemporary witness, Luca Landucci, 'first because children are usually afraid of death and then because the stench was so terrible that no one could get near the corpse.' Jacopo had now been dead for three weeks, from 28 April to about 20 May. 'Don't be late,' the boys would call out to the cadaver, 'a crowd of citizens is expecting you in the Piazza of the Signori.' Prevented from entering that piazza, but determined to go on exhibiting their humour and enjoying their howls of glee, they yanked and pulled 'Jacopo' to his own palazzo, where they banged his head on the door, while calling out, 'Who's in there? Who's inside? What, is there no one here to receive the master and his entourage?'

That afternoon, finally, they worked their way south to the river with their ghastly hostage, moving up stream a bit, and then dumped it from the bridge at Rubiconte, now the Ponte alle Grazie, into the rushing waters of the Arno. As the corpse floated downstream, crowds of people rushed to the bridges to watch it flow past. A day or two later, near Brossi, boys again pulled it out of the water, hung it up on a willow tree, and beat it as though they were beating a carpet, then cast it back into the Arno, to let it continue its grotesque journey down river, under the bridges of Pisa, and out to the open sea.

The travels of Messer Jacopo's body end here, but its fate, surely for years, was to echo in the Florentine imagination. In the blossoming plan to degrade the name and memory of the Pazzi family, no more immediate way could have been found than this, the jeering desecration of the house's head and elder, or rather of his remains, in a city that teemed with religious confraternities, one of whose capital purposes was to see to the proper death, burial, and salvation of members.

The Legal Assault

WITHIN A DAY or two of the ambush in the cathedral, the government had unleashed a campaign against the Pazzi, animated by Lorenzo and the men around him. They set out to annihilate the family, not only by seizing all their liquid assets, merchandise, houses, and landed estates, but also by seeking to erase the signs, name, and very memory of the lineage, except as a line cursed and vile (*nisi per ignominiam*). In Roman law, one of the ancient penalties for crimes against the emperor or the State was the *damnatio memoriae*: the name of the offender was expunged from wherever it appeared in any public document or monument, the purpose being to efface all memory of the culprit. Now a similar but more sweeping penalty, remembered by lawyers and the new classical scholarship, was imposed on the great banking rivals and would-be assassins of the Medici.

The Priors and the Eight would press investigators to make every effort, first of all, to get at the complete wealth of the Pazzi. Florentine bankers and tradesmen were keen account keepers; and so all Pazzi banking and business ledgers suddenly fell subject to government seizure.

These papers would provide lists of debtors, as well as the names of Pazzi partners and associates in trade and banking. Florentine tax and treasury officials had detailed inventories of all their properties in Florentine Tuscany, farms as well as buildings, and a complete record of their credits and investments in Florence's government debt (the Monte). Long before the final verdict and sentence issued against them on 4 August 1478, officials set out to sequester or sell off all Pazzi assets and possessions, including even their household goods and chattels. Already on 5 May, nine days after the plot, horses and mules went up for public sale. Then on 1 June, using the wide premises of Florence's Mint (*Zecca*) as their showcase and sales warehouse, the officials in charge put up for auction Pazzi clothing, furniture, linens, pictures, and other household goods, along with the confiscated chattels of their confederates (the implicated Salviati and Bracciolini), the lot adding up to such a massive array of items for sale that they filled the Zecca 'from one side to the other'. In this symbolic extension of the Pazzi, with their personal effects put out on show as wares for sale to the higest bidder, they were configured as traitors and bankrupts, the most dishonourable of civil conditions.

On 23 May, four weeks after the assault in the cathedral, the Medicean oligarchy enacted a new law, spelling out its intent.

All surviving members of the Pazzi lineage, including distant cousins, had to change their surname and coat of arms within six months, and then register the changes with the Eight, or become 'rebels' *ipso facto*, despite the warrant in statutory law, allowing citizens to kill rebels on sight and with impunity. Again, every public sign or symbol of the Pazzi (their escutcheon or name on a place) had at once to be removed: hacked away, erased, or covered over. From this time on, any artist or artisan who sculpted, carved, gilded, painted, or otherwise depicted the Pazzi escutcheon, with its famous pair of vertical dolphins back-to-back, whether for public or private use on any surface, including even cloth or earthenware, fell subject to a penalty of fifty large (gold) florins for each and every such infraction. In a word, the Pazzi name and all their insignia must disappear from Florence. They were not worthy of it. Next, setting an astonishing ban on Pazzi marriages, the law looked back three generations to the founder of the family's fifteenth-century wealth (Messer

Andrea di Guglielmino) and then forward in perpetuity. Henceforth, any Florentine who married one of his daughters to a Pazzi descended from Messer Andrea, or who took as wife a woman traceable back to the same Andrea via the masculine line, became 'suspect' (*admonitus*) by that very action; and he, along with all his direct male descendants, forever lost the right to hold any public office or dignity in Florence and its lands.

The threat against marriage to a Pazzi woman was most remarkable in running against an article in canon law. It verged, in effect, on denying her the right to marry. No man from her social class in Florence would marry her, and being shorn of their wealth, the Pazzi would have trouble providing her with a dowry to marry honourably abroad. In short, in her fifteenth-century urban setting, she had little hope of marriage. Her best bet would be to settle for entry into a convent.

The bar against the Pazzi name appearing anywhere in public meant that even a certain street corner, the Canto de' Pazzi, was no longer to be known or referred to by that name. This *canto* marked the right angle or meeting point of two streets lined with the houses of the family, the Pazzi compound, and affirmed the presence of one of the most distinguished lineages in that area, as in other similar designations, such as the Via de' Bardi, the Via degli Alberti, or the Piazza de' Peruzzi. Overnight the Pazzi name was meant to be struck from the historical record. This would also call for the melting down of the gold florins that carried the Pazzi coat of arms on the reverse side: visual testimony to the emblazoning privilege enjoyed by Florentine families, whenever one of their members served a term in the Zecca (Mint) Officials. Owing to their financial prominence, the mandate against all public display of the Pazzi escutcheon would impose the recall, at all events in principle, of quantities of circulating florins.

There was yet another way to humiliate them, a method ordinarily reserved for bankrupts. In some cities, though not in Florence, the declared bankrupt had to beat his bared backside against a special stone or post in a public square, in the sight of a crowd of witnesses. Getting the attention of citizens with a few blasts of their trumpets, town criers would call out the name of the bankrupt, as well as the time and place of the shaming event, so as to attract creditors and a curious crowd. In Florence, instead, bankrupts and traitors were depicted in large format on the façades of buildings, sometimes on the palace of the Lord Priors, but more often on the Bargello, the fortress of the chief police magistrate. To underline identities, names were carefully inscribed beside or under images. In the case of traitors, images were also accompanied by scurrilous lines of verse; and any such portrait was likely to last for many years.

None other than the gifted Sandro Botticelli, a Medici favourite, was hired to depict the April conspirators. On 21 July the Eight issued an order to pay him forty large florins 'for his work in painting the traitors'. These lifelike pictures, eradicated after the expulsion of the Medici in 1494, are generally thought to have been painted on a façade of the Bargello, but it was more likely a wall of the Dogana, part of the government-palace complex. The men depicted were certainly Francesco de' Pazzi, Messer Jacopo, Archbishop Salviati, Renato de' Pazzi, and Bernardo Bandini Baroncelli, as well as Jacopo Bracciolini and Napoleone Franzesi. The vivid realism of the images was such as to unnerve friends and relatives, and two years later, acting under continuing pressure from the Pope, the Lord Priors ordered the removal of the Archbishop's picture: it was of course even more scandalous to the Church than to the prominent Salviati lineage.

The draconian law of 23 May was so extraordinary that over the course of the next three years, being practical men and responding to the needs of diplomacy, Lorenzo and his circle were forced to backtrack and to tone down their hounding of the Pazzi women, but they did not relent in matters concerning the family's wealth, the suppression of their civic symbols, or their political obliteration.

The sentence against the Pazzi brothers and cousins, imprisoning them for life in the tower of Volterra, was commuted in April 1482 to a penalty of perpetual exile outside Italy. And the ban against marriage to the Pazzi women was lifted, although no ambitious or right-thinking family in the ranks of the Florentine patriciate would have dreamed of making such a suspect match. Florence was a stage for all the city's upper-class families; they kept a sharp eye on one another; and that supreme triad – family, politics, money – was an infrangible unity. To tamper with one was to touch the others as well.

Botticelli's defamatory pictures of the conspirators were to have their political and moral opposites in sculpted images of the victorious

Fig. 7 Bust of Lorenzo, probably after a model by Orsino Benintendi and Andrea del Verrochio.

Lorenzo de' Medici. In the aftermath of the April Plot, the images were commissioned by some of Lorenzo's friends and relatives. Collaborating with Verrocchio, the wax modeller Orsino Benintendi sculpted three life-size figures of Lorenzo (Figure 7), idealised of course but – Vasari claimed – looking very much like him. They were put on display in different churches, as though to assure the local populace that, being very much alive, there he was amongst them.

What 'ordinary' Florentines thought about the April Plot and the Pazzi is not a simple question. The immediate passions roused by the conspiracy certainly drove some men out into the streets to shout support for Lorenzo, to dismember corpses, and to flaunt body parts. But nothing is known about their numbers, and still less about whether or not they were representative. The men who cried out, 'Long live Lorenzo who gives us bread', came from the city's large numbers of beggars and the ranks of the poor. They were not political citizens and had no voice in government.

It was a commonplace among informed Florentines that very few people knew what really went on in the secret councils of state at the highest level. This was the business of the leading citizens. Of these, all the known Mediceans must have sided with Lorenzo in April 1478. But there were also the citizens who belonged to the silent and fearful opposition. A small percentage of these very likely sympathised with the Pazzi, if not necessarily with the sanguinary part of the plot itself. Others again, if allowed to vote in secret, could act for or against Lorenzo, depending upon the tug of current matters. In these circumstances, even after he appeared to consolidate his authority in the 1480s, Lorenzo was unable to construct so great a legacy of good will that it would serve to secure his political heir: his son Piero would fall from power in less than three years.

CHAPTER EIGHT

Assaulting the Body: 'Cannibalism'

WHY WERE THE men of the Italian Renaissance ready to tear into the bodies of enemies and criminals, suspects and the hated, with an alacrity that may seem to us cruel or even barbarous?

I interrupt the narrative in order to deal with a question that nags at the conspiracies of the opening chapter and at the butchery of the Medicean reprisals. The discussion that follows will be suggestive and provisional. In matters of the sort before us, we can only ask for so much precision as the subject will allow.

Capital Punishment

THE FIERCE CIVIL wars of the thirteenth century, fought both between Italian cities and within their walls, lay in the distant past; so also the brutalities of the fourteenth century, with its rapacious companies of foreign mercenaries. But the fifteenth century was not altogether free from alarming acts of violence. Sown with more cities than any other part of Europe, Italy's urban life, underpinned by layers of ancient familiarities, could at times erupt in explosive furies.

Up and down the Italian peninsula, to draw blood by an act of violence was at once more serious in law, because it attested to the gravity of the assault and so was more severely punished. Blood was the measure. Similarly, for a judge to impose the penalty of whipping until the body oozed blood was a mark of condign severity. Here already the sign of blood began to take on meaning that went beyond the matter of its mere appearance.

Symbolic overtones came forth easily from that red substance, but being ambiguous or polysemous, they muddled the sharp differences between religious and penal connotations, all the more so in that the imagery of blood had a prominent place in the rituals of everyday life – in the spectacle of public executions, in the staged mutilation of criminals, the occasional sight of (or talk about) self-flagellants, and most especially in ubiquitous images of the bleeding Jesus Christ and martyred saints, as intoned in prayers or seen in the great splash of religious art. Where crime was concerned, the punitive spilling of blood was the exacting of payment for evil done by theft, murder, forgery, perjury, rape, heresy, and treason. In the case of Christian martyrdom, whether by decapitation, nails, arrows, or fire, blood was what some saints had shed for the love of God. And Christ himself, as prayers constantly repeated, had paid with his blood to redeem us, to 'buy' us back from sin and ruin. Thus a laud of the period has Christ affirming,

> I am He who is the true way,
> Who bought you all back:
> Alas, woe, I bought you back
> With my blood and sweat.

And Lorenzo de' Medici, in a prayer to Jesus, tersely observes: 'About your blood you were never a miser.'

The blood of criminals and the blood of martyrs was incommensurable; there was no moral match or relation between them; and yet there was. For the one was universally seen as payment for wicked action, while the other, spilled in the sacrifice of atoning martyrs, was payment for the original sin of all men and women.

Every city had its regular 'place' or 'field of justice', an open space with a scaffold for condemned criminals; and frequently too there was a chapel nearby, where those who wished could pray for the soul of the condemned. The place of justice was a place of infamy, usually located outside the city walls, far from its 'sacred' centre; but not in Venice, where the convicted were famously hanged a stone's throw from the ducal palace, between the 'two columns' in the square (*piazzetta*) beside the Grand Canal. Public executions might also take place at various points within the great urban cluster, such as the windows of the main criminal court or at the site where the crime had been committed, unless it was a holy place. When capital punishment was inflicted in the middle of the city, the rationale was to show citizens and spectators that justice could be swift and pitiless, and that the state was a barrier against sin.

In Florence around 1400, when a second-hand clothes dealer, Bartolo Cini, killed a member of government in the Old Market by striking him on the head with a sword, he was quickly arrested. The next day, with the encouragement of the Lord Priors, the deciding magistrate had a gibbet erected in the same marketplace. Shortly before the execution, to alert the populace, the customary bell of capital punishment was sounded and Bartolo, mounted on a cart, was drawn through the streets of the city, while being repeatedly pinched with redhot pincers. His ride came to an end in the Old Market, where he was hanged in the sight of all, and there his body hung until nightfall. A hundred years later, the rite was still fully in use; it continued up to the seventeenth century. On 27 June 1498, an unnamed man was hanged in the Old Market, at the very point where he had murdered a man the day before, 'and he was gripped by hot tongs', wrote a contemporary diarist, 'as he was borne through the city on a cart. Justice was beautifully and swiftly done.'

When a murder was exceptionally wicked, the killer might be carted, completely naked, to his own neighbourhood, then on to the site of the crime and to other central points, while wearing his sinning, severed hands tied around his neck, each dangling by its thumb, and the stumps of his arms pinned up to the level of his eyes, so that he could see them. In one Florentine case, the man was finally turned upside down and thrust head first into a watery ditch until he was dead. Only then did the executioners take his body out to the place of justice, where it hung for six days 'as an example to other evildoers'. It took the pleas of his relatives to get the corpse back for burial. All Florence, it seems, had been happy when the murderer in question, Busechino of San Frediano, was tracked down and caught in the countryside near Pistoia, because his crime had been especially treacherous. His victim, a second-hand clothes vendor and possible pawn-taker, was believed to have saved Busechino from the gallows on two different occasions.

Capital punishment in the heart of the city, then, was usually reserved for crimes of a more heinous sort, including plots against the state, but it was also doled out on occasion to strike back at audacious cases of theft and forgery, at hardened criminals, or even at foreigners, who included people from other cities. The Venetians sometimes staged their executions at the Rialto, the financial and commercial heart of the city, or in the great central square of San Marco, having first borne the convicted criminal, chained to a raft, up the Grand Canal. On 24 August 1504, in the Square of San Marco, such 'a reprobate was burned to death for having raped a little girl four years old'. A few years later, in a bloodier ending on the same site, Gasparo d'Arquà was quartered and the quarters were then 'hung up on the scaffold'.

But ordinary executions, terminating at the 'place of justice', had, if anything, a more echoing ritual. The cart ride out of the city to the gallows looked to the model of Christ's Calvary, His punishing walk to Golgotha. Had He not after all perished on a public gallows, a criminal between two other criminals, in front of soldiers and a crowd of people, as shown by countless pictures of the Crucifixion? The memory of this event was also recalled by a religious confraternity found in all Italian cities, whose mission was to comfort condemned prisoners and to accompany them on the way to their execution. In Florence, this society of hooded men, known as the 'Black Company in the Confraternity of St Mary of the Cross at the Temple', went about their duties attired in black and numbered fifty men at the time of the Pazzi Conspiracy, when they were under the control of the Medici family and their partisans. Lorenzo was a member of the order, but seems not to have marched with them in their processions to the gallows. During the march, with two of them walking beside the cart, one on each side of the condemned criminal, the hooded men in black (the *Neri*) sought to comfort him or her with reminders of Jesus Christ's Passion, with calls to repent, cries of compassion, and the incitement to triumph over terror by means of prayer and a vision of the suffering Christ.

Characteristically in Florence, this mortal Calvary began outside the criminal court of the Podestà (see Map 1), situated behind and just to the north-east of the battlemented palace or 'castle' of the Lord Priors. With the condemned prisoner usually unable to walk, hence borne on a cart that was sometimes spotted with blood, the march of death would wind up north along the Street of the Crossbowmen (*Balestrieri*) to the cathedral. Here it would turn left around it and into the square between the cathedral and the Baptistery, proceed south into the Via Calimala and the Old Market, then on to the New Market. The procession soon turned left and down the Via Vacchereccia, leading directly into the Piazza dei Signori, the principal public and government square. From here cart, criminal, guardsmen, hangman, confraternity, and gaping crowd proceeded east along the street that hugged the southern façade of the government palace, then north again behind this fortress. And by now the procession had largely circled the heart of the old upper-class city: that oval within which the cathedral and the palace of the Lord Priors were the identifying (and tallest) points of spiritual and earthly power, Church and State. Now the woeful march moved east again, along the Borgo dei Greci, to the rectangle in front of the church of Santa Croce, the favourite site for jousts, and ever east again, on the north side of the church, in a parallel to the river, along the Street of the Malcontent. The procession continued all the way to the massive city gate known as 'The Gate of Justice', whence it filed directly out to the killing field. Here the Black Company had both a cemetery and a chapel where the condemned person could pray, hear Mass, and take communion.

But the dry outlines of this itinerary omit all the sounds and drama that issued from the cart, the Black Company, and the throng of spectators. A whole spectrum of emotions was being enacted there. Scenes were sometimes ugly, as when crowds raged against the condemned, spitting and shouting abuse; or, instead, they might look on in horror, and every rare now and then some wild attempt might be made to free the sinner. Occasionally too there was a mournful, shocked silence on faces in the crowd, such as on 10 April 1465, when the daughter of Zanobi Gherucci, a mere *fanciulla*, hence only some ten to thirteen years of age at most, was carted through the streets of Florence and out of the Gate of Justice to be beheaded, convicted of having killed the infant daughter of the goldsmith Bernardo della Zecca. The court found that she had thrown her into a well to steal the string of pearls and silver oddments worn around the infant's neck. But what the exact circumstances were, who knows? A week or two later, a counterfeiter, accused of forging small silver coins, was also beheaded, and we can be reasonably certain that there was little if any sympathy for him. In a harsh age from our modern Western viewpoint, easy money of that sort could not elicit much compassion; nor did perjury and the forgery of documents, for which the penalties could be – if the laws were strictly applied – the bloody loss of the tongue and the sinning hand. The branding of the face was also practised, but more on members of the lower classes and notorious criminals, as though to stamp them for ever with the mark of their degraded social and moral station.

What exactly did the members of the Black Company say to the convicted person on his or her march of death? Many of their utterances were both ritualised *and* spontaneous, but the main themes were caught by the Bolognese lawyer, Gregorio Roverbella (*c*. 1410–88), who belonged to Bologna's Confraternity of St Mary of Death. He produced a prayer in verse 'For those who are on their way to justice', imagining that he himself was such a man. What we have, therefore, is an imagined voice speaking the prayer; and although the woe is muted to fit the verse form, we must think of the words as being uttered in an agonised and tearful passion, with the speaker often surrounded by a shouting, insulting, murmuring, or moaning mob of witnesses. Here are parts of the prayer:

> Mercy, O highest God and everlasting,
> . . .
> Here I am, dear Lord, at the final step
> That every man must take
> In this thieving, base and sighing world.
> . . .
> I deserve the hellish and eternal fires;
> . . .
> I repent my criminal ways,
> And with this sobbing face and torment,
> I think about your mortal woes [on the Cross]
> . . .
> Now fill me with such a fire of love for you
> That by the treasures of your passion
> I may bear this weight with valour.
> . . .

O Lord, snatch me from this weeping
And take me up to gaze on that sweet face
Offered to the martyrs and to other saints;

. . .

My soul, come to the ends of the earth,
Cries out for your divine help, so
That you may put it among the blessed.
Here's the bitter gall, here the hard bite
That Peter and great Paul and all your others
Faced and suffered for your love,
And you yourself went through it here among us
With that high example of your Holy Cross.

The string of moving commonplaces is meant to insert the prayer into the liturgical tradition, while also working to reinsert the convicted sinner into the Christian community, to win him back to a decent humanity. And by likening the impending execution to the martyrdom of Christ and certain saints, the closing lines bring in Calvary as the paradigm for the horrific march of death.

If Florence had staged only one or two executions a year, could we have said that the spectacle was, after all, uncommon? Perhaps so, although any such case could turn into a gruesome affair and stir up a frenzy of collective feeling. On 29 May 1503, an enraged crowd of spectators terrified the Black Company and stoned the city's hangman to death, because he had so bungled the beheading of a young man, a vendor of banners and flags, that the attending mounted captain had been forced to complete the task by clubbing the youth to death. And by then the ground around the immediate site was awash with blood, because the official executioner had made three different attempts with his sword.

Over the fifty years from 1451 to 1500, the people of Florence saw an average of nearly eight executions (7.94) per year, not counting the 80 to 100 men hanged or cut to pieces in the wake of the Pazzi Conspiracy; and the real average was certainly higher, given the gaps in sources. For the same period, Ferrara, a city under princely rule and with a population about two-thirds the size of Florence's, was witness to an average of 4.88 official killings a year. If we increase this Ferrara figure by a third, the

Florentine average is still higher by a factor of 1.44. In other words, when compared to a 'tyranny' (to use a term favoured by republican humanists), there was nothing softer, more humane, or more 'civilised' about republican Florence. Our burghers knew how to deal out stern justice.

'Cannibalism'

WAS IT THE case, as contemporary chronicles and other sources now and again report, that in rage and vengeance people could tear at human flesh with their teeth? The plots against Count Girolamo Riario, the Medici brothers, and the Duke of Milan all ended with incidents of this sort. The image sometimes served as a metaphor to sum up a pitch of feeling, such as when two members of the Lampugnani clan swore that if they had known of the conspiracy, they would have 'eaten' the assassins of Galeazzo Maria Sforza 'with their own teeth'. Here was a species of cannibalism as symbolic action, an act of speech that *wants* to be the action itself. Very occasionally, however, the thing itself must actually have taken place, as in the reprisals at Forlì, after the assassination of Count Girolamo Riario, for the action is too often reported in descriptions of explosive violence. In the peninsula's great rural and mountainous expanses, where the civilities of urban restraint (such as they were) receded, the blunt deed was perhaps more likely to occur. There too the march of mercenary armies was always more frequent, oppressive, and cruel. When their employers failed to pay up or were slow to do so, soldiers plundered crops, set fire to farm buildings, seized livestock in numbers large enough to deplete localities, killed or held people to ransom, and molested or raped women. From the Veneto to central Italy, looking out to that world with a mix of slight pity and more contempt, the urban upper classes often regarded peasants and country folk as a little less than human.

In papal territory one day, in February 1437, in the low mountains of Acquapendente, near the south-western frontiers of Tuscany, three young shepherds began to talk about how men are actually hanged. One thing led to another, and they decided to try a harmless experiment.

Jesting, while wishing to see how the procedure truly worked, one of them put a rope around the neck of another, looped it over the branch of an oak tree, and the third man then pulled the second one up from the ground, as the first one tied the loose end to the tree. This at least is the chronicler's description of the event. Suddenly a wolf appeared, scaring the two jesters and putting them to flight. Returning after the wolf had gone, 'they found their hanging companion dead, so they untied and buried him'. On the following Sunday, the father of the dead youth, as was his custom, went out to see him, taking along a portion of bread. Unable to find the boy, he naturally turned for help to the two companions, 'and pressed them with questions, until one of them told him what had happened'. Grabbing hold of that one and forcing him to go to the place where they had buried his son, the father 'killed the young shephered there with a knife, cut him open, pulled out his liver, took it home, invited the father of the murdered shepherd to a meal, and proceeded to serve him his son's liver.' The striking, ambivalent symbolism of this deed collects around the fact that the liver, rendered edible, was degraded to being the part of an animal, while yet continuing to bear – in accordance with the folklore of the age – some of the moral qualities, such as the force or courage, of the 'de-livered' shepherd.

Once they had finished the meal, the avenging father informed the other that he had just eaten his own son's liver. Then and there the outraged father killed the confessed killer of his son, 'and similarly the screaming mother killed the mother of the hanged boy'. By now a fatal sequence of passion had been ignited, 'one killing off the other and the other yet another, with the result, we gather, that by the end of February, that is, in less than a month, about thirty-six people had been killed, including men, women, and children'.

The symbolism to one side, there was nothing typical about this string of revenge murders. While not giving a single first or family name, the chronicler Graziani, a reliable reporter, rushes through the bare bones of the drama, recording it because it strikes him as unusual. But he does not treat it as a wonder and he does not moralise; he accepts it, as if he somehow understands. And although the motor force of the action is clear enough in the thirst for vengeance, we must ourselves insert the whole cultural context of the bloody proceedings.

Driven by a burst of persisting rage when he cuts out and serves up the liver of the murdered youth, the first revenger does something that comes too readily and almost, it appears, naturally. There was some whispered tradition here, however incoherent and irregular, of doing the like in cases of revenge for the killing of one's closest kin. Action of this sort surfaced as a topic in folk conversation, even if it was rarely done. What is more, the subject also floated in the seconding, mimetic mental world of late-medieval Christianity, which made a point of underlining the imagery and lessons of martyred flesh. Would the nearest of kin not see a murdered son or father as something of a martyr? And would they not suddenly see him as good? In pictures as in prayer, the religious culture of the age praised Christian martyrdom every day. It was a message of bloodletting, with stories of the dramatic rending of human flesh carried right into the household, such as in prayers to Christ or lauds for St John the Baptist, St Sebastian, St James, the bleeding St Francis, St Agnes, St Margaret, St Barbara, and so on.

The stories and their images offered a narrative of maximum pain, of the cutting-up or puncturing of the body. To save humanity from evil, Jesus Christ had been put to death in one of the most painful of all ways, a crucifixion. And many martyrs proved their devotion to Him and to heaven by a consenting death through a ritual of blood or fire. Since no ordinary man or woman could attain eternal life through personal merit, supreme pain and the assistance of the Church were introduced as the means. Real saints, in any case, lived lives of physical abnegation, and the agonised suffering of the body in this life was the surest gateway to the next life.

There is no suggestion here – not at all – that the imagery of martyrdom in itself led people to cannibalism, real or mimetic, such as in moments of extraordinary stress, especially in view of the message of loving charity and forgiveness in Christian doctrine. Martyrs were heroes, not tortured criminals and not kinsmen killed in acts of revenge. However, the visual programme of Christian martyrdom did not come *in itself*, nor in a mere bed of pleas for brotherly love. It came embedded in a larger real world of political violence and in a setting in which revenge, even when toned down in the fifteenth century, continued to be the duty of the male animal. All men and women were educated in the symbolism of torn flesh.

Like every other city in Italy, Florence was a honeycomb of parish churches, convents, and other religious establishments. Moving from east to west, or north to south across the Arno River, one could easily cross the entire city by foot in about thirty minutes. Yet it had sixty-two parish churches, not including other religious houses, and about 100 religious confraternities. Lorenzo de' Medici was inscribed in at least seven 'brotherhoods', while other men might belong to three or four. Many confraternities were founded as flagellant companies; and in Venice, where they were known as the 'Great Schools', they were the richest and most prestigious of such associations. Members met periodically to scourge themselves in group assembly; and although such self-flailing had become ritualised by the late fourteenth century, we may assume that there were also times when individuals broke through the formalities of ritual and acted to inflict pain, even on occasion to the point of drawing blood. The fact that Venetian nobles and rich men in the 'Great Schools' were allowed to pay large sums of money for the privilege of being excused from scourging themselves indicates that the procedure could be painful, indecorous, or at least inconvenient. If nothing else, the call to punish the body in memory of Christ and the martyrs, or to correct and cleanse the soul, was always in the air: in talk, in dogma, in pictures, in belief. Thus a prayer by the Florentine poet, Bernardo Giambullari, invites the suppliant to consider Christ on the cross:

> Look at the gashing wound on his side,
> Put there by those dogs,
> All of his face a sheet of blood,
> And his hands and feet punched with holes.

If pious men in the flagellant companies were willing to hurt themselves, they were all the more ready, it would seem, to hurt those whom they believed to be evil.

Since religious views regarding man's nature permeated the culture, when the ensuing readiness to punish or deprive the flesh – the classic way of atonement – was combined with the ferocity of politics, as in the plot against the Medici, or in retribution against conspirators real and alleged, the brutality was at once heightened, because politics in

Italy, urban politics, was the ground *par excellence* of 'no mercy'. It had been so since time out of mind. For nearly 300 years, political differences in the cities had frequently been settled by means of mass exile and executions. Though it is true that the fifteenth century saw far less of this, politics remained a vocation for the strong and the bold: one in which – in serious struggle – the winners took all, while utterly destroying the opposition. There was no such thing, not even in Venice, as a legitimate political opposition. Debate and discussion among men at the head of government or those around them, debate within the ruling group – this was certainly admissible; but there must be none outside the established elites, where men could probe questions more deeply or even alter them. Political elites were meant to speak with one voice. Consequently, when the need for revenge, or the sudden will to exterminate, entered politics, there were no restraints: every atrocity was possible. The advice of a political revenge poem of the period says this to the would-be revenger: lie low, and watch and wait for your chance,

> Till Fortune turns around to serve you,
> Then out with your list of all their crimes,
> And never fear, just grab on with your teeth,
> Cut, chop, tear, break and beat,
> And never more go crouching to those crazy bastards.

CHAPTER NINE

A Soldier Confesses

Confession

THE PLAN TO kill the Medici brothers was the plot of three ambitious and resentful men: a banker, a new prince, and an archbishop. But it spread as though by a mad logic, to draw in a surprising company: the Pope, the King of Naples, and the Duke of Urbino; next, a professional soldier, a merchant banker, a man of letters, priests, two bishops, a cardinal, a businessman, more top captains, and at the last minute an assorted crowd of mercenaries. In the final hours, twenty to thirty innocent men — relatives, companions, servants of the conspirators — would also be implicated and then murdered in the bloody reprisals.

The plot is best unravelled by picking it out of the confession of the soldier at the heart of the conspiracy, Giovan Battista, the Count of Montesecco, a hired 'lance' from a hill town some eighteen miles south-west of Urbino. Bred to the profession of arms, this petty nobleman typified the many captains recruited from that Adriatic part of Italy, the Marches and the Romagna, for centuries the breeding ground of hungry mercenaries. Because of their violence and frequent looting in wartime, professional soldiers often had foul reputations among country people. But since war, like military security, was the business of professionals, many of the best of them also being feudal lords, rulers honoured and paid and cosseted them. Relying on detailed contracts, they would keep mercenary captains on retainer, or hire them for periods ranging from several months to a year or more. Some fifteenth-century battles were bloody, with many hundreds of men killed and wounded, not to mention the slaughter of horses, as at the Battle of Molinella (25 July 1467), near Bologna, which pitted the Count (later Duke) of Urbino against the outstanding soldier in Venetian pay, Bartolomeo Colleoni. But many more engagements were not nearly so fierce; and it was always the case that the top captains — Orsini, Sforza, Fortebracci — risked the lives of their troops as little as possible. Without trained and seasoned men, a captain was worth little.

As a result of hearsay and his published confession, Montesecco passed into Florentine reports of the day as a soldier of sober judgment and honour, despite being wholly entangled in the coils of his bosses, Count Girolamo Riario and the Count's uncle, Pope Sixtus IV. Actually a papal soldier, Montesecco had served in Rome as Captain of the Apostolic Palace Guard and as chief officer of the Roman fortress, Castel St Angelo.

Dated 4 May 1478, eight days after the bloody attempt in the cathedral, the soldier's confession, as highlighted in the following extracts (his own words appear in italics), has been translated literally. This explains the abrupt transitions and jerky shifts between direct and indirect discourse. Since Montesecco penned his statement in fear of execution, however controlled his flow of words, he was in no state to offer a single word of description regarding his meeting places with the ringleaders. But when in Rome, holding talks in the 'quarters' (*camera*) of the Count Girolamo or of Archbishop Salviati, it is clear that the site was somewhere in the papal palace, where the Count and Salviati had chambers at their disposal. Sixtus liked to have his relatives and loved ones near him. In this and in other senses, the great shadow of the Pope is never absent from the soldier's statement.

Montesecco confessed to having first heard of the plot in Rome, in the Archbishop of Pisa's Vatican rooms, where he was made to take an oath of secrecy in the presence of one other man, the Florentine merchant banker, Francesco de' Pazzi. It was most likely the late summer of 1477. Revealingly, the three men did not meet in the Roman palace of the Pazzi family — and Montesecco never refers to it — which was located near the bridge of St Angelo, in the Via del Canale del Ponte. This was also the residential area of bankers from Siena and Genoa, and the sight of a leading papal soldier, arriving at (or leaving) the house of the top papal banker, would have occasioned talk and rumours.

Speaking first, the Archbishop told the soldier that they were planning to force a change of government in Florence. *I answered that I would do anything for them, but that being a soldier in the pay of the Pope and the Count [Girolamo Riario], I couldn't enter into their plans. How can you think, they replied, that we would get up to something like this without the Count's consent?*

Priest and banker, good friends of the Count, went on to argue that Riario's new state of Imola and Forlì would otherwise *not be worth a bean, because Lorenzo de' Medici nourishes a mortal hatred against him . . . and after the Pope dies, he will do everything he can to hurt the Count and to take that state away from him.* The soldier asked why Lorenzo was such an enemy of the Count, and they answered by going into details regarding the papal treasury, the Archbishop of Pisa, and other affairs, *all too long to write down here,* Montesecco claimed.

When the confession was published three months later, after Florence decided to send out copies to other Italian states, the causes of Lorenzo's hatred had no need to be detailed: they were too well known and too shaming to spell out in a public document. Lorenzo had hoped to lay hands for Florence on the Romagnol city of Imola. Instead, against Lorenzo's will, Pope Sixtus had bought Imola from the Duke of Milan for 40,000 ducats, intending it as the heart of a new mini-state for one of his favourite nephews, Girolamo Riario, for whom he had also arranged a grand marriage with the Duke's illegitimate daughter, Caterina Sforza. Consequently, the little city now also looked, confusingly, like part of her dowry. Moreover, the Medici Bank refused to lend the Imola purchase money to Sixtus, so that he was forced to borrow most of the sum from the Pazzi Bank in Rome – part of the reason Sixtus dismissed the Medici as his chief bankers and put the Pazzi in charge of papal revenues. Two other quarrels also inflamed the anger between the parties. The Pope accused Lorenzo of having helped to block his efforts, back in 1474, to take Città di Castello, a fortified town in papal territory, away from the soldier and anti-papal rebel Niccolò Vitelli. More recently, as has been noted, Lorenzo had strenuously opposed the papal appointment of a Florentine citizen, Francesco Salviati, to the archbishopric of Pisa, because he wanted one of his own creatures or relatives there, and feared that Salviati was next in line for a cardinal's hat.

Montesecco's first interview with the banker and the Archbishop ended when the soldier agreed to obey Count Girolamo's order in all things concerning *his [the Count's] honour and profit and theirs.* About two weeks later, the Count himself summoned Montesecco, and Archbishop Salviati was again present. The Count recalled, *The Archbishop tells me that they've discussed a certain matter with you. Well, what do you think? My lord, I answered, I don't know what to say about this thing, because I don't understand it yet. When I do, I'll tell you what I think. The Archbishop: Come now, haven't I told you that we want a coup d'état in Florence? Indeed you have, yes, but you haven't told me how [you plan to go about it], and not knowing this, I don't know what to say about it.*

The soldier's words seem to come forth in so serene and orderly a manner, that the historian Gino Capponi believed that his captors had promised to spare his life if he made a complete confession. The statement continues:

Now the two of them came out frankly and began to talk about Lorenzo's evil intentions against each of them, and what dangers the Count and his state would face after the Pope's death, and how by overturning the said government [of Florence] we would be arranging things for the Count so that he could never again be hurt.

When Montesecco again asked about how they planned to achieve their desired *coup,* they replied by talking in general terms about the power of the Pazzi and Salviati families in Florence. Then, quite abruptly, something in the original confession seems to have been suppressed, a passage which very likely introduced the names, implicating them, of the King of Naples (Ferrante) and the well-known patron of the arts, the warrior Duke of Urbino, Federigo da Montefeltro. The Count and the Archbishop finally admitted that *the only way was to cut Lorenzo and Giuliano to pieces, to have soldiers ready, and to go into Florence. And [to do this] we'd have to raise troops secretly, so as not to plant suspicions.*

My lords, I replied, look again at what you want to do. I guarantee that this is something big, and I don't know how it can be done, because Florence is something big, and the Magnificent Lorenzo is, I gather, much liked there.

The Count responded at once, claiming that Archbishop Salviati and Francesco de' Pazzi held the opposite view, namely, that Lorenzo *enjoys little grace and is much hated [in Florence], that once they [the two Medici brothers] are dead, the Florentines will raise their hands up to heaven [in thanksgiving].*

Now the Archbishop spoke up: *Giovan Battista, you've never been to Florence. We know more about Florentine affairs than you do, and we know all about the good and bad will that Florentines bear Lorenzo. So don't worry about our plan. As sure as we're sitting here, it'll work. All we have to do is fix on the way. And what is it? To warm up [recruit] Messer Jacopo [de' Pazzi], who is colder than an icicle, but once we have him, the whole thing will be on its way. And don't doubt it for a moment.*

Could this churchman, Archbishop Francesco Salviati, have been so certain of the outcome? Here is a sketch of the man.

He was born about 1443, to one of Florence's foremost political families. The Salviati name ranked with the first dozen surnames in Florentine public life. Not more than six or seven others surpassed their record of terms in the Lord Priors over the course of the fourteenth and fifteenth centuries. His grandfather Jacopo and his uncle Alamanno were two of the men most often seen in the political councils of their day; and the house had marriage ties with the Pazzi, Medici, Vettori, and other prominent families, so that Francesco could even claim that he was related to the Medici by ties of marriage. Orphaned but yet fashionably educated in the new humanist vein, the young Salviati, an ambitious spender, resolved to 'make it' in the Church. He settled in Rome in 1464, leaving numerous friends and acquaintances back in Florence, including Marsilio Ficino; and he was later on to know Poliziano, who would claim that Salviati was a flatterer, a gambler, and a bold, intriguing sensualist. His great luck (or misfortune) in Rome had been to strike up a friendship with Francesco della Rovere, the future Pope Sixtus IV, and with his nephews, Girolamo and Pietro Riario.

When the young Pietro, a wealthy cardinal, died in 1474, vacating the archbishopric of Florence, Salviati expected to succeed him in this post, but he was thwarted by Lorenzo de' Medici, who helped to persuade Sixtus to confer the dignity on Rinaldo Orsini, a Roman nobleman and indeed Lorenzo's brother-in-law. Later in the year therefore, without consulting Florence or Lorenzo, the Pope chose Salviati for the archbishopric of Pisa, the celebrated seaport now under Florentine rule. Governing circles in Florence at once decried the move as unfriendly.

Now everything changed decisively for Salviati. The concerted Florentine campaign to obstruct his appointment to the Pisan dignity, added to his close ties with Sixtus and Count Girolamo Riario, turned him against his 'Magnificent' co-citizen. His resentment and hatred, however, cut deeply, for never once did he seem to falter from the plan to kill the Medici brothers. He talked two close relatives into the conspiracy: his own brother Jacopo and a first cousin Bartolomeo (alias Jacopo), both of whom would be executed on the day of the disastrous plot. The Archbishop's feelings against Lorenzo were also fuelled by ambition: his devotion to the papal family was partly governed by his desire to keep in the Pope's good graces. He hoped to be made a cardinal.

There was an additional twist. Jacopo de' Pazzi's mother was one of Salviati's aunts, and Jacopo seems to have financed his ecclesiastical career. In 1477 therefore, in his conversations with Jacopo about Lorenzo de' Medici, the Archbishop was drawing on family bonds and obligations.

We return to the confession. Informed of Jacopo de' Pazzi's refusal to join the conspirators, Montesecco then put the overwhelming question to the Count and the Archbishop, only to have it brushed aside: *Very well, and will all this [coup and double murder] please the Holy Father? The answer was: we'll always make him do whatever we want. Another thing, His Holiness hates Lorenzo; he wants this more than anyone else. Have you talked to him [asks Montesecco]? Of course we have, and we'll arrange to have him tell you too, so that you fully understand his will.*

They turned next to thinking about how they would raise and move troops without stirring up suspicions, and the confession now broaches their idea of concealing their own men among troops in the Todi, Perugia, Montone, and other areas. Papal mercenaries had recently — September 1477 — reconquered the Castle of Montone from the wife of Carlo Fortebracci, a Florentine protégé and anti-papal rebel, who at that point was actually in Florence.

Soon after this, Francesco de' Pazzi, then residing in Rome and directing the Pazzi Bank there, went to Florence to ferret out military information and to talk to the family elder, his uncle Messer Jacopo, who opposed the whole idea of the plot. Francesco continued to feel that if they could but win him over, they would be able to hand him the pivotal part of the conspiracy: taking to the streets to arouse the populace against the Medici, and the complete capture of the government palace. But we must assume that he would never have approached Messer Jacopo with the idea for such a murderous plot, and then kept at him about it, if Jacopo, in conversation over the years, had not himself revealed intense feeling against Lorenzo.

Count Girolamo next used the illness of his neighbour and deadly rival, the Lord of Faenza, as the excuse for sending Montesecco to Florence on a minor embassy to Lorenzo, with a view to having him spy things out there. The soldier also carried a message of strong, pretended warmth and friendship for the Florentine *signore*, claiming that *despite the things that had come between them, [the Count] wanted to cast all that aside . . . and to have him [Lorenzo] as a father.* Not to be outdone at the game of courtly diplomacy, Lorenzo's response was so spontaneously friendly and loving, that Montesecco marvelled, especially after what he had heard regarding his hatred for the Count. Fearing for his life and seeking mercy, the soldier very likely exaggerated the Florentine's winsome humanity in his confession, but we may well believe that Lorenzo went through his charade of loving friendship with impeccable grace. This was the way of high diplomacy in Quattrocento Italy.

After his interview with Lorenzo, Montesecco went on for lunch to the Inn of the Bell, bearing letters of accreditation from Count Girolamo and Archbishop Salviati. He sent a message to Messer Jacopo de' Pazzi, who quickly turned up at the Inn for a meeting. *We withdrew in secret to a bedroom and I conveyed greetings and good wishes to him from our lord [Pope Sixtus], from the Count, and from the Archbishop. I then presented the letters. Having read them, he asked: What have we to say to each other, Giovan Battista? Are we supposed to talk about a matter of state? Yes, I said, absolutely. He replied: Look, I don't want to hear anything you have to say, because those gentlemen are racking their brains to make themselves lords of Florence. But I understand things here better than they do, so don't talk to me about this business. I don't want to listen to you.*

Having just touched on 'this business', Messer Jacopo was apparently observing and assessing Montesecco, and indeed desiring to hear more. This ex-holder of the city's highest office, Gonfalonier of Justice (1469), had no legitimate offspring, but in the 1470s, as the sole survivor of his generation, he had nine nephews, four nieces, and thirteen grand-nephews and nieces, all children and grandchildren of his two brothers. His nephew Francesco, the banker at the heart of the Conspiracy, was, as we have seen, a brother-in-law to Bianca de' Medici and so to Lorenzo himself.

In the mid 1460s, Messer Jacopo had been a supporter of Piero de' Medici, Lorenzo's father, while also spending a good deal of time in

France on banking business. Long active as a banker, tax farmer, and head partner in a firm for the production of luxury silks, he had been as far as England on business at least once, and was no idle *rentier*. For a year or two after holding the exalted Gonfaloniership, when still only forty-eight years old, 'he was one of the most influential members of the oligarchy'. And like Luca Pitti, he had been knighted by the Lord Priors for his services to Florence, in a follow-up to his knighting by the French royal prince, René of Anjou. Thus, in the decade of the April Plot, Jacopo de' Pazzi was naturally seen as the family elder and the main bearer of its fame. The Milanese ambassador reported in 1471 that he was 'very well liked among the people [of Florence]'. However, a scorching travesty of the man began to rule the historical picture after the Conspiracy, when Lorenzo's sparkling protégé, Poliziano, produced a sketch of Jacopo in his incisive Latin, casting him both as a miser and wild spender, and as an arrogant, insolent, mulish creature, pallid, weak, a cheater of poor workers, and a notorious blasphemer and gambler. He has Jacopo tossing his head, talking with unstable gestures, and paying day labourers with rotten pork. These alleged actions and vices are all better struck from the record.

Machiavelli, instead, underlined Jacopo's generosity with poor folk. And the fair-minded Guicciardini brought out the gambler in his sketch, but more interestingly so. Explaining his initial reluctance to join the conspirators, the great historian puns on his doings as banker and gambler: Messer Jacopo was held back from the plot by the fear or prospect 'of how much wealth and what a great position in life he would be putting on the gaming table (*tavoliere*)'.

So then, Francesco de' Pazzi, Count Girolamo, and Archbishop Salviati had picked Messer Jacopo the knight as their key figure for the political climax of their plot. They needed his name, dignity, and know-how; and Montesecco, the military expert, bearing a message from the Pope himself, had been sent to Florence to persuade him. In fact, he suggests, he managed to talk Jacopo into listening; but it appears that the knight was already eager to hear the latest word, while yet affecting at first to spurn the whole enterprise.

Montesecco: *I bring encouragement from our lord [the Holy Father]. I talked to him just before I left. In the presence of the Count and the Archbishop, His Holiness said that I should urge you to get on with the Florence matter, because he has no idea of when there may be another siege like this one of Montone,* [i.e., action against a papal rebel in neighbouring Montone] *with so many armed men ready, together, and so close to Florence. And since it's dangerous to delay, he wants to move you to take action.*

Montesecco's confession was witnessed and undersigned by the chief Florentine magistrate (the Podestà) and, unusually, six men in holy orders. There was nothing random about this choice of witnesses, owing to what the soldier said about Pope Sixtus. The presence of so many priests was meant to be remarkable, as Montesecco read out his confession to them, once it was all down on paper. Moreover, confessing under pressure, he darted from one topic or venue to another, and having just warned Messer Jacopo of the dangers of delaying, he passed suddenly over to the papal role.

Here are his words to Messer Jacopo: *His Holiness definitely wants a change of government in Florence, but without anyone's death. And when I told him in front of the Count and the Archbishop that these things cannot really be done without the death of Lorenzo and Giuliano and perhaps others, His Holiness said to me: I want the death of no man, not for any reason. It is not part of our office to consent to any person's death, and though Lorenzo is a scoundrel and behaves badly with us, yet on no account would I wish to see him dead. But a change of government, this yes. Then the Count responded: We will do what we can to see that this doesn't happen, but if it should, Your Holiness will forgive those responsible. The Pope answered the Count and said: You're an animal! I tell you I want no man dead, but I do want a change of government. So I say to you, Giovan Battista [Montesecco], that I greatly desire a polit-ical change in Florence. I want that government taken from Lorenzo's hands, because he's a villain and a wicked man and has no respect for us. Once he's out of Florence, we'll be able to do as we wish in that republic and this would be very much in keeping with our plans. [Here] . . . the Count and the Archbishop . . . said: Your Holiness speaks the truth. When you have Florence in your power, you'll be able to do what you want with it, provided it's in . . . [new] hands. Then you will set laws for half of Italy, and everyone will long to be your friend; therefore be pleased to see everything done to achieve this end. His Holiness said: I have told you what I do not want. Go and do what you think best, as long as death doesn't come into it. . . . . [The Pope] then concluded by saying that he was content to give all favour and the support of troops or whatever else might be necessary to attain our ends. The Archbishop answered by saying: Be pleased to have us piloting this boat, for we shall steer it well. And our lord said: I am pleased. With this we all got up from his feet [where they had been kneeling] and withdrew to the Count's quarters.*

Can it be said that we have a sketch here, however fragmentary, of the complex Sixtus IV?

Theologian, writer, ex-professor of holy writ, former General of the Franciscan Order, hence a man wedded to personal poverty, Francesco della Rovere had been known for his unworldliness. He had even written learned treatises *On the Blood of Christ* and *On the Power of God*; and when they elected him Pope, the College of Cardinals had been won over by his pious reputation, despite the fact that he had made lavish gifts in some quarters and that one of his nephews had made promises to leading cardinals. But from the moment he became the Vicar of Christ on earth, we see a man profoundly of this world: a nepotist devoted to his extended family, doting on his siblings and nephews, arranging marriages, and suddenly steeped – no doubt rightly so for a Renaissance pope – in power politics not only in Umbria and Romagna, but also all along the frontiers of the Papal State. Painted about 1477, the famous fresco (now on canvas) by Melozzo da Forlì (Figure 8) shows us the saintly old man on the extreme right, flanked by his cosseted nephews. Above him, shown in the robes of a papal protonotary, is Cardinal Pietro Riario, son of the Pope's sister, Bianca, who married a Riario. In the middle, beside the Corinthian pillar, is Cardinal Giuliano della Rovere, son of the Pope's brother, Raffaele. With his back to Cardinal Giuliano is the rather pretty Count Girolamo Riario, another of Bianca's sons, shown wearing his chain of office. And next to him on the far left, also wearing his official chain, is Cardinal Giuliano's brother Giovanni, Prefect of the city of Rome, lord of the papal lands (vicariates) of Senigallia and Mondavio, and married to a daughter of the Duke of Urbino by arrangement of his uncle, Pope Sixtus. Although Sixtus was deeply committed to the building up of the Vatican Library, none of them looks at the humanist Platina, who kneels to the Pope under the images of the Count and the Cardinal, because he is there as a servant, not first of all as the new papal librarian. The work has been described as 'a shameless celebration of nepotism, a self-congratulatory purchase of pictorial and humanistic "immortality".'

In plotting with Count Girolamo and Archbishop Salviati, Sixtus

Fig. 8 Melozzo da Forlì, *Sixtus IV Appointing Platina.*

naturally declared – and did so repeatedly – that he wanted no blood-shed. Holy wars aside, his entire conditioning and vows drew him back from any programme of willed killing, and he had his conscience to live with. But by the autumn of 1477, he had been the crowned head of an Italian state for six years and plunged head-over-heels in worldly politics. How then did he square his determination to engineer an outside *coup d'état* in Florence, to be achieved with the decisive help of papal troops, with his desire to have it without blood? Did he know nothing, this Pope and quondam professor, about security at city gates and govern-ment palaces? Nothing about armed bodyguards, professional merce-naries, and the lethal sharpness of steel weapons? Nothing about the ways in which his contemporaries, elites and princes and his own nephews, clung greedily to their lofty stations? He knew Padua, Pavia, Bologna, Siena, Florence, and Perugia: he had studied, taught, and preached there. In his orisons, therefore, this vigorous debater must have prayed for a bloodless miracle in Florence, for a miracle there is what a peaceful *colpo di stato* was going to require. Yet after the event, after that bloody April of 1478, he was to show a fierce and hard personality in the propaganda war with Florence and in his deployment of armies, interdicts, excommunications, and an urgent diplomacy, as he fought to overthrow Lorenzo and all the claque and clique around him. Time and again Lorenzo refused to go to Rome to seek his pardon and have the ban of excommunication lifted, because he feared that if he went, he would never leave the Eternal City alive, for all Sixtus's grand words and promises.

We pick up Montesecco's confession again just after the audience with Pope Sixtus and the declaration, thrice repeated, that he wanted Lorenzo's government overturned but not the death – murder really – of the two brothers.

Having repaired to the Count's rooms in the Vatican, the three men went on discussing *the matter in detail and we concluded that the thing could not possibly be done without . . . the death of the Magnificent Lorenzo and his brother. And when I said that this would be a bad thing to do, they answered that great things can be done in no other way . . . . It was finally decided that I would have to come here [to Florence] to talk to Francesco [de' Pazzi] and Messer Jacopo, so as to learn from them exactly how [our mission was to be accomplished].*

The soldier journeyed twice to Florence to meet the two men, and one night they were able to talk at length, but no fixed plan emerged. The details kept changing. They knew that they would need soldiers, but not before the day of the ambush; that Archbishop Salviati would also have to be in Florence; and that Messer Jacopo would make his contribution outside the government palace and in the streets. But everything else was fluid or uncertain, even the question of whether or not Lorenzo and Giuliano had to be together when the murders took place. Messer Jacopo, for one, being anxious about a simultaneous double murder, did not want them both killed in the city. *He felt*, said Montesecco, *that it wouldn't work. Whereas Francesco held that it had to be done . . . [with the two together], and he was always thinking that he would have the pluck to do it and that he'd need few other men alongside [to help], so long as the two were in the same place — in a church, at a game of cards, or at a wedding party.*

The fleeting image here of a daring and determined Francesco lends weight to Montesecco's testimony, for on the Sunday of the attempted murders, he was Giuliano's most rabid assailant, stabbing him with such energy, as we have seen, that the terrible wound which he himself suffered may have been self-inflicted in his frenzy. Poliziano, who knew the man, describes him as short, thin, pale, and with blond hair; and Guicciardini, calling him 'bold, restless, and ambitious', adduces a trio of adjectives that were perfectly in accord with Montesecco's confession and the events of the fatal day. Francesco, indeed, was an unquiet personality and an entrepreneur, not the sort of banker who sat sedately at a business table.

Well before the end of 1477, both by letter and word of mouth, Lorenzo had heard rumours of plots – no surprising thing in those years. Besides, the ever-watchful Eight were supposed to have eyes and ears everywhere, primed for the possible dangers by the knowledge that the Medici had sown a good deal of hatred and fear, which of course remained muted. But if Lorenzo took any of the stray rumours seriously, he gave no sign of it. He did little to alter his habits and movements, though it became more and more difficult to find him and Giuliano together on social occasions, at all events in the sight of strangers. By February 1478, with the Conspiracy greatly enlarged, the plotters themselves began to worry about the dangers of its reaching the wrong ears. Montesecco in particular became increasingly uneasy, as he travelled between Rome,

Florence, and Imola, in the last of which he had 100 soldiers under his command, held in readiness for the race to Florence. But the unpredictable movement of other mercenaries, notable along the edges of southern Tuscany, caused the ringleaders to keep putting off the tempestuous moment. In March, Montesecco again had meetings in Rome with Count Girolamo, Francesco, and now also with two other captains, Giovan Francesco da Tolentino and Messer Lorenzo Giustini. The latter was a sworn enemy of Lorenzo de' Medici, who had thrown Florence's weight behind the anti-papal rebel and *condottiere*, Niccolò Vitelli, in a deadly struggle with Giustini for the lordship of Città di Castello, a fortified town some ten miles east of Arezzo. Giustini was on the papal payroll and had the wholehearted backing of Pope Sixtus.

As late as March, Count Girolamo and Francesco de' Pazzi expected action in both Rome and Florence. *And when [again] I asked about the way [to overturn Florence's government], the Count told me: Lorenzo is meant to come to Rome for Easter. As soon as we hear that he has left [Florence], Francesco will also leave to carry out his part and the job will be done on the one who remains [Giuliano in Florence]. We shall think of what should be done to the other one here, and he will be dealt with so that the whole thing is nicely arranged before he leaves us. I asked: will you have him killed? He answered me: No, certainly not. I don't want him to suffer anything unpleasant here, but things will be well taken care of before he leaves. I asked the Count: Does our lord [Pope Sixtus] know about this? He told me: Of course he does. Then I say: hell, he's really consenting to something big there! The Count answered me: Don't you know that we can make him do whatever we want, as long as things go well? And we held to this line of things for quite a few days, about Lorenzo's coming or not coming. Then, seeing that he was not going to come, they decided that action had to be taken most definitely before May was upon us . . . . And as I've said many times, this thing was always being talked about . . . and [we agreed] that things could simply not go on this way or the whole affair would be discovered, because it was already on so many tongues.*

The Count's assertion that they could bend the Pope to their wishes seems an extraordinary claim, but it is well to remember that Sixtus had spent most of his life as a scholar and unworldly friar; that once he was handed power and steeped in the materialism of politics, his nepotistic devotion to his family opened him up to their endearments, flattery, and manipulation.

Fear of exposure moved the plotters to action at last. *It was resolved that Francesco should come here [to Florence], that Giovan Francesco da Tolentino and I should repair to Imola, and Messer Lorenzo [Giustini] da Castello to . . . [*something here is deleted from the confession, probably naming the Duke of Urbino*] in order to complete the arrangements, then on for him to Città di Castello. And we were all to be fully ready to act on whatever orders should come from Messer Jacopo, the Archbishop, and Francesco . . . . And this command was given to us by the Signor Count in Rome. In the end, the Bishop of Lyons also came [into the affair] and he repeated the same command, that we should be ready to meet every request of the above-named men. . . . We heard nothing more until that Saturday at the second hour of the night [10:00]. Then on Sunday they again changed the plan. And this is the way these matters were handled, although we were always told to look out for the honour of our lord [Pope Sixtus] and of the Count. Thus on Sunday morning, 26 April 1478, in Santa Liperata [the cathedral of Florence] that was done which has been made public to the whole world.*

Notes for the Confession

THE VILLAINS OF Montesecco's confession are Pope Sixtus, his nephew Count Girolamo, Francesco de' Pazzi, Archbishop Salviati, and the head of the Pazzi family in Florence, the knight and merchant banker Messer Jacopo. What the soldier confessed added up to so grave an indictment of Lorenzo's enemies, that three months later (August), in the midst of war with the papacy, Florentine political leaders printed and circulated the confession, in a campaign to denigrate and subvert the interdicts that Sixtus had imposed on Florence, Pistoia, and Fiesole. Priests here had been ordered to suspend their pastoral duties, while wagging tongues touched daily on the scandal of the excommunication both of Lorenzo and of the heads of Florentine government during the months of April and May. Montesecco's confession, however, has large shadows; it implicates only the ringleaders; information about the King of Naples and Duke of Urbino is suppressed; motives are either ignored or made too general; all minor confederates in the web of secrecy are passed over in silence; and the soldier himself, having his own axe to grind, keeps hinting that the plot was harebrained. But then he had scarcely been under orders to a hare.

One of the keys that never emerges from his testimony — we need the advantage of hindsight for this — is the immensity of the Pope's nepotistic ambitions. Within three months of his coronation, some of his nephews were drawing payments from the Apostolic Camera. Within the year, he bought houses in Rome for his sisters, who lived up in the Genoa region, and had them move to the Holy City. But most unusual was the fact that of the thirty-four cardinals created by him during his pontificate, both with and without the consent of the College of Cardinals, no fewer than six were nephews of his, three of them having been elevated to the red at a single go in 1477, and two in December 1471. Sixtus, in short, was ready to countenance any charge of infamy, any denunciation of his cascade of favours for relatives, so long as he could successfully raise them above other worldly creatures by means of lands, offices, dignities, church incomes, and audacious (social-climbing) marriages. In this unfolding spectacle, Lorenzo and Florence were too much in the way, especially along the path of the Pope's plans for Count Girolamo in Romagna. The swagger of Sixtine ambition is articulated in that delicious group portrait of nepotism by Melozzo da Forlì. Aimed at consolidation by his reclaiming of towns and fortresses that had been turned into autonomous mini-states, his policies for the Papal State may even have been driven by the force of his nepotism.

Although unnamed in the confession as published, Ferrante of Naples and the Duke of Urbino were involved as shadowy but crucial presences from the very start. Florence had a treaty of alliance with Venice and Milan, and the wily King Ferrante had taken offence by choosing to see it as a threat to his pact with Pope Sixtus. Eyeing Siena and the lands of southern Tuscany, he was seeking to have a voice there, and the northern alliance appeared to send him a warning. As for Federigo of Urbino, he was both in Ferrante's pocket and in the Pope's — soldiering for them both. But Sixtus had raised Federigo's little principality to a duchy in August 1474, thereby putting him most particularly under a special debt. In a ceremony of prostration, which involved his kissing of the Pope's hands and feet, the new duke had sworn an oath of fidelity. This alliance, moreover, had been reinforced by a marriage: one of Duke

Federigo's daughters, Giovanna, was wedded to a papal nephew, Giovanni, son of Raffaele della Rovere, brother to Pope Sixtus. Blood, marriage, and politics had been profitably linked.

Most absent from Montesecco's picture – yet it keeps ghosting in – was the force of anti-Medici resentment which Archbishop Salviati and Francesco de' Pazzi expected to harness in Florence, once the plot was unleashed. Whether or not the level of resentment had been rightly calculated, it has to be counted as an element which propelled them into action, because it was central to their planning and to Messer Jacopo's decision to join them.

The soldiers, Giovan Francesco da Tolentino and Lorenzo Giustini, who were prepared to lead their troops into Florence, were mercenaries in the pay of Pope Sixtus and Count Girolamo. They were doing a job. Political ideology and soldiering never mixed in Renaissance Italy. No professional soldier ever refrained from marching on a republic because he cherished 'liberty' or republicanism, nor ever refused to move an army against a city under princely rule, because of an ideal belief in the principle of monarchy. Patriots (Machiavelli for one) occasionally railed against the treachery and the expense of mercenaries, but theirs was a feeble voice raised against a torrent. Although the vital social foundations for citizen-armies *had* existed in many thirteenth-century Italian cities, notably so in Florence, politics undermined that resource in the fourteenth century. In the fifteenth century, while local militias of poor men were sometimes called up in emergency situations, as happened in the wake of the Pazzi Conspiracy, no prince or republican elite would have trusted standing, well-armed troops made up of local citizens. War was the business of a profession, including numerous feudal lords in the Papal State and the duchy of Milan. But just as humanists had their pens out for hire, whether to despots or republican oligarchies, so, as military 'technocrats', Tolentino and Giustini sold their services to the highest bidders, or to princes with whom they had long-term ties. Seen in this light, doubts about the feasibility of the April Plot, as strongly implied by the professional Montesecco, must be taken with a grain of salt. He is trying to save his life and reaching out, in his confession, to say flattering things about Lorenzo. Yet the truth is that he travelled repeatedly between Imola, Rome, and Florence, to help draw the conspiracy together; and he carried his commission out 'to the place of doom', fully conscious of the fact that his life was at stake. His alleged refusal to kill Lorenzo with his own hands did not release him from his position at the centre of the plot.

Citing a claim by Lorenzo himself, Piero Parenti observes that on the morning of the tragic walk to the cathedral, Montesecco began by accompanying Lorenzo, linking arms with him and seeking his friendship, intending, perhaps, to reveal the plot. Some superior or servitor, however, then got the soldier to give up his place to Cardinal Sansoni Riario's brother, a more important gentleman. The suggestion is that Lorenzo afterwards speculated about the occasion. But if indeed Montesecco verged just then on exposing the plot and his bosses, here would have been a fine example of the treachery sometimes laid at the feet of mercenaries.

It seems surprising, at first glance, that Archbishop Salviati was able to talk two members of his family into taking part in the plot: his only brother Jacopo, and a first cousin named Bartolomeo but also known, confusingly, as Jacopo. Surprising because these men also knew that they were dicing with death, the more dangerously so on the morning of 26 April, when they joined the train of the Archbishop, almost certainly in the possession of weapons concealed under their cloaks. Poliziano's booklet on the conspiracy dismisses the brother as a depraved nonentity and the cousin as a shrewd businessman who was fond of the company of whores and low-life people. Maybe so, but in view of the capital dangers before them, we must suppose that these two men were convinced that the operation would succeed. What then had the Archbishop said to them? It could only have been (a) that Pope Sixtus himself was solidly behind the plot, (b) that King Ferrante and the Duke of Urbino were also behind it, and (c) that the conspirators had the armed manpower to succeed. These must have been the very reasons – and they were fundamental – that served to recruit the reluctant Messer Jacopo de' Pazzi. Perhaps too, like Messer Jacopo, the Archbishop's brother and cousin were driven by resentment of Lorenzo and belief in the practicality of an urban uprising against the Medici – belief based on a sense of the city's having a silenced political opposition. The last two of these motives, rancour and the promise of political change, were important because they also moved the other Florentines who joined the conspirators.

The one man of letters enticed into the plot seems to have been driven by the hope of a change in government, and he certainly knew the Florentine scene. This was Jacopo Bracciolini, the son of Poggio, one of the liveliest and best-known humanists of the age. Poggio's Latinity and literary brilliance had first established the family in Florence, and Jacopo, whose mother sprang from the Buondelmonti, old Florentine magnates, was brought up reading the Latin classics. The elder Bracciolini managed to break into politics and opened the way for his son in public life. But in the mid 1460s, the learned Jacopo fell in with the anti-Medicean reformers and emerged — unless he was maliciously charged — as one of the more outspoken of them. He was banished from the city for twenty years and sentenced to pay an astounding fine of 2000 gold florins. These penalties were quickly reduced to ten years and 1000 florins; and later on he was allowed to return to Florence, where he made a point of courting Lorenzo and even took part, lavishly dressed, in the fancy Florentine tourney of 1469. In 1476 he issued an Italian translation of his father's Latin *History of Florence*. This was followed in 1477, or early 1478, by his commentary on one of the six parts of Petrarch's long poem on *Triumphs*, the one on the 'Triumph of Fame', which is all about 'men of iron' and moral 'valour', including 'intellectual heroes'. Jacopo dedicated this short work to Lorenzo de' Medici. Yet in 1477, drawing upon his numerous connections, he was also taken on as secretary to the new cardinal and papal nephew, Raffaele Sansoni Riario. Already in touch with them, this appointment brought Jacopo Bracciolini into closer contact with the conspirators, the Archbishop of Pisa and Francesco de' Pazzi, who promptly drew him into their bloody business, unless, indeed, he had been recruited first and then attached to the cardinal.

Poliziano's picture of this man is another travesty. He would have us believe that Jacopo was a debt-ridden, evil-tongued, intellectual show-off, who readily sold himself and his paltry talents, and so was obviously seeking place, favour, and money from the chief conspirators. The world of politics disappears: Jacopo is cast as an intellectual prostitute. In fact, he was a serious writer and student of the classics, with marked republican views, though he was also attracted by the notion of a 'civil principate' and the hope that princely rule could be enlightened.

As time and more thought revealed the complexities of the plot to the conspirators, the web of machination spread. The slaying of the two brothers would trigger the action, and the next two steps – so it was assumed – would follow almost of themselves: seizing the government palace and summoning 'the people' out into the streets of Florence. But since professional arms and violence would also be at the fulcrum, these required the recruitment of skilled men. However, the last of the big-name Florentines among the plotters, Bernardo Bandini Baroncelli (Figure 9), was not a man of this sort. In his curt dismissal, Poliziano calls him a shameless and evil bankrupt. Though not much is known about him, he clearly had close connections with Francesco and Jacopo de' Pazzi, and was even, possibly, a Pazzi employee. The Milanese ambassador referred to him – mockingly perhaps – as their 'cashier'. But Valori reported that he was 'by nature most discerning, with a quickness of spirit and body'. He had nearly 1000 florins invested in one of the Pazzi banks; his wife had brought a very considerable dowry of 2600 'large' (full value) florins to their marriage; and he had lofty connections both in Naples and Rome, where his widow Giovanna was afterwards able to enlist the support of the Cardinal of Rouen, Guillaume d'Estouteville, in the legal struggle to salvage her dowry from the debacle of the Pazzi Conspiracy.

Put into a wider context, Poliziano's 'bankrupt' Bernardo turns out to have had a close relative, Pierantonio Bandini Baroncelli, who ran the Bruges branch of the Pazzi Bank for some years. Like the Mozzi, Bardi, and Peruzzi, the Baroncelli were an honoured Florentine clan, often associated with banking. Holding a solid place in the political life of the city, they were long concentrated, like the Salviati, in Florence's eastern (Santa Croce) quarter. When one of the Baroncelli households sided with the anti-Medici faction in 1433–34, they and all their male descendants were banished from the city. Prospering in Naples thereafter, and enjoying the King's favour, they won the sympathies of the Baroncelli back in Florence; and Bernardo himself spent some time in that southern city, where he had access to King Ferrante. Indeed, it was thanks to Ferrante's personal intervention that Bernardo, after killing Giuliano de' Medici, was able to flee as far as Constantinople. Intriguingly, too, one of his cousins, Maria Baroncelli, was married to Tommaso Portinari, the

Fig. 9 Leonardo da Vinci, *Bernardo Bandini Baroncelli Shown Hanged.*

former head of the Bruges branch of the Medici Bank. All in all, then, Bernardo had superior connections.

Two priests were recruited late in the proceedings: Antonio Maffei da Volterra, a clerk in papal service, and Ser Stefano da Bagnone, parish priest of the village of Montemurlo, which lay in the middle of lands owned by Messer Jacopo de' Pazzi. Maffei joined the conspirators, it was alleged, in revenge for the sacking of his native Volterra in 1472 , a merciless assault for which the Volterrans, who had rebelled against Florence, blamed Lorenzo the Magnificent. As for Ser Stefano, Poliziano informs us that he was Messer Jacopo's secretary and tutor to his bastard daughter Caterina. He also held a benefice in the parish church of San Procolo, where Messer Jacopo surely enjoyed favour, because it almost touched the southern flank of the enclave of Pazzi houses. These late recruits were drawn in to carry out one of Montesecco's prime tasks. Although his confession makes no mention of this, contemporary reports affirm that the soldier had made a commitment to kill Lorenzo with his own hands. With the passage of time, however, the plot kept changing, and when at last it became clear that the killings would have to take place at High Mass in Santa Maria del Fiore, Montesecco reneged on this part of his commission by pleading that he was unable to combine murder with sacrilege. It was also suggested, in a fine example of Medicean mythmaking, that he had got to like the Florentine *signore* too much. In the event, the two priests stepped in and agreed to spill the necessary blood. And so we are left with a mystery here: the readiness of a professional like Montesecco to put one of the bloodiest parts of the action into the hands of two priestly amateurs. It was a moment of strange confusion or inattention on his part, above all because the failure of the plot was very likely to end in his own death.

At the end of his confession, Montesecco glancingly introduces a mysterious figure, the Bishop of Lyons, who is shown confirming the fact that Messer Jacopo, Archbishop Salviati, and Francesco de' Pazzi were the heads of the Conspiracy. This man was a certain Thomas James, who was clearly indebted to Pope Sixtus and the Riario family. But interestingly, the soldier never refers to Antonio di Piero de' Pazzi, Bishop of Sarno and Mileto, who had conducted at least one mission to France for the Pazzi and Pope Sixtus. Sarno was about eighteen miles due east of Naples, and Antonio had been picked for that diocese by King Ferrante and Pope Sixtus in the summer of 1475, shortly after these two princes began to cast about for ways to terminate Lorenzo de' Medici's authority in Florence. Nephew to Messer Jacopo, first cousin to Francesco, and supported both by Sixtus and Ferrante, the Bishop of Sarno, then of Mileto, had almost certainly ended in the camp of the conspirators, although not a scrap of proof was offered when he was charged with having had full knowledge of the plot. The Eight decreed that he be 'confined for life to his new diocese of Mileto', but Florence had no way of enforcing the sentence.

Now enter a seventeen-year-old student, whose presence in Florence turned out to be a pivot in the action: Cardinal Raffaele Sansoni Riario. His mother, Violante Riario, was the daughter of Sixtus IV's elder sister Bianca, thus making the youth a grand-nephew of the Pope. But not for him, in his studies, anything so lofty as theology, his grand-uncle's subject. The family knew what they needed. This young prince, who was eventually to hold sixteen archbishoprics, had been dispatched to the University of Pisa to study canon law, which would give him a grasp of the legal rights and responsibilities of the Church and its different orders, and be a step to top-level administration. On the appointed morning in the Florence cathedral, however, he would have no need of legal subtleties on suddenly finding himself in the thick of a plot, once the frenzied screams and cries began to resound in that vast space. Yet it was his special visit to Lorenzo's city, slyly choreographed by the conspirators, that was turned into the springboard for the attempt to murder the two brothers. Since he was required, as a cardinal, to keep a large train of servitors, particularly when travelling, the ringleaders planted armed men in his retinue. One of these turned out to be the humanist Jacopo Bracciolini. Given their need both of soldiers and overwhelming surprise, they could not afford to pass up the Cardinal's large company. We can almost hear them advising the inexperienced youth on his first trip to Florence, informing him that his entry into that city, to be entertained by the Medici and perhaps even to negotiate with Lorenzo, had to be made with all due dignity. He must be accompanied by a large troop of servitors and attendants. This pitch carried the more force in that Pope Sixtus had invested the young man with the powers of a papal legate, making him an emissary with the right to treat top-drawer diplomatic questions.

It is likely that Giovan Francesco da Tolentino and Lorenzo Giustini, the captains elected to conduct troops into Florence, were first approached in late September or October 1477. They would strike from the outside. But the prime movers inside the city, Archbishop Salviati and Messer Jacopo de' Pazzi, also needed soldiers in their entourages, and most of these had to be hired at the last possible moment, in order to guard the secret of the plot and to keep from rousing suspicions. About twenty fully-armed political exiles from Perugia arrived on the scene, assistants to the Archbishop and to others. They would all end as torn bodies in the great square of the Lord Priors. The reprisals that immediately followed the foiled plot were so swift and complete, so many foreigners were killed, that it has never been possible to assign a final figure to the numbers slaughtered or executed. From eighty to a hundred victims over the course of the first three days (26–28 April) would seem to be about right.

Despite the failure of the conspirators, it may be easily argued that the plot was driven by an accurate sense of what was practical and feasible. If Lorenzo had been killed along with Giuliano, or if Archbishop Salviati and Messer Jacopo had managed to take the government palace, and the additional companies of papal soldiers had entered the city, there can be little doubt that the conspirators would have forced a change of government in Florence: a change made, to be sure, with the zeal and assistance of hundreds of alienated citizens and returned exiles. The restoration of peace, the brandishing of promises, and the further courting or enlargement of the political class would have served, in time, to deliver many more supporters to their ranks. With the Medici of Cosimo's branch gone, no other Florentine family had the wealth or name or charisma to rally and lead the remnants of the Medicean opposition.

CHAPTER TEN

Raging: Pope and Citizen

Of Gods and Men

ONCE THE PLOT had failed, Lorenzo faced his most dangerous enemy in a raging Pope Sixtus IV: a fierce antagonist, even if a former mendicant friar and an intellectual. But after the murder of the young Giuliano and the Count of Montesecco's confession, the Medici lord's closest aides – such as the Bishop of Arezzo and Bartolomeo Scala – were also in a fury, arguably the best of passions for a vigorous defence of Lorenzo. The King of Naples could press Florence and Lorenzo with troops and foreign alliances. The Duke of Urbino could command armies against Florence. Sixtus, however, Vicar of Christ on earth and the head of Christendom, had a web of diplomatic contacts all over Europe, in addition to vast revenue from a wealth of sources. He could call not only on squadrons of cavalry and infantry, but also on the weapons that entitled him to claim the high moral ground. And those weapons were not words alone; they were also direct action, such as in papal bulls that imposed excommunications, interdicts against cities and countries, and the hounding of Florentine merchants abroad. Therefore, once the conspirators against Lorenzo had the active support of the Pope, little wonder that they had such faith in their plot.

An outstanding debater and preacher, Sixtus had a brilliant career behind him as a professor, theologian, and General of the Franciscan Order. He knew all the tricks of argument, rhetorical and logical; and he held – as a tenet in theology – that being the Vicar of Christ, he could not submit to the arbitration of any mortal creature. Now, using these talents in papal bulls and with the other resources at his fingertips, he must have seemed invincible in his clash with Lorenzo, who, in law, was only a citizen of Florence, not its prince, for all his usurped authority. Moreover, as an unflinching nepotist and the secret father, possibly, of one of his alleged nephews, Sixtus was stirred by nothing so much, it seemed, as the material interests of his own family. Here was another spur to his struggle with Lorenzo, who stood obstinately in the way of his family ambitions in Romagna. The Florentine chieftain feared papal power in the region and had his own clients there, on Florence's eastern borders, just where Sixtus was seeking to camouflage his nepotism by claiming that he was doing no more than seeking superior control inside his own Papal State.

Yet Lorenzo held an important card, one not altogether appreciated in the rest of Europe, and this was the habit of dynamic alliance-making among Italian states, a vigorous tradition that ran back for 350 years. Since the papacy as a temporal power was looked upon by neighbouring states with as much suspicion as any other, Lorenzo and his Florentines would be able to count on foreign alliances in their stand against the Pope's armies and interdicts.

The drama itself drew colour and detail from the fact that the fight between the old Pope (aged sixty-four) and the young citizen (twenty-nine) had a personal touch. It was not an affair of unknown faces, impersonally conducted. They had met several times back in the autumn of 1471, not long after Sixtus's coronation in August, when Lorenzo headed an imposing Florentine embassy to Rome, sent out to congratulate and honour the new pope. In the course of their meetings, Sixtus had put both the monies of the Apostolic Chamber and the Tolfa alum mines, near Città Vecchia, under the control of the Medici Bank, officially now the Pope's new 'Depositary', which was charged chiefly with receiving and disbursing funds. In addition, apart from allowing him to buy some antique cameos and medals for modest prices from the collection of the previous pope (Paul II), he also made a personal gift to Lorenzo of two ancient marble busts, representing Augustus and Agrippa.

A few months later, in February 1472, Sixtus even granted a special plenary indulgence to Lorenzo, Giuliano, their mother Lucrezia Tornabuoni, and their paternal grandmother Contessina. But it happened that Lorenzo wanted something bigger and more worldly: he may have broached the subject of a cardinal's hat for his brother Giuliano, but did not begin to press this suit until 1472. Reacting pleasantly but making no promises, Sixtus did not reject the request, particularly since the mighty Orsini family of Rome had figured among his most vigorous supporters for the papal tiara, and Lorenzo's wife was an Orsini. Being as political an animal as Lorenzo himself, he understood that the keen desire to have a cardinal in the Medici family was nothing if not politics. Given their slippery position in the Florentine republic, the family was in grave need of the influence and dignity of a Church magnate. In any final reckoning at Florence, only some kind of 'higher' power — combined of course with the force of arms — would enable the Medici to paint their unconstitutional authority with the colour of right; and in this work, arms alone might not be enough.

By 1475, however, such an honour had been made impossible by Lorenzo's acrimonious relations with Sixtus, and any hope of a cardinal's hat would now depend upon relations with the next pope. Lorenzo's fearsome task for the moment was to grapple with the consequences of Florence's bloody reprisals against the conspirators: war, excommunications, interdicts, and the expulsion or harassment of Florentine merchants and bankers in Rome, Naples, Siena, Urbino, and other towns.

With papal troops already illegally present in Florentine territory on 26 April 1478, it was only a matter of weeks before war between Florence and the Pope turned into outright aggression and became a public fact. In June the republic set up its war magistracy, the Ten, and Lorenzo, on being elected to it, took major government office for — surprisingly — only the second time in his life. But election to the war-office Ten would alter little for him or others on the Florentine political scene, save to provide a frame for his actual authority. Aside from the fact that important political decisions were often made in the Medici Palace, he used to stride into council chambers now and then to watch men cast illegal 'exposed' votes (see pp. 52–3), to see whether or not they were backing his measures. In this fashion, he piloted two petitions through council favouring his friend, the poet Luigi Pulci, one securing a high office for him and another removing his sentence of exile to Vernia. He perhaps also used the same method to secure the legislation that deprived Giovanni de' Pazzi's wife, Beatrice Borromei, of a great inheritance.

For Lorenzo, at least, the consequences of the April Plot seemed to lurch out of control. By the middle of May all Florentine merchants in

Rome were being closely watched, and by the 24th, after all had been arrested and briefly jailed, they were forbidden to leave the city or to send goods and money out of it. In the eyes of Pope Sixtus, Lorenzo and the Florentine government had been guilty of sacrilege, a kind of spiritual high treason, in the horrors connected with the window-hanging of the Archbishop of Pisa, by countenancing the murder of innocent priests (young men in Cardinal Sansoni Riario's train), and by imprisoning the Cardinal. The bull of excommunication was dated June 1st, printed and published on the 4th, and then sent out to the leading princes of Italy and Europe, together with supporting papal letters. The news reached lesser places by moving through the Church's great web of bishops. Papal nuncios were also dispatched to the Emperor, the King of France, and Venice. Stigmatised as 'sons of iniquity', Lorenzo, the Eight, two sets of Lord Priors, and their advisors were denied all Church services and sacraments; and Christians were meant to avoid all ordinary social intercourse with them, lest their impious contagion spread. This anathema was to go on until such time as they released the Cardinal and met other conditions laid down by Sixtus. On 8 June the Pope offered 'a plenary remission of sins and other indulgences' to all men who took up arms against Florence. On the 22nd he put Florence, Fiesole, and Pistoia, under an interdict, ordering the local clergy to suspend all religious services for the laity, on pain of incurring censures themselves. He claimed to have the support of the College of Cardinals.

The bull of excommunication rehearsed Lorenzo's other acts of infidelity and disobedience, including his mulish opposition to the appointment of Salviati as Archbishop of Pisa, his meddling in the papal lands of Imola and Città di Castello, and the material assistance which Florence had given to the anti-papal rebels, Niccolò Vitelli and Carlo da Montone. The next move came from King Ferrante of Naples, who dispatched an embassy to Florence in strong support of the Holy Father and threatening the city with a cruel war and total destruction, unless the Florentines expelled Lorenzo from their midst. Every effort was made to distinguish this 'tyrant' and ill-famed citizen from the free republic: Florence had but to get rid of him, or turn him over to Sixtus, and all would be well.

On 12 June, when Lorenzo finally met with the city's most influential citizens to discuss the threat of war, he faced a throng of Mediceans

— men whose commitment to the Medici house was beyond question and whose families had long gleaned material benefits from that loyalty. Addressing them in his most eloquent and moving manner, he told them that he was ready for exile or even death, if such action would bring peace with the enemy. He had, after all, received more favour from Florence than any other citizen, so all the more must he be ready, from love of country too, to put the common good above his own. Moved to tears, the assembly's reaction was unsurprising. Their destinies were tied up with those of the Medici; they were compromised, at all events thus far; and so they closed ranks with Lorenzo by assuring him that the safety and welfare of Florence and of the Medici were identical. To defend one was to defend the other. Fully aware of King Ferrante's ambitions in southern Tuscany and of the Pope's designs in Romagna, they saw to it that on the next day (13 June) Lorenzo was elected to the war-office Ten. He had resigned in fact, on 18 May, from the powerful political and criminal police, the Eight; and four days later — with all but a tiny handful of arms' permits revoked in the city — he was granted the right to have eight private guardsmen around his person, all men of his own choice. In June, the Eight increased this number to twelve, and guards were also assigned to his family.

In the second week of July, papal and Neapolitan troops, commanded by the dukes of Urbino and Calabria, pushed deep into Florentine territory in the far south-east, near Montepulciano, then quickly swept up to the north-west, passing above Siena, to lay hands on Radda and Castellina in Chianti, two of Florence's fortified towns. The Florentines were able to claim no more than a slight, diversionary victory near Perugia.

The battlefield, however, was also on paper and in the minds of men. Lorenzo and Florence lost no time in getting letters of self-defence out to princes, friends, and possible allies. Milan immediately responded with a dispatch of small companies of troops; Venice expressed outrage over the excommunications and interdicts; Giovanni Bentivoglio of Bologna hurried to Florence with his soldiers; and Louis XI of France, taking Florence's side at once, denounced the Pope, sent emissaries to Italy and, seeking to undermine papal authority, soon began to press for a general Church Council. King and Pope, at any rate, had been at loggerheads for some time.

Turning up in Rome with a deathly-pale face, the fruit — it was said — of numerous threats of execution, the young Cardinal of San Giorgio had been released by the Florentines on 4 June, but the papal censures against Lorenzo and his 'accomplices' were not suspended or annulled, despite papal suggestions that the release of the Cardinal would bring their removal. In June and July, all Medici banking and other assets in Rome and Naples were seized; and some of the Pope's July letters now referred to Lorenzo as 'a heretic'. The feisty Sixtus was not intimidated by King Louis's warnings, the threats of a Church Council, or the Florentine call for the withdrawal of all obedience to him. If anything, he stepped up his railing against Lorenzo and Florence.

In any war of words, Renaissance Florentines were second to none. Lorenzo had reacted to the Pope's censures by quickly 'mobilising his secretaries, inciting his cohort of loyal followers, and orchestrating a massive anti-papal campaign'. He even turned to leading jurists of the age (Bartolomeo Sozzini, Bulgarini of Siena, and Francesco Accolti), to get them to examine the legality as well of the excommunications as of the interdicts imposed on Florence and the other cities. They concluded that the censures had no validity, that the whole question could be appealed to a Church Council, and that the clergy therefore should continue with their care of souls and go on administering the sacraments — legal arguments that Lorenzo and the Florentine government lost no time in circulating. Part of the case in law surely rested on the force of two canon-law decretals, holding that priests are not in ecclesiastical dress when they are caught in the act of bearing arms and disposed to commit murder. They thereby forfeit their clerical privileges. However, in the reprisals that followed the April Plot, five or six priests at least were killed, despite the fact, so far as we know, that only two were armed.

A scornful letter to Pope Sixtus from the Lord Priors, dated 21 July 1478, already asserted that 'your charges make us laugh', while referring to him repeatedly as 'friar Francesco [of Savona]'. They also call him a 'Judas in the seat of Peter,' throwing out 'poison like a net from your boat, in order to catch good fish'. But the most blistering attack of all, the *Florentina Synodus*, issued from the pen of Lorenzo's former tutor and continuing favourite, now Bishop of Arezzo, Gentile Becchi. In 1472, within a year of Sixtus's coronation, so soon, Becchi had produced an acerbic Latin epigram, nailing him both for his flagrant nepotism and theft of the Church's riches. It must have rankled:

> Sixtus scattered jewels and silver vessels.
> A treasure spent, he parceled out the state.
> The state gone, the towns remained: he's giving these away.
> O tiara, beware: he's asking, 'What am I anyway?'

Becchi now drafted a document, dated 23 July 1478, alleged to be the report of a Florentine Synod, a meeting of high-ranking clergymen in the cathedral of Florence, supposedly called to consider the excommunications and the plot against the Medici. Whether or not such a synod was ever held remains a trifle uncertain, though it was most likely an outright fiction. No evidence relating to it, administrative or financial, has ever been found, despite the fact that the Florentines of Lorenzo's day were compulsive record keepers. The point of the Synod, real or invented, was clear enough: it was to issue a scathing reply to the papal indictment, to print it post haste, and to circulate it.

Mocking, angry, jeering, and abusive, *Florentina Synodus* scoffs at Sixtus's charges in the bull of excommunications. It opens with a rush of images, calling Pope Sixtus 'Vicar of the devil' and a pimp who has prostituted his own mother, the Church, by selling its rites and offices, in order to nourish 'pigs with golden truffles'. Archbishop Salviati 'was never a Christian' but 'an agent of insurrection'. At the moment of his rabid violence, which called for a swift defence, he was an armed criminal, not an archbishop. If the Priors had not defended themselves and he had seized the government palace, he would have had them hanged. The innocent Lorenzo has been put outside the Church, excommunicated, because he did not allow himself to be murdered, as his brother was; and the same curse has been laid on the Lord Priors of March–April because they refused to let themselves be thrown from the palace windows. Well then, the Synod curses the curse and excommunicates the excommunications.

The Synod's invective passes to the details of the plot itself, to the Count of Montesecco's confession, and to the eleven points raised against Lorenzo in the excommunication, including his material support for the anti-papal rebels Niccolò Vitelli and Carlo da Montone, while all the while deriding and trashing Sixtine pretensions. There is no greater killer than one who happens to be a pope and a theologian. How can a simonist and heretic give voice to the Holy Spirit? This man now wants to wash his wicked stains with excrement and to accomplish with words what he failed to do with the sword. 'Accomplices' he calls Lorenzo's friends. Who rose up against 'the parricides' and 'traitors', if not the entire city? Who dragged Jacopo de' Pazzi's corpse through the streets of Florence, 'a crowd of accomplices or a crowd of little boys?' And again, 'Who sang out the ditty, Death to the Pope, Death to the Cardinal, Long live Lorenzo who gives us bread!'?

The charges continue. Sixtus is not the Vicar of Christ but the vicar of Count Girolamo Riario. He is like all 'those little women who, being whores themselves, call others fornicators'. The Cardinal's aides in the cathedral were armed, so how could they have been men in holy orders? Sixtus has debased the Church, swung it round to evil worldly ends, violated trusts, and used the money of Christians to wage a private war. 'We show wounds and slaying, he comes up with words and false accusations.' He does not say that the servants of the two prelates carried weapons, were set on seizing the government palace, were instigating rebellion, and holding swords to the throats of the Lord Priors. 'Priests' is what he calls killers, and he is now bent on adding poison to the wounds, spears to the sword, and an army to the band of hired assassins. Since Florentines cannot turn to the Pope for justice, they must have recourse to the Emperor, to the King of France, and to all Christian princes. To these they appeal against a man who became pope by means of simony. They also accuse him of murder, treason, and heresy. Since he is the Vicar of the devil, the Synod condemns him to the devil and calls on the Lord to deliver Christians from the false shepherds who come as sheep, when they are nothing but ravenous wolves. The document even makes a glancing reference to the interests of humanism by admitting to 'a gasping and broken [literary] style, because grief mutilates our discourse'.

This diatribe against Sixtus was followed on 11 August by a 'Defence of the Florentines' (*Excusatio Florentinorum*), an open letter of the Lord Priors, drafted and signed by the humanist and top government secretary (chancellor), Bartolomeo Scala. Levelled at the Pope and his censures, and summoning the support of Christian princes, the letter touches on particulars of the plot and reproduces verbatim the whole of Montesecco's confession. It is directly addressed to the Habsburg Holy Roman Emperor, Frederick III, and to the King of France, but it was also printed by the same press that issued Becchi's *Florentina Synodus*, and was then sent out to as many princes and cities as the government deemed useful. Scala points out, among other matters, that the leading men of the city were the very ones who saved Cardinal Sansoni Riario from the fury of the mob, which had been eager to tear into him too.

Recently arrived in Italy, the newly-invented printing press fuelled the energies of propaganda in both camps, and it is likely that broadsides did the rounds, in addition to the main texts, which were soon suppressed and destroyed, and so are now exceedingly rare incunabula. The most famous account of the April Plot, *Coniurationis commentarium*, written by the poet and scholar Angelo Poliziano, was produced sometime between May and mid August 1478, and rushed into print, to be followed by two more printings between 1480 and 1482. Poliziano, we have seen, was with Lorenzo in the cathedral's new sacristy, in the hour following the murder of Giuliano. Virulent and mendacious, his account, a work of inane history and incendiary propaganda, reduces the motives of the conspirators to little more than a paste of malice, vice, and greed, while keeping the utmost silence about the roles of Pope Sixtus and the King of Naples. Although it was to fix the historical record for centuries, the Venetian historian Giovan Michele Bruto, writing in the middle of the sixteenth century, already rejected Poliziano's account as childish history, because he saw that the conspiracy was deeply political. If nothing else, the ensuing Pazzi War, bringing immediate anxiety to Florence and a frantic diplomacy, plagued the opponents – but especially Lorenzo and his friends – for the better part of twenty months, until the raw power of Lorenzo's enemies once again became decisive, forced him into concessive negotiations, and brought the war to an end.

Although conducted chiefly in Latin, beyond the understanding of all but a minority of men, the verbal assault on Pope Sixtus made Florentines uneasy. By introducing spiritual weapons – he had no other choice – the Pope himself had made the war of words just as important as marching troops. Lorenzo's defenders were forced to respond in kind, but they could look back to a strong precedent and draw courage from it. A hundred years before, during its 'War of the Eight Saints' against the papacy (1375–78), Florence had used similar means, polemic, to fight Pope Gregory XI. The memory of this clash now belonged to the tradition of anti-clericalism, which was most found among the educated and was richly nourished by the Great Schism (1378–1415), with its shocking scandal of two and then three rival popes, each hurling abuse at the others. This background held the intellectual ancestry of the philippic, *Florentina Synodus*, and the lineage for the figure of the anti-clerical cleric. Who could best know and point out the shortcomings of priests, if not priests themselves? Stepping into this tradition, the author of *Florentina Synodus*, the Bishop of Arezzo, Lorenzo's former tutor, was able to release a stream of scurrilous abuse, unmatched even by the diatribes of the Protestant Reformers fifty years later. Forced to deal with Pope Sixtus IV as a mere earthly ruler, but seeing him as all the more vile and unworthy because of his exalted spiritual pretensions, he would spare no vulgarity or insult. In order to show that he was nothing but a nepotist and grubby worldling, the Bishop had to bring Sixtus down to earth and even into the dirt.

Yet the churchman's savage roughing up of Pope Sixtus was really meant for the world of high politics. The fact that Poliziano himself does not mention Sixtus in his account is an indicator of the religious delicacies that lay in the line of fire, although we can be sure that the Pope's name was on every tongue in conversation throughout Florence. The Pazzi War had broken out within seven weeks of the assault in the cathedral, and Florence was facing papal troops. In this setting, the prop-aganda battle was easily joined without open reference to the great names, as shown at the level of street performances, in the public recitation of an anonymous poem 'On the Death of Giuliano de' Medici'. Florence and other Italian cities had occasional performers known as 'bench singers': rhymesters who would chant or speak out verse chronicles of recent or horrific events, usually at a well-known site and to a crowd of listeners.

Done in several hundred lines of *terza rima*, the poem in question – actually a narrative of the April Plot – began to do the rounds in Florence no later than October 1478, when a printed version was already available for sale. It includes a stinging indictment of the Pazzi family and of 'Salviato', the late Archbishop of Pisa, while also announcing that the Conspiracy involved 'others of great condition,/ but better not to speak their names'. No opportunity to praise friends or to accuse enemies is lost. The poet seizes the occasion to sing the glories of the Medici, 'that saintly house', and of Giuliano, 'a radiant sun' who 'had come down to earth from the choir of heaven'. There is also of course an accolade for Lorenzo, who is ruled by 'kindness and charity,/ supreme knowledge and an old man's gravity'. He 'keeps justice' in Florence 'on the straight and narrow' and 'supports his people', the Florentines. As the lines weave toward a conclusion, the poet implores God to place Giuliano 'in the College of your Holy Martyrs'.

A second poem on the murder of Giuliano was also printed and attributed to the major poet, Luigi Pulci. It was written to console Giuliano's mother, Lucrezia Tornabuoni. The focus here is more truly on the murdered man, who 'was a warming fire in the winter and a fresh breeze in the summer'. But the poem also fulminates against papal Rome, and although Pope Sixtus again goes unmentioned, he and his cardinals are the targets of the poet's rage. Rome, he says, is 'the new wife' of the god of the underworld, Pluto; it is a Babylon 'teeming with poisonous tigers and snakes' and 'greedy for the blood of human flesh'. Dante and Petrarch railed 'against you . . . O schismatic synagogue!' Go then, and 'ride with the horsemen of the devil.'

Lashing out at the top men in the Church, Pulci – if he was the author – steps directly into the city's current of anti-clericalism and has no qualms about addressing his attack to Lucrezia Tornabuoni. She, indeed, was known for her piety and was herself the author of a small body of religious verse.

The Medicean regime forced the Florentine clergy to go on meeting their religious obligations to the laity, and while having their moments of anxiety, neither Lorenzo nor other political leaders in Florence seem to have suffered much from any denial of rites or services. Nevertheless, the censures produced shame and discomfort, not to mention the fact that they nourished enemy propaganda. For all its worldly ways and airs, Florence was a religious city, even deeply so; only sixteen years later, Florentines saw the start of the Savonarolan era, with its religious processions and episodes of astonishing fervour. A growing anxiety snaked through the city, as plague broke out in the summer of 1478 and the war passed into a second year, apparently holding no realistic prospects of a peace, and turning ever more destructive for citizens, such as the patrician Vettori family, who had rich possessions in the Tuscan countryside (Val d'Elsa), lying in the path of ravaging soldiers. The consequent fears drew forth a swelling voice of complaint among the many who often believed that war and epidemic disease were a sign of God's displeasure. In March 1479, Florentine citizens began secretly to post up squibs and other anonymous jottings against Lorenzo. All the while, too, Sixtus kept it up: he went on insisting that if Lorenzo would go to Rome, humble himself, and seek his forgiveness, a general solution would then come almost of itself.

Anxious about the interdict, war costs, threats to Florentine merchants in foreign lands, and fearful of a discontented populace, the Ten and the Lord Priors were none the less forced to impose war taxes. They also found more monies for their war chest by dipping, in a roundabout fashion, into the stored-up assets of citizens. Payments to all shareholders in the government debt were suspended and rerouted into the pockets of soldiers. Within weeks of the conspiracy, and with Lorenzo at first disbursing money from his own pocket, Florence had hired an extra 3000 mercenaries.

In a letter of 1477, while fully recognising the impiety of the wish, Lorenzo had asserted that for his purposes three or four popes would be better than one; and in the summer and autumn of 1478, he could have wished for nothing better. In private, surely, he raged against the Pope, particularly as his letters betray signs of desperation over personal shortages of cash throughout that period and later. He was pushed to dun his debtors for the repayment of loans, including the lords of Mantua and Milan; and he bullied his unhappy young cousins, heads of the collateral Medici line, into lending him many thousands of florins. Most of the money needed and raised he spent on soldiers, and some of it came from digging into his own cash reserves, at the very time when his bank branches at Bruges, Milan, Venice, and Avignon were teetering on the edge of failure. In one way or another he would be fully reimbursed. With the help of his agents in government and devious theft from the public till, as we shall see, he was to make up for any losses.

In the meantime, right through the crisis, Florence had trouble with its allies: Venice, Milan, and Ferrara. In the opening months of the war, none came forward with enough soldiers to enable Florentines to feel secure, as Neapolitan and papal troops raked its southern frontiers. Milan faced a revolt in Genoa, its seaport colony, fomented by King Ferrante and the uncles of the young Duke of Milan. Venice, worried about the advancing Turks, offered much advice and a flow of words, but was short in deeds. And the Duke of Ferrara, Ercole d'Este, ruled too small a state to be of much use. In his incarnation as a *condottiere*, he himself needed cash and in fact, in September, became captain general of Florence's allied forces.

Despite some additional help from allies, the following year brought more defeats for the republic and a fresh outbreak of plague. Florence lost two great fortresses to enemy action in the south, Poggio Imperiale in September and Colle Val d'Elsa, a major market town, in November. Enemy soldiers were never more than eighteen to twenty miles away from Florence's walls, and occasionally their forays took them in much closer. But the productive countryside was the prime sufferer, especially around Cortona, Arezzo, Certaldo, Vico, Colle, Castellina, and Poggibonsi, where soldiers shattered the rhythms of agricultural labour by means of arson, no less than by looting food supplies, goods, and livestock at will, and then no doubt disposing of much of their booty in Sienese territory. The little republic of Siena, a traditional Florentine enemy, had thrown its support behind Pope Sixtus and King Ferrante of Naples, and one of the two enemy commanders, the Duke of Calabria, Ferrante's son, was actually billeted there.

The crisis peaked and Lorenzo was driven to the wall. Day after day for months, working as the *maestro* of the war-office Ten, he did nothing but direct policy, sweat out decisions, and write or dictate countless letters. He was desperately overworked. Complaints and murmuring against the regime gained momentum. Trade in wool and silk, the backbone of local industry, had declined sharply. Business travel and employment suffered. The premises of Florentine cloth merchants and banks had been shut down in Rome and southern Italy. To top it all, bread prices had been rising since about 1473. Rioting broke out in the streets of Florence, caused in part by the menace of famine. And at the end of the summer (1479) Lorenzo was finally stricken by a stubborn fever. But now he had suddenly to face the worst possible turn in his relations with allies.

The Journey to Naples

WHEN THE YOUNG Duke of Milan died in late July, his disgraced uncles (Ludovico and Ascanio Sforza) and a large company of Milanese exiles were able to strike an agreement with his mother, the regent Bona of Savoy. They returned to Milan in September. In October, Lorenzo's agents discovered that Count Girolamo Riario's top captain, Giovan Francesco da Tolentino, was in the Lombard city, urging Ludovico Sforza to break with Florence, to repay certain favours, and to send Milanese troops into Pisa's hinterland, so as to squeeze the Tuscan republic from the west, while Neapolitan and papal troops marched up from the townships already conquered in the south. They would thus be rid of Lorenzo 'within a month'. When news of Tolentino's embassy arrived in Florence late in October, the ruling group was shocked, and for the moment Lorenzo and his circle turned anxiously to Venice to implore help. In early November, on the regular diplomatic front, Lorenzo and the Sforza lords of Milan continued to swear mutual love and loyalty, yet each city was moving out along a separate course, Milan paying more than courtesies to King Ferrante, and the lords of Florence courting the Venetian republic.

But it was not so for long. In the middle of November, Lorenzo was told by his old friend, Filippo Sacramoro, the Milanese ambassador to Florence, that Ludovico Sforza wanted a reconciliation with Ferrante and could not understand all the Florentine fuss about keeping faith with Venice, which after all had shamelessly failed Lorenzo in his hour of need. A week later, Lorenzo was confronted with an ultimatum: if he insisted on maintaining his ties with Venice, then Milan would push off independently, even if 'with some pain', and seek a peace 'with his majesty the king, as is called for by nature and need'. Meanwhile, Pope Sixtus and his nephew Count Girolamo Riario remained unshakable in their insistence that Lorenzo journey to Rome to beg forgiveness. For them this act of submission was the key to peace. In a lateral connection, the emerging lord of Milan, Ludovico Sforza, now brought up the suggestion that Ferrante himself was ready to accept Lorenzo's primacy in Florence.

If Ludovico clinched an agreement with the King of Naples, this would draw Milan away from Florence, leaving Lorenzo at the mercy of King and Pope. In late November, therefore, forced into an about-face, Lorenzo and the Ten agreed to cut their ties with Venice, to betray the Romagnol lords by abandoning them to the wishes of the Pope and Ferrante, and even (however painfully) to settle for reimbursements, if Florentine castles and townships in enemy hands should not be returned. Solemn agreements with Venice were about to be torn up; Milan and Florence were breaking faith; and though continuing to speak of honour and loyalty in their future talks with the Venetians, they would justify their bad faith with the usual diplomatic arguments — the necessity of peace, defensive needs, altered realities, and the offer to invite Venice into the new arrangements as an equal partner. But the stickiest question still remained for the Florentines: how was a deal to be got with Pope Sixtus and (behind him) Count Girolamo Riario, without the sacrifice of the quasi-lord of Florence?

Lorenzo now saw the need for a diplomatic stroke: he would journey to Naples and personally court King Ferrante. The move struck contemporaries as sensational, and it has often been the occasion for awe and praise of Lorenzo's courage, patriotism, genius, luck, and statecraft. None of these can be taken away from him: he was a vastly gifted man, and seen to be so even by his enemies. His letters, as he set out for that southern kingdom, reveal his grit. It was also clear, however, that all other routes had been closed to him. The costly war and the inevitable Florentine defeat would bring him and his government down, along with at least thirty-five or forty other leading Florentine families, all of them deeply compromised with the Medici. And all of them would be punitively targeted by the new government, as scores of exiles returned to the city, while the many who had long been silent at home suddenly found their tongues again and the thirst for revenge took over. Across the years, the confiscated lands and houses of exiles, amounting to hundreds of thousands of florins, had been put up for auction and sold, often to staunch supporters of the Medici.

With his grasp of politics and its ceremonial trappings, Lorenzo saw that the trip to Naples would have to be both a flourish and a grave undertaking, not just an act of expedience. All Florence longed for peace. When, therefore, Duke Alfonso of Calabria captured Colle Val d'Elsa on 12 November and offered a truce twelve days later, Florence snapped it up thankfully, allowing the Duke to repair to his winter quarters in Siena. Some minor battlefield action would go on, but the spring promised to bring back full-scale military operations, and this time Milan would be neutral or even, conceivably, on the other side. In late November the Venetian ambassador to Florence noted that citizens were 'riotously' crying out for peace and against hardline Venice, which insisted that the Florentine alliance with the Venetians be strictly observed and that the Romagnol lords be protected from Ferrante and Sixtus. Menacing, anonymous notices were affixed to the entrance of the ambassador's house, inviting him to get out of Florence. None of this escaped the spies and informers of the Eight.

Lorenzo made his plans in secret. He had been thinking about a trip to Naples for some months. In private communication from the enemy side, the Duke of Calabria, a close acquaintance to whom he had addressed some verse, had been urging him 'to throw himself into the arms' of King Ferrante. And having put out feelers to the King, Lorenzo got the Florentine merchant banker, Filippo Strozzi, an old Naples hand, to hurry down to that southern seaport to consult Ferrante, so as to prepare the way. Strozzi was well known in the royal household. The whole affair now moved with amazing speed. On the evening of 5 December, addressing the war-office Ten and a select group of forty prominent citizens (not the Lord Priors), Lorenzo informed them of his decision to go to Naples. He had made up his mind: either he was about to sacrifice himself, and even so they might have to fight on, or he would be able to negotiate an end to the war. His conscience told him that he owed such a dangerous trip to the city. At dawn the next morning he stole quietly away and made for Pisa. Some days later, off the Pisan coast, at a point between Vada and Piombino, he was met by two Neapolitan galleys and they set sail on the 14th. Arriving in Naples four days later, he was lodged, after a week or so, in the palazzo of the former Medici Bank, which had been fully redecorated for him on orders from the King, in part with furnishings from the court itself. Since the Medici name was everywhere synonymous with wealth, Lorenzo's good sense did not fail him: he arrived in Naples laden with gifts for members and friends of the court.

Spreading quickly through Italy, news of Lorenzo's dramatic visit to Naples elicited wonder, anger, and doubts. Although ambassadors were informed of his journey and official letters had gone out at once to all the parties concerned, Lorenzo and King Ferrante suddenly appeared to be operating behind everyone's back. The encounter flaunted the King's betrayal of Pope Sixtus. Venice could not but feel cheated and lied-to by Lorenzo. Count Girolamo Riario was furious. The lords of Milan, feeling that the lead and opening moves in any Florentine rapprochment with Naples belonged to them, were humiliated and annoyed. And Florence's Lord Priors, at first surprised, quickly resigned themselves, most of them hoping and praying that Lorenzo's escapade would climax in his return with a solid peace. In a letter to the Lord Priors, written the day after his departure, Lorenzo concluded: 'The Lord God perhaps desires that since this war began with my brother's blood and mine, so too that it should end by my hands. What I most desire is that my life and death, and what is good and bad for me, be ever for the benefit of our city.' They responded with hope and courtesy, but the voices of underground protest already had something else to say. Within days of his exit from the city, copies of an anonymous scribble had been scattered in the streets of Florence, cryptically declaring, 'And yet the tyrant has gone.' A month later, in early January, Pope Sixtus was still in such a fury that at one point the Neapolitan ambassador to Rome was afraid to approach him with new instructions from the King. As for the meaning of the mysterious scribble? Possibly this: Well, all right, despite being a tyrant, he has chosen to leave the scene of his crimes. What now? Shouldn't we be taking some action?

There was nothing pusillanimous about Lorenzo and Pope Sixtus.

Until the spring of 1479, and for some points right up to Lorenzo's flight to Naples, the Pope's demands remained uncompromising: that is,

(1) that Lorenzo and Florence humbly sue for his forgiveness, (2) an indemnity of 100,000 florins, (3) immediate removal of the shameful fresco depicting the hanged Archbishop Salviati, (4) the building of a special chapel in commemoration of the murdered priests, and (5) the perpetual celebration of masses for their souls. However, if Florence would hand over three fortresses in Florentine territory – Borgo San Sepolcro, Castrocaro, and Modigliana – then these could serve as substitutes for the indemnity. While the third demand was possible, the others were not, neither for Florence nor for Lorenzo. They carried too great a load of shame and put the life of the chief citizen in danger.

Having fewer resources at hand than the Pope, Lorenzo was forced to rely more fully on his genius. His talks with King and court in Naples raised him to the summit of his intellectual and courtly powers. There, no delegating of jobs was possible, no dealing by letter and emissary, and there was no time for reflection. Nor had he the input of the politicians back in Florence. He was entirely on his own, fighting for his life and for the political survival of the Medici house.

Ferrante was notoriously astute and treacherous by reputation, though this meant little more than the readiness to spin right around and to sacrifice allies – no rare dexterity in Renaissance Italy. Apart from having the military muscle, he also had gifted and seasoned advisors, such as Diomede Carafa. Lorenzo, therefore, in conversations with the King and his courtiers (men of the sort who could be dangerously bored), had to be quick, clever, imaginative, and likeable too: he had to move them by his talk and winsome manner. For what had he really to offer the rulers of that southern kingdom in the way of auxiliary troops or substantial political advantages? All the more reason for him to arrive in Naples bearing gifts and what must have been a large fortune in cash, while also being set to curry favour with the Duchess of Calabria, born Ippolita Maria Sforza, daughter of the great northern soldier of fortune, Francesco. He had first met her in Milan, back in 1465, at the time of her proxy marriage to King Ferrante's son, Alfonso; and if courtly verse was one of her tastes, he could certainly talk about that with more felicity than almost anyone else in the world. Not surprisingly, keeping a kind of open house in the Neapolitan palazzo of the Medici Bank, he offered a flow of luncheon and dinner parties, where he must inevitably have sparkled. The Naples trip would turn out to be hugely expensive, as his contemporary biographer observed; but there was also an expense of nerves, for as one of his aides in Naples noted, Paolantonio Soderini, he was 'like two men: full of grace and confidence during the day, presenting himself as light-hearted and self-assured, but at night he would complain wretchedly about his and Florence's *fortuna*'.

The critical moments were in Lorenzo's frequent, almost daily, discussions with the King or his courtiers and ministers. His letters to Florence and to others during those weeks, like the letters of the foreign ambassadors who watched him in action, touch only the main diplomatic topics and problems. In this sense, they broached one aspect only, however fundamental, of a whole process and ceremony in which word and manner, face and gesture, spirit and quickness also carried persuasion. On a quite different front, meanwhile, Ferrante was dealing with a formidable and angry Pope Sixtus, who was himself ready to conduct secret negotiations with Venice. The King had thrown his support behind the new Sforza lord, Ludovico il Moro, by having assisted both his exile's return to Milan and his reconciliation with the regency, after the troubled years that followed the assassination in 1476 of Ludovico's brother, Galeazzo Maria Sforza. But the King also had to beware of a stronger Milan; and he was keeping a wary eye on France's Angevin claims to Naples, particularly since the French had contacts everywhere in princely and republican Italy.

Lorenzo seems to have played one card with a good deal of success: again and again he promised Ferrante that he could deliver a Florence that would be loyal to him, the King, for as long as Lorenzo retained his primacy there. He also raised the realistic possibility of Florence's suddenly turning away from Naples to make a new alliance with Venice, an allegation that was strongly seconded by the new lord of Milan. Did the King want this? Lorenzo had strong ties with Louis XI of France, here too suggesting another possible resource for Naples.

Yet just as important, and perhaps more so, was the fact that Lorenzo's ways and words won the King over: Ferrante got to like him, and liking him, was more ready to listen to his claims. This large and artful side of Lorenzo, however – the stuff of novelists and great French diarists – could not be distilled into the diplomatic correspondence. There wasn't even, as yet, a modern literary form for the expression of such a person-ality. We have to imagine and re-imagine Lorenzo's most appealing qual-ities, so as to gauge their effects on Ferrante, who even resolved to get Pope Sixtus to drop his demand that the Florentine *gran maestro* go to Rome and beg his forgiveness. In the end, as it turned out, he failed to win this concession from Sixtus; but Lorenzo believed that he would succeed, and he left Naples thinking that Ferrante's commitment on this point had pulled him 'back from the dead'.

One of Lorenzo's greatest attractions must have been in the felicity of his words and conversation, in his case a remarkable feat, because his voice was rather unnatural, owing to blocked nasal passages that also eliminated his sense of smell. Yet as a poet, short-story writer, and critic of refinement, he naturally looked for the most effective turns of expres-sion, and equally so in his role as a public figure. This care was filtered into the language of his letters. But being all of a piece, he doubtless cultivated an engaging manner in his daily speech as well, as we may infer from a letter of 26 November 1484, addressed to his twelve-year-old son, Piero. The youth was on his way to Rome, in the company of six Florentine ambassadors, all bearing congratulations for the new Pope Innocent VIII, and he was to make a stop in Siena, to convey greetings to three of his father's Sienese friends. Lorenzo urges Piero, when he talks to them, to 'use your own words, well put, natural, and not stilted or forced; and don't try to seem too learned. . . . Use courteous, sweet, and serious expressions with them and with all others. . . . Calling on all due manner and politeness, conduct yourself seriously with your peers.'

There can be little doubt that Lorenzo himself had long sought to live by the verbal parts of this instruction. In his *Life* of the Florentine lord, Niccolò Valori turns Lorenzo's eloquence and ease with words into one of the biography's recurring themes. He knew him well and was the familiar of some of his intimate acquaintances.

Ferrante kept Lorenzo in Naples for nearly two-and-a-half months, while at the same time dealing with Pope Sixtus and Milan by means of letters and ambassadors, and also expecting, at first, that a long absence from Florence would end in disaster for his near captive – a quick solu-tion for the contending parties. Faced with money problems and an unruly baronage, the King himself was eager to treat the outstanding matters: Pope Sixtus's demands, the lords of Romagna, and relations with Milan and Venice. He was also spurred on by the fear of enemies in France and concern about a stronger government in Milan. But he remained a canny negotiator, always keeping the angry Sixtus in mind and knowing that he had Lorenzo and Florence in a corner. The give-and-take of negotiation went on till the very day of Lorenzo's departure, 28 February, when he left for Gaeta, to set sail for home on 5–6 March. No agreement had yet been finalised, and matters seemed to pass into the hands of two Florentine ambassadors at the court of Naples. Lorenzo could afford to stay away from Florence no longer, despite a last minute plea from King Ferrante, which reached him by letter in Gaeta. He had received anxious tidings from home in February, reporting that criticism of the regime had bluntly surfaced, with voices even speaking out for an opening up and expansion of the oligarchy.

On the very day of his disembarking at Pisa (13 March), after a stormy voyage, the peace was signed in Naples. Pope Sixtus had angrily agreed to it. But most of the outlines were already known in Florence, and Lorenzo returned to a hero's welcome, as all the foreign ambassadors, and more than 100 of the most eminent citizens, rode out of the city to meet him, in a ceremonial practice more often reserved for royalty and princes. Lorenzo was to say afterwards that 'There was no man in Florence, whatever his condition, who did not come to touch my hand and kiss me.' The Medicean joy of the moment converted a harsh peace into a triumph, though in the weeks to come something bitter would break through the honeyed surfaces. King Ferrante was now the sole arbiter in the question of when and if the captured Florentine lands would be returned to Florence. The Duke of Calabria had to be paid a sizeable military stipend for an unspecified period. As a pointer to the continuing influence of the Pazzi family, one article laid it down that the brothers and cousins imprisoned in Volterra had to be released. Sixtus's censures against Florence remained, including the excommunications; and Lorenzo was still awaited in Rome to beg the Holy Father's forgiveness. The interdicts affecting Florence, Fiesole, and Pistoia were lifted for a few days in April, in order to satisfy communicants at Easter.

It was a hard peace for Florence, but there was one positive result: foreign armies would no longer threaten its walls, or plunder and move

Fig. 10 Medal commemorating the Pazzi conspiracy, by Bertoldo di Giovanni.

rampantly over the productive lands of Florentine Tuscany.

Lorenzo's luck held out. 'Dame Fortune' – as many a contemporary would have said – came to his aid less than five months later. Early in August the Turks stormed Otranto in the far south of Italy, killing about 12,000 people and taking another 10,000 into slavery. All at once King Ferrante faced a military crisis; the Duke of Calabria was pulled out of Siena; and Pope Sixtus was forced to organise action against the infidel, even while hating to offer any kind of assistance to the King. Dropping his hard line against Florence, Sixtus now let it be known that if the republic would dispatch a large embassy of citizens to seek his pardon in Rome, even without Lorenzo, they would have it, along with the removal of the excommunications and interdicts.

No more had to be said. The spectacle that followed was a sight for the chroniclers of ceremony. In late November, obviously echoing the number of the apostles, twelve of Florence's foremost citizens, including two of Lorenzo's relatives, arrived in Rome, entering two hours before sunset and keeping a low profile. On 3 December, in the portico of St Peter's, they appeared before the Pope, who was flanked by many cardinals and other prelates. Seeming to throw themselves down at his feet, and 'showing every sign of great humility', they begged his pardon for all the errors and offences of their country and declared themselves ready to suffer any penalty. Intoning special words for the occasion and touching each of them lightly on the back with his staff, he absolved them (and all Florentines) of their past sins, admitting them back into the Church with the benefits of all its holy rites and services. They were no longer disobedient schismatics. When news of the lifting of the censures reached Florence two days later, there was jubilation: bonfires were built and all the city's bells rang out. The official absolution, however, was not published until the end of the following March.

CHAPTER ELEVEN

The Pazzi Cursed

Fierce Formalities

INFAMY AND ERASURE from the public record, a moral and political curse: this was the aim, as we have seen, of the law enacted against the Pazzi in May 1478; but they had to be despoiled too, stripped of all their worldly goods, or how could a temporal curse be complete?

Florentine political leaders needed no lessons in the stifling of stubborn dissent, not to speak of armed mutiny. Now and then, as at Perugia and Bologna, noblemen charged into the streets to cut down the political enemy with swords and the help of crossbowmen. The Venetians, employing more civil means (criminal law), used their magistracy of Ten to sniff out dissent and to try, torture, hang, or exile the trouble-makers. Authority in the Venetian lagoon must not be challenged. At Florence, in policy designed to destroy the opposition, the Eight, an early 'totalitarian' police like the Ten in Venice, had recourse to spies, secret informers, torture, confession, and exile. When Archbishop Salviati and his companions planned their assault on Lorenzo and Giuliano de' Medici, they knew that the Eight would be waiting in the shadows.

Created in 1378 to root out the revolutionary aspirations of workers in the woollen-cloth industry, the Eight gathered strength during the fifteenth century and came to look like the city's chief crime fighters. Under the government of the Medici, strong resistance to the swelling powers of this office sometimes surfaced in the councils, as citizens tried to get crime back to the ordinary courts and to eliminate the political fears stirred up by the Eight. But the Medicean party, using a strategy of intimidation, was nearly always able to defeat such efforts.

The Eight who took office on 1 May 1478, five days after the Conspiracy, included Lorenzo the Magnificent and one of his great friends,

Sigismondo della Stufa, who was with him in the north sacristy on that bloody Sunday. At the last minute, clearly, the names of those drawn for the new office term had been reshuffled to make room for these two men. Moving in at once to direct the proceedings against the conspirators, the Eight – which saw a turnover of personnel every four months – had been the focus of anxiety for Francesco de' Pazzi and the Archbishop of Pisa, who feared that time would expose the plot. More worrying still for the conspirators, as for the silent Medicean opposition, was another practice encouraged by the Eight: the secret and anonymous denunciation of thieves, enemies of the regime, homosexuals, clandestine prostitutes, tax dodgers, and other wrongdoers. These denunciations were deposited in *tamburi*, special wooden boxes affixed to the front of the city's main churches and under lock and key. As an invitation, the practice of anonymous accusation was made more attractive by the offer of rewards for successful convictions. Knowing that their identities would be kept a secret, the anonymous informers could step forward to claim their reward money by matching up something in their possession or knowledge with corresponding evidence in the original disclosure and denunciation.

When the April conspirators fell into the hands of the Lord Priors and Eight, they were given a summary trial there and then, or so the government later claimed. Evidently, the actions and guilt of Francesco de' Pazzi, of his uncle Messer Jacopo, and of all the others caught in action were too flagrant and conclusive to require added proof. But the case also raised a question that was altogether murky, concerning the guilt of the other Pazzi: that is, of Francesco's two brothers, a nephew, and seven first cousins, including the esteemed and likeable Renato, who was also hanged. Francesco himself confessed nothing; and nothing in the way of damning evidence was extracted from Renato, or it would have been showcased and noised about by his accusers, so eager were they to establish the justice of their case. Announcing their sentence months later (4 August 1478), by routeing it through the court of the Podestà in a semblance of 'due process', the Priors and the Eight stated that 'the traitor' Messer Jacopo had 'confessed without torture', implicating 'the entire Pazzi family', and doing so in the presence of many of the principal citizens. He claimed, allegedly, that they had all known about and approved of the designs against Lorenzo.

By executing him on the spot, the Eight and Priors sealed Jacopo's mouth forever, but apart from a single sentence in the verdict, they did not produce his testimony, nor were the other exiled and jailed Pazzi cross-examined. Certainly no testimony of theirs was ever brought forward: they were condemned without a trial. And no effort was made to take depositions from the Pazzi women – their wives, sisters, and daughters, who were also punished. They were denied Florentine marriages and forced to sue or fight for their property. But we are in the hard fifteenth century, in the thick of customs very different from our own, and have no business whisking modern notions of human rights and justice into the past by sleight of hand. The Eight were not a true court of law. They were a special-powers commission of high and swift 'justice' or retribution. They observed no ordinary judicial procedure, and they could ride above the statutory law. Our only modern parallel is the secret military tribunal, endowed with the power of capital punishment and offering no right of appeal. Late in 1478, being fully aware of the unusual constitutional standing of the Eight, and concerned to make their mandate more acceptable, Lorenzo's regime codified the rules governing the office and required that their decisions pass through Florence's highest criminal judge, the Podestà. In fact, although they could assemble anywhere, they normally held their sessions in the Palace of the Podestà. But something about the new code seemed to tie their hands, and the Eight who took office at the start of 1479 destroyed the register holding the collected rules.

Since the case against the whole family was all but closed *de facto* by the end of Tuesday, 28 April, the seizure of Pazzi goods and possessions began at once. The heads of government resolved to 'go all out' to destroy the wealth of the house, along with every remaining scrap of its political and social standing in Florence. On the evening of that very first Sunday, they were already tracking Pazzi merchandise on the high seas. In the following weeks they began to put up for auction and sell all Pazzi goods and chattels. And if Messer Piero's manuscripts of classical authors – he was the Pazzi ambassador knighted in France – did not all go in the auction, this was surely because the knowing eye of some influential and learned citizen had already singled them out for purchase. Again, Florentines knew all about the independent property of women when it was linked to trousseaux and dowries; yet in the frenzy to confiscate and destroy, no regard was shown for the richly-dowered women who had entered into the Pazzi family by marriage. Their property was also seized, held, or sold, so that for months and even years thereafter, by exerting private influence or acting through lawyers, they were forced to nag at the Eight and to dun two other commissions for the recovery of their possessions.

As early as 16 May 1478, the Eight found themselves ruling that six items of clothing and a belt, which their office had sold to a used-clothes dealer, was the property of Maddalena Serristori, widow of the late Jacopo de' Pazzi, and should be returned to her. Her branch of the Serristori was one of the city's richest families. On 3 June, again, the Eight ordered the return of a table cloth to its owner, Lorenzo's sister 'Bianca, daughter of Piero de' Medici'. It was decorated with 'the arms of the Medici and formerly of the Pazzi'. She was married, as we know, to the exiled Guglielmo de' Pazzi.

By 23 May, a few days after the gruesome frolicking with Jacopo de' Pazzi's battered corpse, the Lord Priors, as we have seen, had outlawed the Pazzi name and coat of arms. This included, of course, their association with the holy-fire cart and their celebrity at Easter; and harsh penalties were set against any Florentine family which should in future dare to contract a marriage with the accursed house. But what has never been glossed is the fact that even then, with the effects of the plot still very much in the air and the city under a strict arms control, there was keen opposition to the draconian measures. For the act got through the first council (*consilio populi*) by a vote of 162 to 55, only some 18 votes short of a defeat. In the second council (*consilio comunis*), the vote was 123 to 43, a 13-vote margin of victory. While in the *Cento*, the council which had been strong-armed into existence by the Medicean party in 1458, the bill carried by a vote of 82 to 32, topping the two-thirds majority by a bare 6 votes. So, there was some secret and stubborn dissent at the core of the oligarchy itself. In the circumstances, in view of the pervasive tincture of fear (fear of the Medicean magnates), the vaunted hatred for the Pazzi was not, after all, so universal. A substantial political minority wanted to see the family treated with more reason and justice, or was simply determined to frustrate a vindictive leadership.

In the autumn of 1478, an anonymous poem about the April Plot (see p. 183) encapsulated the movement to vilify the Pazzi, working its way into the life of the times by its sale in the new printed format – it was very likely peddled in the streets – and by being publicly recited 'to all you kind listeners'. The poem gives a voice to one of the dominant moods of the day. Catering to a pro-Medici audience and identifying this family with everything that was good for Florence, the author accuses the Pazzi of treachery on the scale of Judas's betrayal of Jesus, although Antenor and Brutus are also thrown in for good measure. He claims that the Pazzi were 'all vile men of a tricksy and base condition', 'ingrates' eaten up by 'envy and ambition', and (more succinctly) 'the hidden snake in the grass'. In less than four generations, they had risen, he asserts, from being 'servants and lenders of dice' to a position which enabled them to contract the highest and most noble marriages in Florence; and all were 'reverenced and honoured'. Yet all the while they were 'cursed and ugly traitors'. The poem's bill of indictment finally concludes with a curse: 'If any seed of theirs remains,/ be it more widely scattered than the Jews.'

Seizure and Confiscation

As GRABBING THE property of 'traitors' had been practised in Florence since time out of mind, there was no hesitation about what had to be done. All the property of the Pazzi must be inventoried and accounted for. This meant not only houses, lands, shares in the government debt, and all personal effects, including of course jewellery, but also cash, assets abroad, rents, office furniture, all goods in stock, and all debts owing to them. Hailed by trumpet and town criers, Pazzi debtors were ordered to come forward to declare their debts and be ready to pay them. After a certain lapse of time, any debtors who had failed to identify themselves were to be considered guilty of fraud and made subject *ipso facto* to arrest, fines, or prison. Similarly, all creditors were invited to make themselves known, and as Pazzi assets and monies came in, it was rightly expected that the government would seek to satisfy their claims.

Orders went out for the surrender of all Pazzi account books and business papers: ledgers, cash books, inventories, the lot. For in Florence, characteristically, proof of debits and credits was treated as valid when in the form of properly recorded account entries; and judges and arbitrators customarily relied on these in the settlement of disputes. The result was, interestingly, that breaking into shops and houses to steal account books and business papers was one of the more common forms of Florentine theft, and the records of the Eight often provide the details concerning times, places, and descriptions of the items taken.

A special office in charge of the properties of rebels, the Tower Officials soon took over from the Eight, as they normally did in such cases, and up to the spring of 1480, they handled most of the business connected with the vast Pazzi estate. More than 400 creditors submitted claims, and they came from every walk of life, ranging from farm workers, masons, and brickmakers, to goldsmiths, lawyers, leading merchants, and amateur classical scholars – Alamanno Rinuccini, for one. He claimed 150 florins on deposit with 'Renato de' Pazzi and Co., bankers in Florence'. Stationers also stepped forward to urge their claims, providing testimony to the heavy use of paper in the different Pazzi households, especially for business purposes. In May 1478, Renato de' Pazzi's widow, Francesca di Messer Giovanni Martini, a Venetian lady, submitted a claim for one of the largest dowries ever seen in Florence, 6000 florins, matched only by the sum attached to Clarice Orsini (if it was ever paid out in full), when she arrived in Florence to consummate her marriage to Lorenzo. The Venetian lady was also suing for her trousseau, jewellery, and the gifts made to her at the time of her marriage.

Although there is no sustained trace of this in the records, it is clear that Lorenzo intruded into the work of the Tower Officials, who perhaps reasoned that having most suffered at the hands of the Pazzi, he was entitled to a voice in the break-up of their estate. He saw to it that the late Renato de' Pazzi's house was held in reserve for sale to the Duke of Ferrara at a price of 4000 florins. And in September 1478 the Duke, then commander of the Florentine army, was in fact lodged in the house. Lorenzo himself took possession of Messer Jacopo's gracious palace and his villa at Montughi, attested to by the fact that these became part of his daughter Maddalena's dowry, when she was married to Franceschetto Cibò in 1488.

Did any of Piero de' Pazzi's finest books, or other precious objects from the different households of the hated family, end up in the Medici collection, either taken outright or purchased at auction for modest sums? Lorenzo had two very rich cousins, Giovanni and Lorenzo di Pierfrancesco (see the Medici genealogical chart), and we know from his dealings with them, as from his treatment of certain artists, that he was not averse to holding on to the property and money of others. At the time of the Pazzi War, as guardian of his cousins' income, and holding more than 20,000 florins of theirs in thirteen bags, he spent the entire sum, although he was already in hock to them for more than 60,000 florins. Aged fifteen and eleven at the time, the two boys were furious with him and in due course would be found on the side of the secret political opposition. When Lorenzo was finally forced to settle with them in 1485, Giovanni and Lorenzo di Pierfrancesco de' Medici claimed 105,880 florins, including interest, but their magnificent cousin worked the debt down to 61,400 florins, paying it over in the form of numerous farms and landed estates, including the Medici villa at Cafaggiolo.

The surest proof of Lorenzo's meddling in the administration of the sequestered Pazzi estate stems from the fact that within two weeks of the Conspiracy, he was writing letters to the cardinals of Rouen, Mantua, and Pavia, assuring them about their Pazzi credit claims. On 14 May, he endorsed a third letter to the Cardinal of Rouen, the rich and powerful Guillaume d'Estoutville, saying that he was holding a store of Pazzi silverware for him, clearly in satisfaction of his claim. In 1479, he dispatched an agent to Bruges to liquidate that branch of the Pazzi Bank. In July 1480, he ordered the manager of the Medici firm in Lyons to surrender to the Capponi company there 'the goods in his hands that had belonged to the Pazzi'. And in June 1481, Lorenzo was still campaigning to seize Pazzi assets in Bruges, where a branch of their bank had been the main outlet for the sale of papal alum. Here, however, the cursed family continued to enjoy the influential long reach of the King of Naples.

Meanwhile, something had gone wrong with the handling of the confiscated estate. In February 1479, the great northern captain, Roberto di Sanseverino, a depositor in one of the defunct Pazzi banks, was having trouble collecting his claimed amount. The officials in charge were failing to come up with the needed funds. Though they compiled a record of Pazzi debtors, this part of their work seems to have been lost. Many debtors took their chances and refused to declare themselves. Some of the major creditors, most of them in the cloth industry, remained unpaid; and Pazzi investments in the French salt tax had yet to be identified and estimated. The government therefore concluded that the Tower Officials were too ill-equipped to handle the complexity of the claims for and against the estate, with the result that at the end of 1479 the job was put into the hands of a new commission, 'The Syndics on the affairs of the Pazzi'. Once again, however, the Lord Priors had to clear the matter with their three legislative councils, and this measure also met resolute resistance, barely obtaining the required votes. Given the opportunity to cast their ballots in secret, members of the political class, circling around the core of the Medicean oligarchy, either feared that the new commission would be corruptly dominated by Lorenzo's henchmen, or they were making a last-ditch effort to hedge that part of the Pazzi estate which had not yet been reached by the grasping hands of partisan government.

Of the six Syndics, three represented Pazzi creditors, while the others were commissioned to represent the Commune (Florence). Owing to quarrels over operating expenses and the question of whether or not they would be salaried, the Syndics did not actually begin work until the spring of 1480. In the end, the government provided them with salaries, two clerks, an attorney, and footmen as needed; but they were restricted in their expenditures to a budget of 600 florins per year, and their funding was to come entirely from the Pazzi estate. All this, probably, to mollify critics.

Many secrets now came tumbling out, concerning debtors in particular but also the Pazzi themselves. No successful effort had been made to track down the family's assets abroad, not from reasons of sympathy for the cursed house, but because the operation was too complex. Apart from the Bishop of Sarno and the exiled Guglielmo, with his (half-Medici) sons, most of the surviving Pazzi males were no longer in the picture; they were prisoners in the high fortress of the hill town of Volterra.

The Syndics began work on 19 May, and by the 27th they had given Pazzi debtors eight days to declare themselves. On that day too they issued a list of eighty debtors, having already dispatched a herald 'to all the usual places', to trumpet and make the announcement regarding the debtors named. A few days later, they sent out letters to merchants in Bruges, Valencia, and Ragusa (Dubrovnik), demanding payment of their debts to some of the different Pazzi companies. In late June, out in the Valdisieve region of the Florentine dominion, they held an auction for the sale of cows, oxen, calves, pigs, sheep, and goats. In early July they issued warrants for the arrest of twenty-seven debtors, some of them the bearers of proud old names, such as Rucellai, Strozzi, Adimari, Baroncelli, Frescobaldi, Gualterotti, and minor Medici. Later still they would send agents to Volterra, Valencia, Bruges, Avignon, Lyons, 'and other places', with orders to conduct on-the-spot inquiries. In the meantime, they were poring over a mass of sequestered papers and account books.

Taking two years to complete their commission, the Pazzi Syndics met two or three times a week, compiling a rich record of entries regarding payments, arrests, pardons, land seizures, and sales, or containing verbatim testimony and whole copies of letters. It turned out, for example, that Renato de' Pazzi, a major partner in two different cloth firms, had been heavily involved in the Florentine wool trade, and that his younger brother Niccolò, posted to Avignon, had been fully engaged in the family business there. As confirmation of more and more Pazzi properties was received, these were periodically sold off at auctions. In early September 1480, and again in October, the Syndics announced the sale of properties that had once belonged to Lorenzo de' Medici's brother-in-law Guglielmo. The lot included two farms, numerous land parcels, four houses, and a villa. In Florence proper, the jewel of the sale was a *palazzo* in the heart of the Pazzi enclave, probably Messer Jacopo's, and the Magnificent Lorenzo got it. The palace had a vaulted courtyard, a loggia, an orchard, wells, a stable, 'and other buildings and appurtenances'. So bare a listing fails to reveal the fact that the palace carried the prestige of name and place, and that Pazzi land also meant wine, olives, wheat, fodder, flour, fruit, firewood, and the fixtures for raising poultry. Cartloads of most of these, as needed, were hauled into the city for the owners. No Florentine family of means ever paid the food prices (with their hidden taxes) paid by landless men; and like many of their peers, the Pazzi even had their own flour mills.

Early in 1481, the Syndics began to lay out the details of one of their main targets, Messer Jacopo de' Pazzi's involvement in the French salt monopoly, a business which had also attracted his father. They had sent two well-informed Florentines to Lyons in August 1480, to make detailed inquiries and prepare a report, despite the fact that the Tower Officials had already tried to sort the matter out. The company in question was a Florentine banking partnership in Lyons, linking Messer Jacopo, Francesco di Niccolò Capponi, and Francesco di Lutozzo Nasi. One of their most profitable activities was to buy up consignments of royal salt for its subsequent resale in lesser quantities. Messer Jacopo and Capponi were the prime investors in the saline part of the bank, which also naturally took in funds from depositors. Buying in cash but also lending money and selling salt on credit, the firm had debtors and creditors, including the King of France, the King of Naples, French notables, and Florentine merchants. Active in Avignon too, the three partners had done large volumes of business in recent years, adding up to hundreds of thousands of florins. But this was now all in the past.

Having digested the reports of their emissaries, and concluding that the final accounts of the Lyons company would show assets of more than 14,000 French *écus,*the Syndics closed this part of their commission by ordering Capponi to pay the sum of 11,500 florins. He was to route this money, on paper, to Raniero and Lorenzo Ricasoli, who were themselves in debt to the Lyons partners, and the funds proper would then be remitted to Pazzi creditors. Amidst the fog of business procedures and hidden interests, it is impossible to make out who exactly won and who lost in the overall salt enterprise. On learning of the Conspiracy, King Louis XI had immediately suspended the Pazzi operation. But men of influence were bound to be the most successful, and litigious merchants such as the Ricasoli were better survivors.

Acknowledging the possibility of mistakes in their findings, owing to their likely acceptance of false information, the Syndics worked until May 1482, but made arrangements for creditors to be paid over the course of the next two years, or even beyond that if the need arose. The snags and long delays sprang partly at least from the rush to seize and disperse the estate, as illustrated by the plight of the Pazzi wives and widows, in their struggle to reclaim dowries, although these, supposedly, were well protected in law. The Lord Priors and Eight had acted with such speed, just hours after the assault in the cathedral, that there was no time for the Pazzi to conceal much, not even jewellery and cash. The women would have been searched, and the men were all arrested.

A witness to the vindictive desire to smash and grab, Renato's widow had lodged the first claim for her 6000 florins with the Tower Officials on 22 May 1478. Two months later, driven to hire an attorney, she had made an appeal to the city's top magistrate, the Podestà, listing the Pazzi farms and properties that her father-in-law had entailed to guarantee repayment of her dowry, if she should be widowed. Since she was also to press for legal expenses, the exertions of her legal counsel must have been unrelenting. She was not, however, dealing with a law court, but with two commissions (Tower Officials and Syndics), each of them acting under the aegis of executive authority and outside the whole system of courts. Not for another three and a half years, therefore, would her claim be satisfied (25 February 1482), when the Syndics, moving to pay her off at last, had their town criers announce the sale of thirty farms, numerous land parcels, two villas, and some farm workers' houses.

In the four years after the Conspiracy, the most surprising aspect of the seize-and-settle proceedings was in the fact that officials should have had so much trouble meeting the claims of creditors. The clothing alone of the Pazzi would have been worth thousands of florins in what was then a lively and lucrative used-clothes trade. At one point, for example, not surprisingly, a single pair of Pazzi sheets was sold for eight florins. Was it the case, therefore, that the pertinent auctions were pegged at the lowest possible sale prices in the supposed name of speed? Were certain buyers favoured? When added up, the claims of Pazzi creditors could not possibly have amounted to anything like the magnitude of the estate, which must have been in excess of 150,000 florins. After all, lesser folk in Florence, cloth merchants mainly, still had fortunes in the range of 20,000 and 30,000 florins. Although the Eight and the Lord Priors had at once fixed on a sum of 40,000 to 50,000 florins of Pazzi debt, the source of this estimate remains a mystery. They cited no record. Yet if we accept the sum, the question arises, what happened to the rest of the estate? With its scale of traffic, the Lyons banking and salt operation took care of that company's creditors. Any Pazzi assets in Rome, associated with the Curia, were almost certainly retained with papal help. And something for the family was probably salvaged in Bruges. But where was the rest? In Florence's government coffers? Surely not. Florentines were not in the habit of putting the republican commune ahead of private business creditors, unless political vendetta was wheeled into play. Of the hundreds of original claims, the overwhelming number involved small tradesmen's sums, many for less than two or three florins.

The Syndics closed their proceedings by labouring to raise an additional 11,000 florins to pay off remaining Pazzi creditors. To accomplish this, in what must have seemed a desperate shuffle, they turned first to the exiled Guglielmo and the four young men in the tower of Volterra's fortress, to dun them by letter and agent both for the funds and for testimony that would facilitate the collecting of more debtor monies. Did they fear that the surviving Pazzi had a cache somewhere of hidden gold? While it is true that Guglielmo would soon use his freedom to try secretly to rescue assets and properties, what remained was a pittance of what there had been, unless Rome remained a repository for large Pazzi assets, saved with the helping hand of Pope Sixtus. Florence itself seems not to have had the benefit of any part of the sequestered wealth.

It looks very much as if the affairs of the Pazzi estate were put into the hands of trustees who were careless about certain claims and debts, or were willing witnesses to corruption and clever thievery on a considerable scale. Florentine literature of the fifteenth century bristles with the denunciation of cunning greed and the high incidence of legal theft.

Francesco de' Pazzi was hanged on the day of the plot. His uncle Jacopo and first cousin Renato were hanged two days later. His brother Guglielmo was spared, but only after Bianca de' Medici pleaded for his life with Lorenzo. In the weeks following the April Plot, until Lorenzo could get over his shock and rage, he must have been driven to associate his brother-in-law with the plot, because the Florentine sense of family solidarities and blood ties favoured the presumption that all the men of the immediate kin group shared in its vices and virtues. Exiled from the city, Guglielmo was confined to one of his wife's properties, but by September 1480 he was being quietly allowed to move around, although Florence remained out of bounds for him. Did he ever approach it in secret, to gaze upon its tiled roofs and spires, his mind echoing with Dante's words about the yearning to glimpse 'the tower at least of the true city [heaven]'? Or did he remember instead, acrimoniously, the more famous lines about 'the sorrowing city [hell]' with its 'lost people'?

Renato's brother Andrea, seized after his flight from Florence, escaped with his life: he and his younger brothers Niccolò and Galeotto were sentenced to prison in perpetuity and soon transferred to Volterra, where they were afterwards interviewed by agents of the Syndics. Guglielmo's brother Giovanni was also dispatched to Volterra, to be imprisoned for life in the same tower.

Once the cursed Pazzi were removed from Florence, and members of the wider clan were forced to change their surname and coat of arms, it only remained to confiscate property and satisfy creditors. Or so it seemed, though it was soon clear that the Pazzi name and nimbus endured and that the Eight would also have to wrestle with more intangible matters. The family had secret sympathisers in the city, as shown by voting patterns in the large councils, when the Priors moved to enact measures against them. And there had to be other men like Alamanno Rinuccini, whose sympathy swelled, as we shall see, and turned into admiration. But even when citizens entertained no particular liking for the Pazzi, if they resented or hated the Medici, the ruling circle could not rely on them for support in action against the cursed family. Renato's free brother Antonio, Bishop of Sarno and Mileto, had escaped the wave of reprisals. He would be succeeded in 1482 by another Pazzi bishop in the Kingdom of Naples, Andrea di Giovanni; and bishops were never without influence. More significantly, the weight of papal influence in favour of the Pazzi persisted, in addition to King Ferrante's enduring support. Let's not forget that in order to meet the conditions of the peace that closed the Pazzi War, Florence was compelled to commute the life prison terms of the four young Pazzi to sentences of exile.

But the Eight were not without powers of intimidation for their distant foes. Apart from being watched, political exiles, including those whose sins reached all the way back to 1434, had to be in continual contact with the Eight. They were required to notify the Eight on a regular basis – often monthly, but it could be weekly – of their presence at the site to which they had been banished. And the document dispatched had to carry a notarised public seal. Failure to meet this injunction was a crime that turned the delinquent into a 'rebel', who now became subject not only to the seizure of all his remaining properties but also, in Florentine law, to the danger of being killed on sight with impunity. The killer might then qualify for a reward.

There were additional threats. All verbal contact between exiles and Florentines was monitored. No letter could legally go out of the city to an exile, unless it was first read by the Eight and marked with their seal; nor could anyone from Florence – relative, friend, or business associate – go out to meet an exile without the previous consent of the Eight. Equally, no correpondence from exiles was allowed into the city, unless it passed first before the eyes of the Eight, who could also deploy spies wherever Florentine exiles resided. No effort or money was spared to keep an eye on important exiles, such as the Albizzi, Acciaiuoli, Neroni, and Niccolò Soderini; and at critical moments, the Eight might have as many as forty servants and agents at their disposal. When mothers or wives dared to meet or write to their exiled men without the Eight's approval, the penalty, if they were caught, was two years in a prison in-famous for its appalling conditions (*le Stinche*), plus a fine of 200 florins.

Revenge and resentment in Florentine politics lived on by passing from father to son over the filament of property. The loss of political favour menaced land and capital, stirring up fear, anger, and undying resentment. This explains the 'totalitarian' precautions of the Eight. Fully aware of the woe and despoilment of exile, but identifying its political aspects as evil or treachery, the Medicean oligarchy feared that exiles were forever being tempted to meet, to plot, and to seek the aid of Florence's foreign enemies.

Were Medicean suspicions justified? Extreme measures could make for desperate men. Once an exile passed over to the status of 'rebel' for whatever reason – such as travel without permission, or being spotted with a known enemy – there was in effect a price on his head. So if he had well-placed friends and aquaintances abroad, he might be moved to enter into intrigues against the ruling group back home. What had he to lose? The plot to kill Lorenzo in June 1481 was the work of three Florentines, driven by icy hatred of the man. In the 1470s and 1480s, Neri Acciaiuoli and Giovanni Altoviti travelled around the peninsula, ιooking for funds, military support, and ways to murder him, whether by stealthy steel, poison, or ambush. For years after any exile had turned rebel, the Eight and the Tower Officials searched for every scrap of his wealth – a house in Pisa, or a parcel of land somewhere else – not only to complete his 'just' punishment, but also to remove every resource that might help him in his continuing 'treachery'. Exiled with his father and for the sins of his father in 1466, Neri Acciaiuoli had seen the man reduced to penury; hence he was driven by hatred of Lorenzo. In 1482, Cola Montano claimed that Guglielmo de' Pazzi was in touch with other malcontents, dreaming up new schemes to eliminate the Florentine lord. Seventeen years after Niccolò Soderini's flight into exile and disobedience in 1466, the Eight and Tower Officials were still tracking down and selling his remaining real properties.

In the process of inquiry, however questionable their handling of the Pazzi estate, the Syndics and Tower Officials went through thousands of pages of documentary evidence, in their determined hunt for assets, debtors, and creditors. Striking proof of this came forth years later, in September 1486, when officials drew up an inventory of the Pazzi account books and papers that had been in the hands of the two commissions. They listed no fewer than fifty-six smallish notebooks, eight bundles of papers, and 127 record and account books, of which twelve contained the proceedings pertaining to the confiscated estate. The rest were business ledgers, account diaries, cash books, inventory and possession registers, estate management books, and so forth. All or most of these seem to have been lost.

Something else, very probably, was also destroyed, though the matter is likely to remain a question for all times. There appear to be no surviving portraits of adult members of the fifteenth-century Pazzi family (see Figure 11). In view of new Quattrocento habits, such a house, with its known cargo of pride and riches, would have had some. We know, for example, that between about 1452 and 1462, at least five of the Pazzi girls – two of Guglielmo's sisters, and three of Renato's – went to their marriages with wedding chests depicting classical or more recent love tales, and issued by the workshop of the city's leading painter of *cassoni*, Apollonio di Giovanni. The most likely candidates for portraits were Messer Jacopo, Messer Piero, Renato de' Pazzi, and their wives. I suspect

Fig. 11 The Pazzi altarpiece, possibly by Andrea del Castagno. Two Pazzi children, Renato and his sister Oretta, can be seen at the bottom left and right.

that when Pazzi goods and chattels were seized to be put up for auction, an effort was made to destroy existing portraits, in obedience to the campaign to erase all honourable memory of the family. But if it happened that any such pictures reached the market, then the identifying coat of arms, if any, would have been removed, and they passed out into a name-less anonymity.

CHAPTER TWELVE

Profile: Rinuccini

Alamanno Rinuccini, 1426–99

CITIZEN ELEUTHERIUS, A devotee of liberty, has retreated from Florence to his modest farm and house in the country. Two dear friends of his, Alitheus (truth-teller) and Microtoxus (troubleshooter), arrive for an overnight visit, wanting to know all about why he has abandoned the city and public life, in spite of the fact that the republic needs the active political presence and input of freedom-loving men.

They settle down to a conversation. Alitheus underlines Florence's long devotion to political liberty and defines the meaning of liberty as a capacity for enlightened action. In the give and take of discussion, Eleutherius responds by seizing the opportunity to indict the present ways of political men in Florence, where high office is corruptly doled out or filled by depraved choice, when, instead, public affairs should of course be in the hands of well-born men of good character.

Alitheus picks up the discussion and pitches in against Lorenzo de' Medici for subjecting the city's traditional leaders to a vile servitude. Men are silent in council, afraid to say what they really think. Citizens are apathetic. Justice is often sold, or is in the hands of the powerful. The mighty fill office with their yes-men. By working through the Eight, Lorenzo has even used his heft to release brazen criminals from prison. Taxes favour the elite of prepotent men. How could all this have happened to us, whose plucky forebears overcame neighbouring cities and fought off barbarous tyrants? Alitheus even suggests that in the current Pazzi War, it would be well to dump Lorenzo and return to liberty.

After a night's break from their intent conversation, Microtoxus takes it up again with the argument that the individual has a moral obligation to serve his community, and notes that the ancestors of their host met this duty by standing out as taxpayers and leading servants of the republic. Does Eleutherius not betray this heritage and incur infamy by living only for himself and his solitary rural studies?

Eleutherius replies with an argument from stoicism. Having studied philosophy, he says, he seeks to avoid passion, such as we see it in the quest for riches and vain honours. Pursuits of this sort lead to nothing but anxiety. The one true ideal to live for is tranquillity of mind; this is the way to happiness. Having served in office to meet his moral responsibilities, he came to realise that he was merely helping Lorenzo and his circle of sycophants. So, seeing himself surrounded in effect by criminals in government, he decided that it would be best to give up public life.

Well, but is he likely to change his mind? No, because political corruption in Florence is now so pervasive, that he would end by having to beg for office from base usurpers, although office should be his by right of birth. Given the circumstances, it stands to reason that such begging would be far worse than his abdication and rural retreat. One other point: the current war with Pope Sixtus and King Ferrante is not so much a struggle for Florentine freedom as a war to keep Florence in servitude to Lorenzo. The Florentine lord and his government thus stand indicted.

The foregoing conversation, obviously a historical fiction, is a précis of Alamanno Rinuccini's melancholy political testament, his secret *Dialogue on Liberty*. Rinuccini himself is the citizen Eleutherius who has exiled himself from Florence in disgust. Composed in the year following the April Plot, he intended to publish it when and if the Pazzi War overthrew Lorenzo. In fact, the short work did not see the light and was not printed until after the Second World War. Urbanely rational and denuded of everything Christian, the *Dialogue* conforms to a purely 'pagan' line of reasoning. Its argument tracks or echoes Cicero, Plato, Aristotle, and the Stoics, rather than the early Church fathers or any medieval scholastic.

What do we know about the author?

The most articulate witness to an underground of political opposition, Alamanno Rinuccini was a close observer of the Florentine scene – ambitious, passionate, and well-educated. He knew Lorenzo and all the men of letters around him, passed as a friend, held a variety of high public offices, and seemed to approve of the ruling circle. In private, however, by the time of the April Plot, he was gnashing his teeth, as he saw *il Magnifico* gathering all power to himself and treating Florentine patricians as his servants. In response, Alamanno came to nurse a secret admiration for the Pazzi, and deeply regretted the failure of their conspiracy. Animated by 'a manly and generous spirit', he notes in his memoirs and *Dialogue*, the Pazzi took on 'the just and honest task of liberating their country'. It was 'a most glorious action (*facinus gloriosissimum*)', an attempt 'worthy of everlasting praise', but 'alas, they were defeated by *fortuna*'.

The Rinuccini family came up in the 1200s, and won their place in the history of Florence during the middle of the fourteenth century, when Alamanno's great-grandfather, Messer Francesco, a merchant and knight, was to have five different terms of office in the Lord Priors, a possible record. He was also immensely rich, ranking for years as the city's foremost taxpayer. From then on, and down to the 1430s, despite plunging in political importance, the Rinuccini family always appeared near the head of Florence's taxrolls. They lived not far from the Pazzi and Albizzi enclaves, in the eastern quarter of the city.

Although brought up to go into trade and banking, in the customary fashion of many upper-class Florentines, Alamanno was schooled in Latin and Greek, not only because the family took pride in its literary inclinations, running back to his famous grandfather Cino, a poet and polemicist, but also because an education in the classics was by now considered the ideal programme of study for boys from the ruling class.

Alamanno's father inherited a large fortune, but was unable to hold on to it, or to secure it by means of successful business enterprise, owing in part to the destructive property and income taxes of the 1430s and 1440s. Alamanno himself, growing up in difficult times, when cautious but angry talk about taxes was rife, also failed to prosper in trade, or had no liking for it – with the result that later on in life he was often forced to depend upon earnings from public office to supplement his private income from rents and land. The fact was that other interests really claimed his spirit. In the 1440s and 1450s, he attended lectures on rhetoric and philosophy at the University of Florence. Becoming one of the city's best Hellenists, he began to translate Greek works into Latin – Plutarch especially.

But politics – and Plutarch's *Lives* are crammed with it – is our theme, and it was to affect the Rinuccini households always. With wealth like theirs, Florentine families either made the needed strategic marriages and sought out public office, or they were hounded by partisan tax inspectors, who sometimes regarded them as easy prey. In the late fourteenth century, as one historian has noted, the Rinuccini 'ran into trouble with the [republican] oligarchy and were excluded from all major offices for about fifty years'. The reasons for this remain obscure. Racing through his family history in one passage of his *Dialogue on Liberty*, Alamanno glides silently over the long political shadow of this half century, yet it was then that the family were most harried by taxes, along a curve that peaked under the early Medicean oligarchy. By the 1450s, the dwindling fortunes of the main branch of the Rinuccini had reduced the house to the economic rank of middling tradesmen, although their name and social standing remained high: they could still expect to marry well. In his 1447 tax returns, one of Alamanno's uncles declared that many of his properties had 'passed to the Florentine commune because of the great and dishonest tax burdens borne [by us] until now. God give me patience and forgive those who are the cause of this'. Since no fewer than three of Alamanno's brothers took holy orders, it was almost certainly the case – given the mores of the day – that they had done so for financial reasons. The Church could provide secure careers for men of their class and education.

In 1469, Alamanno's net assets of 1569 florins included just enough real estate and investment capital to enable him to live modestly, in part, for instance, by relying on 'time deposits' in the Pazzi Bank: that is, on deposits held for a given length of time, with interest guaranteed at the discretion of the banker, but usually standing at about 7 or 8 per cent. Alamanno's father lived until 1462, and so looking back, our man must have known from domestic conversation all about the family's political problems early in the century, but he says nothing about that time.

Arrested at one point, and then pardoned, for assaulting and wounding his brother Francesco, the explosive Alamanno tried to walk a crooked line between open cooperation with the Medici on the one side and secret opposition on the other. His intellectual standing and old family name, marriage into a big political lineage (the Capponi), and his active courting of the Medici all served to get his name into the select office purses, and in 1460 he was drawn for a term in the Lord Priors, to be followed by terms in many other offices. Indeed, he came close to attaining the maximum honour, Gonfalonier of Justice. It is all the more surprising then that he signed the anti-Medici petition of the republican 'reformers' of May 1466. But he was able to get around this 'treachery', and got himself appointed to the Medicean *balìe* of 1466 (September), 1471, and 1480, all of which sought to gather more power around fewer men. Nevertheless, when ranging over these years in his historical memoirs (*Ricordi*), he accuses Piero de' Medici of armed violence, tyranny, and corruption, and denounces Lorenzo's 1480 *Balìa* as 'tyrannical'.

His memoirs and the *Dialogue* show that Alamanno loathed the Medicean oligarchy of 'unworthy' and jumped-up men. But he was not averse to seeking favour, and he dedicated five of his translations, selected from Plutarch's *Lives,* to Piero de' Medici and to the young Lorenzo.

On the occasion of his major embassy to Rome (1475–76), in a delicate diplomatic moment, he reported Pope Sixtus's anger with the Duke of Milan directly to the Lord Priors, even quoting one of his outbursts to the effect that the Pope would 'excommunicate him [the Duke] like a dog!' Always protective of his Sforza patron, Lorenzo reacted to this report with fury and Alamanno's mission was terminated. Our learned translator was shocked and humiliated, but he went on writing friendly letters to his angry *capo,* Lorenzo, now and then dispatching a gift of game after a hunt. Was such conduct a plain matter of trimming and hypocrisy, of trying to win back favour in order to return to high office? Put into the light of a man's time and place, morality is unlikely to be a simple transparency. Let us put Alamanno into such a light.

Like Venice, little Florence was a whole state and, in its fierce patriotism, almost a nation. Men from the middle and upper ranks – not to speak of their women – were not normally free to move from one city or region to the other, in the hope of taking up new careers or new trades. Such mobility among the propertied and well-off is more a feature of modern society. Of course Florentine merchants went abroad to ply their trades, often for long periods, but they always came back: home was *la vera città*, the real city, where powerful roots, family, identity, marriage, and friends all had their ground.

Unless an upper-class Florentine like Alamanno went into voluntary exile – like a priest, thereby giving up his world – he made his peace with life as it was at home. Since his coveted social destiny was best realised in the large sphere of public life, he accepted that sphere, and despite gnashing his teeth, was likely to desire a life in politics. Hundreds of Florentine family heads were doing as Alamanno was: appearing to cooperate with the Medici. However, like the 400 reformers of 1466 (not counting the many others who were too cautious to sign the republican oath), and like the legislators who resisted Lorenzo's circle in 1470 and 1471 but later cooperated, citizens connived with the ruling clique in the persisting hope of a release from Medicean domination. They watched and waited; they looked for openings that would suddenly admit a wider electorate; and they dragged their feet in council, or logged in their secret votes of dissent.

In 1479, when the Pazzi War began to look like Lorenzo's undoing, and many Florentines decided that his days were numbered, even the loyal Poliziano (not himself a Florentine) despaired and got out of the city. Understandably, then, Lorenzo rushed back to Florence from Naples in 1480, after an absence of little more than three months, fearing that his government faced a grave internal challenge, as indeed it did. His close advisors had been agitating for him to hurry back home, knowing that there were determined opponents ensconced in the political councils.

Alamanno was a keenly political man, rightly marked out for public life by his large family. Outgoing and intellectually poised, he looked like the ideal choice for the task of reinstating the political fortunes of the Rinuccini. And as the product of a classical education, his signing of the oath of 1466 hints at something of the Roman republican in him, also attested to in his warm applause for the Milanese 'tyrannicides' who assassinated Galeazzo Maria Sforza in 1476.

The fact that he dedicated his Plutarch translations to the Medici has seemed to warrant the claim that he honestly favoured them up to the time of his falling out with Lorenzo. Although doubt is cast on this by his republican oath, the fact that he was later selected for the Medicean *Balìa* of the same year strongly suggests that he was wavering, that he was trying to convert his public commitment to the Medici into a private conviction. For some years, as it happens, especially in the 1460s, he was attracted by the Platonic notion of a 'civil prince', of the wise and good ruler who governs with the consent of the people. And perhaps he wedded this idea to the notion of an aristocratic republic with a leading place for the Medici. This shifting vision allowed him both to serve them and to retain an element of ironic detachment, until he lost Lorenzo's favour for top office and turned decisively against him.

Seeking to convey a forceful political message, Alamanno's *Dialogue on Liberty* has obvious 'over-the-top' features, both in idealising the pre-Medicean republic and in its harsh accusations. The attack on the depraved and criminal character of Lorenzo's government is couched in a language drawn from the orator and lawyer Cicero. Peel this away, however, and the unsavoury elements of Medici rule remain: the flattery and corruption that attended Lorenzo's city-wide ties of patronage and 'friendship'. In this short work, Alamanno is trying to square a circle that was partly of his own making. But if we step out of the imagined world of his *Dialogue* and force him out too, he cannot escape the self-incrimination of his own actions. For right through the 1480s and down to the time of Lorenzo's death, he went on holding offices, thereby – if in fact he was the rare honest man – helping to clean the face of a government which he condemned as criminal.

His story is the tormented tale of the generations of citizens who elected to work with the Medici, doing so either by supporting them or by accepting office under the umbrella of their patronage. Many of them believed or hoped that the moment would come for casting out the talented family, but when it came at last, a new script and players had come on the scene, stepping up all the difficulties.

CHAPTER THIRTEEN

Lorenzo: Lord and Citizen

The Mask Falls

O N A MORNING in January 1489, the Duke of Ferrara's ambassador to Florence came upon an unusual scene.

Lorenzo had returned from one of his country villas the day before, and happened to meet the ambassador in the cathedral, where the two spoke briefly. It was not the occasion for a confidential conversation, so they agreed to meet the following day. Going out to the Medici Palace to see him on the morning of the 19th, the ambassador ran into a menacing throng:

> [There was] a great tumult of people in the streets, and the reason was that a young Florentine was being taken to the place of justice for having killed a servant of the Eight some days before. He had fled to Siena, but the Sienese got him back into the hands of the Lord Priors. As the youth was being led through the streets . . . the crowd mutinied, crying out, 'Escape! Escape!' Then they pushed in and tried to pull him away from the hands of the Podestà's guardsmen. Thereupon the mighty Eight themselves arrived and ordered the piazza to be cleared at once on pain of death.
>
> The ambassadors from Milan and Genoa, and Lorenzino and Giovanni di Pier Francesco de' Medici [Lorenzo's cousins], seeking grace for the young man, had gone with their pleas to the Magnificent Lorenzo, who was in the palace [of the Lord Priors] at the moment of the tumult. He offered them consoling words, but then saw to it that the man was hanged in the piazza, dangled from a window of the Podestà's palazzo. He then commanded that four of those who had been shouting 'Escape! Escape!' be seized and each given four

strappados, after which they were banished from the city for four years. This was how the mutiny was put down, and at no point did the Magnificent Lorenzo want to leave the scene until he saw that the crowd had calmed down. . . . I remained in the palace with the Milanese ambassador and other citizens, and it seemed to me that this was not the moment to have a talk with *il Magnifico*.

There was clearly something very remarkable about the case, extenuating circumstances at the least, or neither the populace nor Lorenzo's cousins, still less the two ambassadors, would have been so concerned about the life of the condemned youth. The facts that favoured him escape us. But the extraordinary thing is that in their desire for lenience, the ambassadors and Lorenzo's cousins turned to him, taking fully for granted that his direct intervention in the affair could get the supreme penalty commuted to a prison sentence, the loss of a limb, or even perhaps exile. Lorenzo held no office at that point that entitled him to any such authority in the case. Yet in the eyes of well-informed contemporaries, such power *was* his, and in fact he quickly exercised it, though not as they wished. For all of a sudden, his word alone sufficed to ensure that instead of being taken to 'the place of justice' outside the city gates, the young man was hanged in the middle of the city, where the action would be read both as a lesson and a slap in the face for the unruly populace.

Not content with this, Lorenzo then ordered the arrest, racking, and exile of the four men picked out of the protesting crowd. On the spot, he turned himself into a policeman and high judge: in other words, into a *de facto* ruler. Only lords and princes claimed such exceptional authority in Italian cities, and even they normally exercised the power of justice through regular magistrates, seldom so directly and brutally, as Milanese lords had often done in the fourteenth century.

Like no other vignette or document, this incident provides immediate insight to Lorenzo's power in the Florence of the late 1480s. Suddenly all his disguises fell away, and he stepped forward as lord of the city. As it happened, he was going through a phase of bad physical pain just then, owing to attacks of gout, as reported by the ambassador from Ferrara himself; and this condition was possibly behind his asperity that day. But it cannot be assumed that his usual preference was for a strict and severe application of the criminal code. More often, for the many hundreds of clients in his patronage web, he seemed ready to favour the repealing of heavy sentences. Indeed, Alamanno Rinuccini held that thanks to Lorenzo's butting into capital cases, murderers walked around freely in the streets of Florence.

Strange Happenings

SINCE WE ARE tracking the crooked rise of princely power, let's antici- pate a point about Lorenzo's final years, in order to set a direction.

Up to the mid seventeenth century, some sacred quality was commonly attributed to anointed kings. Men wanted to believe that high worldly authority had behind it some heavenly power. Infused by the voices of the ancient world, some of the poets and thinkers of the Italian Renaissance challenged this view; but the popular mind and many intel- lectuals (Marsilio Ficino for one) linked political power with the super- natural.

Florentine feeling about Lorenzo's standing in the city came to be so strong, that unique incidents had to attend his death. Just before it actually occurred, some contemporaries reported the howling of wolves, others the sighting of a comet, and others still a fight between 'shadows of astonishing greatness', accompanied by 'horrid and confused voices'. A mad woman in one of the city's major churches broke out with a weird prophecy about fire; and it was claimed that three beams of light from Fiesole, the hill town looking down on Florence, passed over the city and hovered above the church of San Lorenzo, which held the tombs of Lorenzo's father, grandfather, the murdered Giuliano, and other family members.

Then an hour or so before midnight, on 5 April 1492, in the thick of a bad thunderstorm, lightning struck the top of the cathedral with such force that great marble stones were dislodged from the dome and went crashing to the ground, hundreds of feet below, in the direction of the Medici Palace. Three days later the ailing Lorenzo died. All Florence had known that he was gravely ill; his whispering enemies had taken pleasure in bruiting the fact. The world was a haunt for spirits, or so it was thought. Some citizens even believed that Lorenzo had worn a ring with a sprite trapped inside, which, on being released three days before his death, had bolted with such energy as to damage the cathedral, standing opposite the spiritual heart of the city, San Giovanni, the baptistery named after Florence's patron saint. His death filled friends and associates with sadness and in some cases perhaps fear, but many Florentines seem to have rejoiced in secret.

Well, but why was Lorenzo associated with the power of a magical ring? Apart from possible pointers in folklore, the answer can only be that most Florentines had heard about his amazing collection of antique curios, incised gems, rings, coins, medallions, marble trinkets, little table clocks, heaps of rosaries, and other small objects of exceeding value. He was famously proud of the hoard, which also included ink wells, buckles, silver tableware, and even show weapons. Such exotic riches stirred the popular imagination, and all important visitors to the city – princes, cardinals, and foreign ambassadors – soon let it be known that they longed to see the collection, although he had been forced to sell many of the antique coins, particularly at the time of the Pazzi War. Inventoried after his death, some of Lorenzo's small collectibles were individually valued at up to 500 florins, whereas his battle pictures of the *Rout of San Romano*, the three large panels painted by Paolo Uccello, were each assigned a value of a mere 50 florins. Coming from among a resilient, practical, but credulous populace, many citizens sensed a transcendent note in Lorenzo's power and at once concluded, as by a natural impulse, that he could call upon the doings of unearthly spirits.

Power

TURNING INTO A bloodbath for the plotters, the April Plot became a boon for Lorenzo. He used Giuliano's martyrdom and the immediate triumph of his diplomacy in Naples to gather his closest supporters more tightly around himself, to unfurl new governing controls, to push back or overwhelm stubborn resistance, and to raise himself above the oligarchy itself. His near contemporary, the great historian and political thinker Guicciardini (b.1483), whose grandfather and grand-uncle had worked closely with Lorenzo at the summit of government, offered a resounding assessment:

> This [Pazzi] uprising . . . so revived his name and fortunes that it may be said, most happy was that day for him! His brother Giuliano died, with whom he would have been forced to share his wealth, thus putting his great estate into question. His enemies were gloriously eliminated by the arms of government, and so too were the shadows and suspicions that he had cast over Florence. The people took up arms for him . . . and on that day, finally, they saw him as lord of the city. To guard [against attempts on] his life, he was granted the privilege of going about with as many armed servants as he chose. In effect, he all but made himself lord of state . . . and the great and suspect power which he had exercised up to that point became much greater still, but now secure. This [type of victory] puts an end to civil discord. With the extermination of one side [or party], the head of the other becomes lord of the city. Those who championed him, from being companions, almost become his subjects. The people as a whole remain enslaved; and the state is passed on by inheritance.

Lorenzo, however, was more than the implied child of fortune. When the Conspiracy broke, he turned it instinctively to his advantage, as he was forced to manoeuvre and dodge in the midst of war, of conflict with the spiritual arms of the Church, and of soaring government costs and rebellious murmuring. Poet, avid reader, art lover, dreamer, and would-be city planner? Yes, all this too, and in the 1480s, for a few years, a disciple of Ficino and Neo-Platonism. But even as he came to imagine that 'Reality' and the patterns of perfection belonged to the plains of heaven, his business on earth was primary. He was first and always a doer, a man of action intent on a goal in which his government and his place in it were number one, and from which the fortunes of the Medici house could not be separated. Yet his very circumstances, teeming dangerously with the resentments and ambitions of others, ruled that his survival was going to require a quick and cunning intellect, supple turns, and even courtliness: in a word, genius. While none of these qualities could be denied him, not even by his most implacable enemies, they would have insisted on adding his arrogance, his lust for power, cruelty, and a vindictive touchiness. Let's have the words of his bitter antagonist, the humanist Alamanno Rinuccini:

> Lorenzo was a man endowed by nature, training, and practice with such enormous ingenuity, that he was in no way inferior to his grandfather Cosimo. . . . He had so able and versatile a mind that whatever he turned to in his pursuits as a boy, he learned and possessed perfectly, and better than others. So it happened that he learned to dance, fire arrows, sing, ride, join in games, play diverse musical instruments, and do many other things, all going to grace and delight his youthful years. And I believe that being inspired by the magnitude of his ability, when he found our citizens timid and of a servile spirit, having been rendered so by his father, he resolved to transfer to himself all public dignity, power, and authority, and in the end, like Julius Caesar, to make himself lord of the republic.

With his nose for shrewd political action, Lorenzo could move fast, too fast at times, as in 1470, when he tried too soon and failed to put tighter clamps on the ruling group. But on his victorious return from Naples, heralding the end of the Pazzi War, he struck at once, his instincts telling him that this was the moment to cash in on the sparkle. During his absence in the southern kingdom, the Medicean clique had been frightened by the swell of discontent in an oligarchy that would not lie down. Now the disloyal rogues had to be taught a lesson: edge them out to the margins, or exclude them altogether, and truly shrink the ranks of the ruling core of the oligarchy.

Within weeks of his return from Naples, going before the three legislative councils, and fronted by a team of docile Lord Priors, Lorenzo and his friends sought once again to deceive the legislators and to finesse the passage of a bill that was tantamount, paradoxically, to a constitutional *coup d'état*. Yet once more, despite being misled and misinformed, two of the councils smelled a rat and came within a whisker of defeating the measure, with the *Cento* passing it by one vote and the Council of the People by two! Were bribes paid out, favours promised, or heads banged in private and in the corridors? We are unlikely ever to know. Told that certain reforms were needed, such as fairer taxes, an overdue 'scrutiny', and the remedy of 'deficiencies' in the name of 'good government', legislators were pressed into consenting to a powerful short-term council (a *Balìa*). Here was the smelly rat, or, more decorously, a Trojan Horse. For having got their *Balìa*, Lorenzo and his men were now ready for action.

The promised tax changes were late in coming and far from satisfactory; the scrutiny of eligible political names was utterly ignored; other matters were brushed aside; but what did see the light within days of the *Balìa's* commencing work was a new council, the Seventy.

Animated by the spoils of patronage and fear of a resentful opposition, the Medici party had worked for years to concentrate power by reducing the ranks of the oligarchy, while appearing to leave the large political class mostly intact. This 'constitutional' policy had paid off. The menace, however, of 'disobedient' well-born politicians remained – ambitious men inside the ruling group. Lorenzo and his advisors, therefore, now put a kind of senate in place, designed to hold the heart and soul of his oligarchy: the group of Seventy, whose members would be sworn to secrecy and expected to serve for life, despite an initial five-year mandate. Here, in their privileged togetherness, Lorenzo would have a body that he could more easily divide and conquer, although he would naturally expect loyalty and obedience. The powers of the Seventy were unprecedented. From 1480 onwards, they would pick the successive teams of Lord Priors; control legislation by functioning as the decisive consultative group, thus stripping the Priors of one of their greatest powers; and staff two new ministries exclusively from among their own members – the Committee of Eight and the Twelve Procurators. The first of these was put in charge of foreign affairs; the second was appointed to handle internal business, including criminal and financial matters.

Yet even as Lorenzo and his friends, still glowing from his Neapolitan triumph, imposed their group of Seventy, the ambassador from Ferrara, speaking of this and other recent changes (3 July 1480), reported: 'I find this people more discontented than ever.' If there was anything to the ambassador's claim, then Florence's first citizen would have to remain on his guard, go on being as manipulative as ever, and sometimes come down with a heavy hand.

Client to the Sforza

LORENZO'S CORRESPONDENCE TOOK up an astonishing part of his life and reveals the lord above all, more than the citizen. Over 20,000 letters addressed to him survive, and there is no knowing how many thousands more were destroyed or lost. Incomplete minutes, kept by his secretaries, disclose that he himself sent out tens of thousands of letters, occasionally spending five and six hours a day in his chambers, both dictating letters and composing them in his own hand. In effect, he headed a foreign-affairs ministry, as he claimed an ever widening control, in the course of the 1480s, over all foreign correspondence. The vast bulk of his letters went out to Florentine ambassadors, governors in Florence's subject territories, town councils, princes, popes, and cardinals, as well as to petty lords, bishops, and some of the foremost soldiers of the day, such as the Vitelli, Orsini, Sanseverino, Baglioni, and lesser lights. Remarkably, for a man of his interests, none of his surviving, published letters deals with poetry and writing, although there are occasional requests to borrow books. In his pursuit of political power and perhaps larger goals, he was to develop a particular fondness for reading history.

His correspondence shows the mighty patron at work, directing emissaries, doling out favours, requesting favours, rendering thanks, or recommending friends, clients, and friends of friends, in letters that wheedle, play, urge, argue, instruct, bully, or seek to charm and finesse. Frequently too, and almost obsessively, his letters of patronage turn on the ceremonial claims of love, as in this composite quotation: 'Do this favour out of the love I know you bear for me, or in the name of my love for you; and treat this man and his business as if I were he and his business mine. Such is the way I feel about him.'

Yet Lorenzo's power in Florence had not the wisp of a basis in the city's constitution. It was founded, instead, on forms of political organisation that had been both negotiated and coerced. And although the structure of Florentine republican government could be bent to yield the like, it could not *rightly* confer the authority which he claimed and exercised. He held power because he was *able* to hold it, and this was possible because a circle of leading men and families – most of them 'aristocrats' – had chosen to hand it to him, to work with him, and if need be (at least in some cases) to go down with him. It was the power of stalwarts and clever politicians, of big shots and patrons, merchants and landowners, 'honourable' knights and doctors of law. They all knew the serpentine ways of public office, political patronage, and secret meetings. Acting without any constitutional right and alleging the dire need for civic harmony, in a setting in which they themselves ranked, arguably, among the chief disrupters, they transferred power to Lorenzo. By elevating him and his house, they elevated themselves and their own families, and also made conditions safer for that part of the patriciate that had most cooperated with the Medici.

But it was also clear that if Tommaso Soderini and company had not gone to Lorenzo's house in December 1469, to acknowledge him as *maestro di bottega* (boss of the shop), the soldiers of the Duke of Milan would have sought to impose Lorenzo on the city. In that case, a united Florentine oligarchy could at once have found allies and stood up to such a threat effectively enough to repel the menace of troops. But it has to be said that the diehard Mediceans would never have agreed to such a large show of unity.

In relations with Milan, Lorenzo was the client always and Galeazzo Maria Sforza the patron, even though that princely house was nearly always the main debtor of the Medici Bank. On his death in 1466, Francesco Sforza owed the Medici 115,000 ducats, security for which lay in pawned jewels and in assigned salt taxes, and over the next year or two, according to the historian of the Medici Bank, this debt would rise 'to the fantastic sum of 179,000 ducats'. The dukes, however, lords of one of Italy's greatest states, had the soldiers to defend the Medici if the need arose, always provided that the Medici retained enough control in Florence to command the city gates. And neither the first nor the second of these points was ever forgotten. Lorenzo now and then must have turned his mind to the spectacle of 'the Milanese artillery train', which in 1472 consisted 'of 16 large cannon', requiring '227 carts and 522 pairs of oxen to transport them'. And behind its cannon Milan could gear up an army of from 20,000 to 40,000 men, including cavalry units of up to 12,000 men.

As a ten-year-old, Lorenzo had first met the young prince Galeazzo Maria in Florence, and then again six years later in Milan, on the occasion of a marriage linking the Neapolitan royal house with the Sforza. They met a third time in the following year, when Lorenzo returned to Milan for the baptism of Galeazzo Maria's newborn son; and on this occasion he presented the Duchess with a gold necklace, bearing a huge diamond. Much more intimate was their fourth and last meeting, which took place in March 1471. The Duke arrived in Florence with a magnificent cavalcade of about 2000 horseman, including 500 infantry, 500 pairs of dogs, and a wealth of hunting hawks. He remained for nine days, he and his immediate circle staying as guests in the Medici Palace. And as fellow citizens looked on, gaping, the occasion necessarily cast an aura about Lorenzo, although a number of informed Florentines, such as Rinuccini, considered Sforza a monster of turpitude.

Letters between Lorenzo and the Duke were of course formal, but also outspoken and sometimes charged with feeling. Time and again Lorenzo declares that he holds his place in Florence because of Galeazzo Maria, that he is there to serve the Duke, to be his 'thing', his instrument, and 'wax' in his hands, so that whatever is good for 'Your Loftiness' (*Vostra Celsitudine*) is good for Lorenzo and Florence. Our first citizen was saying, in effect, that Medicean rule would keep Florence subservient to Milanese foreign policy; and while this use of hyperbole naturally overstated things, the lord of Milan and his advisors took the commitment seriously. They acted on it. This gives the lie to later Medicean charges, claiming that the Pazzi and Archbishop Salviati had laboured to sacrifice Florentine independence by seeking to put the city under the command of Pope Sixtus and the King of Naples. Lorenzo and his associates had already tied Florence to the Sforza cart; and since close ties with Milan went back little more than two decades, to 1450, the Medici circle could scarcely argue that they were merely being loyal to a vital old tradition. That would have been rubbish. In a dynamic, unstable system of Italian states, it was wiser to pursue flexible policies, putting

Florence sometimes closer to Venice, or to the Pope, or even to the King of Naples. In 1470, Lorenzo's differences with the oligarchy were so sharp, that even Tommaso Soderini had to be fought and bought, and much of the trouble sprang from the conviction that Florence had been made a slave to Milan's foreign policies.

Lorenzo himself was to taste the partial truth of this claim in the autumn of 1479, when Milanese policy under the rising new lord, Ludovico Sforza, took an abrupt turn in favour of King Ferrante, forcing Lorenzo into his dramatic flight to Naples, to a King who could well have packed him off to Rome, into the hands of Pope Sixtus and Count Girolamo. In fact, as late as the middle of January 1480, King Ferrante wanted him to go to Rome 'to sue for [the Pope's] forgiveness'. But Lorenzo had answered by saying that he would have to be sent in chains, and that if this was done, the King should also send along a confessor and a lawyer to draw up a last will and testament.

Patron

L ET'S IMAGINE A mighty citizen – or budding prince – 'holding court' as he walked in the streets of Florence, in the great government piazza, or as he paced around slowly in the cathedral. This was routine for the Magnificent Lorenzo down to the time of the April Conspiracy, in a habit never acquired by his father and grandfather, whose ways were more aloof. But the brilliant Lorenzo, with his wealth of words and easy manner, though far from good-looking (Figure 12) and with a raspy voice, enjoyed public performances, liked to be seen, and flourished in company. He believed in his attractions and must have used them often, with spectacular success on his famous embassy to Naples. Ambassadors, friends, favour seekers, poets, and many another were often seen conversing with him in public places. The cathedral and the government square were favourite meeting points. It goes without saying that his confidential and secret encounters – unless they were trysts in the Florentine countryside – took place in the Medici Palace, or in the official chambers of the Gonfalonier of Justice, the Lord Priors, and the Eight.

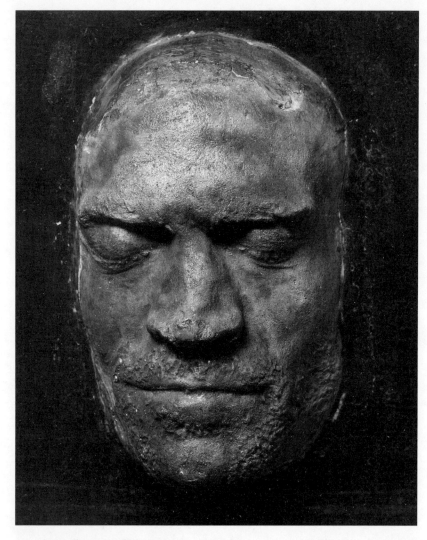

Fig. 12 Death mask of Lorenzo.

His easy public style came to a sharp end in April 1478. Fear set in, and he was now too exalted a citizen. 'Condemning the memory' of the Pazzi echoed a practice that ran back to the lofty position of the prince or emperor in Roman law, as if the attempt on Lorenzo's life had involved 'the crime of violated majesty'. Suddenly the Eight cancelled every permit to carry arms. Town criers were sent out to trumpet the announcement that citizens had to submit lists of all weapons in their households. A tiny handful of select citizens received the Eight's special exemption; and for the first time in the history of republican Florence, a private citizen, Lorenzo, was authorised to move through the city with an armed escort consisting of twelve to fourteen men, some of them mounted, including archers, four crossbowmen, and swordsmen. Lorenzo seems to have preferred armed attendants with colourful nicknames, and surely he dubbed some of them: thus Garlic Saver (Salvalaglio), Black Martin (Martino Nero), Crooked Andrea (Andrea Malfatto), and the chokingly styled Marghutt, who, like another guard called Morgante, sported a ridiculous name drawn from Luigi Pulci's heroic comic poem, *Morgante*. They must have seemed a strange lot as they rode or walked together through the city, some with their swords always menacingly drawn. In fact, Florence had seen something like this, if not nearly so conspicuous, some years earlier (1472), when Lorenzo was blamed for the murderous suppression of a revolt in the Florentine town of Volterra. Feeling threatened, he was seen for a time with a small contingent of soldiers, as he went through Florence, but the supposed danger soon passed.

His new escort of guardsmen was to be permanent, and in raising him visibly above every other citizen, the attendant language of menace and bluster gave him extraordinary status. We must picture him moving through the streets of Florence, or passing out of the city gates into the countryside, always accompanied by that armed company, personal and yet official too. The little cavalcade could never have struck citizens as anything but a sight to stare at. Living in a world in which angels and devils were real for many people, little wonder that some citizens came to believe that he walked about with a powerful genie trapped inside a ring.

Lorenzo's new image had a strange air about it, despite the fact that it expressed a reality. He was the city's maximum 'godfather', and had been so for years. Brought up to be courted, feared, and respected, to dispense favour, to treat with great lords, and to expect a reverential body language from people, he found a ready fit in his new trappings. Unlike true princes, he could not call civil and criminal cases to himself for trial (though we have seen him plunge into a near riot and dispense summary justice); but he could certainly pull strings in the Eight and more deviously in the great Merchants' Court. He could not, like the Council of Ten in Venice or the Este lords of Ferrara, put himself above the ordinary law in alleged emergencies. Instead, he had to work from behind the scenes, through cronies, clients, and fearful or ambitious men – pushing, browbeating, negotiating, and favouring some citizens, while hurting others. For what is usually forgotten about his patronage is its long string of losers, the unchosen, the men who were rejected (rightly or wrongly) by the special favour which he extended to others. Artists and artisans to one side, to benefit from patronage in Medicean Florence was not the reward of merit; it was payment for service rendered, or for knowing how to court the right people.

His unconstitutional status was the very condition that required Lorenzo to caretake a city-wide web of contacts and clients. He had to have eyes at the back of his head, or feel anxious about what others were up to, including his own associates. This also is why there was a continuous flow of requests to and from him, both by letter and word of mouth. In the sorting out of disputes between citizens, he was in great demand and became the city's leading arbiter – happy to be sought after and proud of his judgments. Since this weight of charges was in due course to become too heavy, his brother and even his mother stepped in to help him. He was a religious man, but there was no pious need for him to belong to seven or eight different religious confraternities. In fact, he turned these fellowship cells into his eyes in the city's different neighbourhoods; he even bored into local plebeian sodalities (*potenze*); and through his countless 'friends', he could reach into any corner of Florence. His influence stretched from the Gonfalonier at the crest of Florentine government out to the peripheral parishes near the city walls.

Alamanno Rinuccini claimed that Lorenzo made a habit of pressing mercenary captains (petty lords usually) on Florence as men for hire, forcing up the city's crippling military expenses, in action that cheated shareholders in the government debt and laid heavier taxes on citizens. Since Lorenzo's correspondence shows, indeed, that he intervened often for mercenaries, he could only have done so with an eye to making them clients or dependents, so that he could then call on them in crises, as when he raised the alarm call for Gualterotto da Vernio and

Giovanni Bentivoglio within hours of the April Conspiracy. However, while being exceedingly important, soldiers were only one of the many classes of men whom he cultivated and then pulled into his vast web of supporters. There were also bishops and cardinals, university professors, physicians, famous jurists and humanists, foreign courtiers and secretaries, as well as politicians and statesmen from other cities. This sweep was in part the result of his unquiet and meddlesome genius, but it was also typical of other 'great masters' of the age – cardinals, leading ambassadors, and influential courtiers or statesmen, not to mention learned princes such as Duke Federigo of Urbino and King Alfonso of Naples.

Lorenzo's network of contacts stretched all the way down the social order, to take in servants, workers, peasants, petty tradesmen, and others, in answer to requests that they be pardoned, paid, hired, released from prison, arrested, enabled to collect debts, or any number of other commissions. His mighty foreign friends and acquaintances were continually urging him to step in for *their* local contacts and simple folk, while he, in turn, reached into their cities and provinces to do likewise.

Guicciardini emphasised that Lorenzo was a man so given to suspicion, a sense aroused by the fact of his having to 'keep a free city down', that 'no upper-class marriage was contracted [in Florence] without his leave and participation'. On the face of it, this claim seems exaggerated, but it has yet to be proven so, since Lorenzo was the mediating party or broker for scores of marriages involving prominent families such as the Strozzi, Pitti, Ridolfi, Serristori, Tornabuoni, Martelli, Pandolfini, and many another. Arrangements for these marriages were often made in the Medici Palace, Medici villas, and even in the premises of the Medici Bank itself. Apart from displaying his authority and popularity as a go-between in the marriage market, Lorenzo's abiding interest in patrician marriages was to keep prominent citizens from making their own family alliances – indeed, it was to 'match them up so that they threw no shadow on him'. He was particularly wary of men who could wield power in their own right, and the result was that 'he sometimes pressed young men of quality into taking wives that they would not otherwise have chosen'.

Hands in the Till

Aready in serious troubles during the 1470s, in London, Milan, and Bruges, the Medici Bank began to bleed freely with the outbreak of the Pazzi War, when its assets were seized or frozen in Rome and Naples, and for nearly two years Lorenzo was plagued by the need for cash. With losses of about 200,000 florins, the Bank never recovered its 'imperial' wealth; and although Lorenzo strained to conceal his desperation, it was impossible for him to hide his needs from the eyes of watchful citizens. The city was too small, and in part a ferment of gossip and rancour against him, particularly after the April Plot, when hated war taxes and suspended interest payments to government creditors made Florentines all the more hawk-eyed.

Reliable contemporaries asserted that Lorenzo utilised his agents in government to put his hands into the public till. The estimates of his supposed pilfering varied widely. Cambi put the sum at 50,000 scudi (florins); Piero Parenti fixed on a figure of more than 158,000 florins; and for Rinuccini the theft amounted to 200,000 florins.

It is hard to translate these amounts into purchasing power of the sort that would mean something to a modern reader, but it may help to say that the sums could have put a small army into the field for a short time, or that the total building costs of the mammoth Medici and Strozzi palaces are estimated to have been in the range of about 30,000 to 35,000 florins for each. The round figure of 100,000 florins would have kept 4000 university students for a year, room and board included; and the same sum could easily have been the payroll for a year of some 3500 to 4000 workers at a scatter of big building sites.

But the matter of Lorenzo's theft of public funds is, interestingly, something of a red herring and likely to divert historians from more critical questions. He was obviously not just any man with a private conscience in the Florence of his day. Unofficial head of state, though without the stitch of a legal right, this — his usurpation — was the major transgression and is what calls for study. By comparison, his theft of communal money was a good deal less serious, even if it provoked the anger and outrage of contemporaries. In ordinary legal argument of the age, when a major right was granted, all the lesser ones naturally followed.

While it cannot be ascertained, we may suppose that Lorenzo suffered few stabs of conscience over taking money from the coffers of the Monte. He saw himself, after all, as the city's servant, leader, first patriot, and protecting patron. Being the third Medici in a row to be the shadowy (and then not so shadowy) head man in the state, his political inheritance – he could surely feel – had been thrust upon him, even when he called on the Duke of Milan to stand by with troops at the outset of December 1469. He was forced to reason that to make himself guardian not only of his own family interests, but also of the families whose loyalty had elevated the Medici, was to be doing no more than the 'natural' thing. Buttressed by these justifications, he could not fail to feel that his financial losses at home and abroad were somehow related to his family's public position. Thus in a brief memoir, at one point, he noted that in the years between 1434 and the end of 1471, 'we [the ruling Medici] spent the unbelievable sum of 663,755 florins on buildings and building works, charity, and taxes, not counting other expenses'. A good third to a half of this total sum, it may be ventured, had been paid out in taxes; and as he wrote down the astonishing total, to remember it afterward, it must have served to ease his conscience.

I am suggesting that Lorenzo talked himself into an attitude which enabled him to feel that he had the right to receive secret help from the Monte, because it wasn't really theft. It was payment for a long history of family service to Florence, for having so close a link to the city, indeed, that he could see no distance between himself and the uppermost place in the state. Drawing almost certainly from well-informed talk in his own household, Guicciardini was famously to say that death foiled Lorenzo's plan to make himself Gonfalonier of Justice for life – permanent master, therefore, of the Lord Priors. The allegation is borne out by his life's trajectory, and it also meant that he expected to bequeath the office to his son Piero, in a strategy whose political origins reached back to the late thirteenth century.

A Lordly Trajectory

FOR ALL HIS disguised but compelling authority in the city's ruling councils, Lorenzo was never to have the political security for which he yearned. With its many short-term offices and the persisting Florentine habit of discussion, the republic refused to die, and the danger of plots against Lorenzo persisted. In November 1472, well before the April Plot, there had been serious talk of one with roots among Florentine exiles in Naples; but after setting out, apparently, the would-be assassins were called back. In late September 1480, a religious hermit was suddenly seized at Poggio a Caiano, near Lorenzo's new villa, and accused of planning to murder the Florentine lord. To get the truth out of him, the Eight had his feet burned, 'until they dripped fat. Then he was made to get up and forced to walk on coarse salt.' He died nineteen days later. In April 1481, three well-connected men were suddenly arrested in Florence and executed, charged with plotting to kill the 'tyrant' (their word) Lorenzo. Two of them were born into upper-class families. Their confessed aim was to restore the city's republican liberties. Confiscating all their worldly goods, the Eight then proceeded to hound their close relatives. The charge of lese-majesty was levelled against the three men, as if Lorenzo held the status of a titled prince. At about the same time, according to the testimony of Cola Montano, there were other plots in the offing, connected chiefly with the plans of a Pistoian malcontent and the exile Neri Acciaiuoli, bearer of one of the most prestigious of all Florentine surnames. In 1484 – in a case in which Lorenzo himself sought to suppress the details – one of his own relations, Alessandro Tornabuoni, was exiled to Sicily for life on suspicion of conspiracy. And there is no knowing how many other angry plots were stillborn.

In August 1488, after Lorenzo had quarrelled with the warlord Giovanni Bentivoglio, *signor* of Bologna, his friends began to fear that the soldier might try to have him assassinated in the vicinity of Poggio a Caiano. In May 1490, again, in an episode of tantalising obscurity, two foreigners, one of them from the far south (Gaeta), were arrested in Firenzuola and rushed to Florence, where they were tortured and held for many days. The whole case was kept under a veil of strict secrecy, and to this day the details remain a mystery, although the name of the

King of Naples seems to have been raised; and two other magnates, the Duke of Calabria and Giovanni Bentivoglio, were said to have intervened in the case. The rumour was that the arrested men had been sent out to poison Lorenzo at one of his favourite health spas.

In the persisting shadow of such events, how could Lorenzo count on the future safety of his family, or find the serenity to get fully back to his books and writing? He worked on his poetry in fits and starts; his *Commentary On My Sonnets*, an interesting but uneven exercise, was never finished; nor were the poems *De summo bono*, the *Selve*, and his two eclogues.

Like the Pazzi, many contemporaries had seen that Lorenzo was on his way to a Renaissance dictatorship. What his grandfather Cosimo had won but held with the close aid of chosen families, Lorenzo was turning into a solo performance both by surrounding himself with jumped-up men (his own creations) in the key positions, and by being able, as it were, to hire and fire the aristocrats who held power under the wide arch of his patronage. This solution, however, was putting a growing distance between himself and the whole class of patricians – the Guicciardini, Ridolfi, Albizzi, Gianfigliazzi, Rucellai, and so on. Nothing better illustrates this than his calculated marriage and career policies for his family.

In their climb to power, the Medici made solid local marriages, looking carefully sideways to other political families. These helped to provide the needed network of contacts throughout the city, so that even in Lorenzo's generation, despite the undercurrent of contention between them, the Medici struck a deal with the Pazzi in Guglielmo's marriage to Lorenzo's elder sister. But this generation also held a momentous break: Lorenzo's marriage to a woman from the princely Orsini family. In effect, he was too important for any Florentine girl. The marriage was a frank, indeed crude, statement of political ambition. Here was the likely work of grandfather Cosimo, the patron behind the brilliant career of a distant cousin, Filippo de' Medici, who rose above all other native Florentine clerics, except one, to become the Archbishop of Pisa (1461–74). He was the priest who rounded up 1500 armed men for Lorenzo's father in the crisis of 1466. The single exception was Giovanni Dietisalvi Neroni, Archbishop of Florence (1462–73), who courageously joined his brother, an outstanding politician, by siding with the anti-Medicean 'reformers' of 1466. Regarded at once as a capital enemy, he paid for his republicanism with the penalty of exile from the city for the rest of his life; and Pope Paul II (1464–71) had to put up with this fallout from the world of Florentine politics, reminded of it whenever he encountered the Archbishop, who chose, in his exile, to reside in Rome.

Once the Medici had forged a link with the Orsini in Lorenzo's marriage, there was to be no turning back from the promise of this quasi-princely direction. His brother Giuliano seemed to move naturally along a path that led to one of two lives: that of priest and cardinal, or spouse and dynastic pin in a lordly marriage abroad. There was certainly no plan for him, any more than there had been for Lorenzo, to pursue a life in trade and international banking. During much of 1473, Lorenzo used various means to press his brother on Pope Sixtus, in a campaign to procure a cardinalship for him; but the Holy Father had other fish to fry, as we have seen, so the two brothers then considered a grand marriage for the anxious Giuliano. One of the houses that seems to have been discussed in this connection was that of the Appiano lords of Piombino, on the south-western (maritime) frontier of Florentine territory. They had Aragonese blood ties. But the plan came to nothing, and in 1480 Semiramide, the daughter of Jacopo III d'Appiano, bearing a princely dowry of 10,000 large florins of gold, was married instead to Lorenzo's young cousin, Lorenzo di Pierfrancesco de' Medici.

If Lorenzo's greatest concern was the survival of his house, this became a nagging anxiety after 1485, as his growing gout-pains and ill-health turned into frequent reminders of his mortality. Moved by a vision of Medicean grandeur and destiny, as he had been since his earliest years, he was now tormented by the question of his children's future, and at the top of this agenda was a marriage for Piero, his eldest son.

For this crucial match Lorenzo again turned to Rome and again to the Orsini clan, but now to a mightier branch. In 1487, even before he was seventeen years old, Piero, half an Orsini himself, was married to Alfonsina Orsini, daughter of the late Count of Tagliacozzo and Alba, but ward of the powerful Virginio Orsini, one of the busiest soldiers of the day. To add to its peninsular importance, the wedding was celebrated in Naples, in King Ferrante's castle, where the entire court was present. Lorenzo, meanwhile, had allowed at least one foreign ambassador to think that Alfonsina would arrive in Florence with a dowry of 30,000 florins (matter for sensational news up and down the peninsula), when in fact the sum was set at 12,000 Neapolitan ducats. Having previously made large loans to Virginio, he seems to have written off most of this debt in order to help clinch the marriage. So, had Lorenzo, whose family coat of arms was to become a pawnbroking emblem, half purchased a little princess?

The lordly ambitions of the Orsini marriages – Lorenzo's first and then Piero's – were not lost on fellow citizens, and while Florentines in public said nothing critical or nasty about these matches, the subject rankled. It would not be forgotten.

The remaining Medici marriages and careers move along the trail that was more securely opened up by the 'glorious elimination' (Guicciardini) of the Pazzi.

When Lorenzo died, his third son Giuliano was only thirteen years old, but the models for his life had already been chosen, and this soldier, courtier, musician, and poet would end his days as the Duke of Nemours. He sought to take up arms against the new republic in 1495, 1498, and again in 1500, finally marrying in 1515 and taking Filiberta, daughter of the Duke of Savoy, as his wife.

Since Lorenzo's first-born, Lucrezia, was not married till the age of eighteen (1488), she was most likely a plain-looking girl. Florentines could be ungenerous about the way people looked. Back in the 1460s, all patrician Florence knew that a marriagable Pazzi girl had a cast in one eye, and this defect naturally counted against her. Lorenzo's Lucrezia, as it happened, was married into the most distinguished branch of the Salviati lineage. Flaunting amity between the two houses, this marriage cemented one of those sensible native alliances, while also serving – in conscious Laurentian policy – to remind the city of the Medici's 'bourgeois' origins.

The fact that the worried and ill Lorenzo was rushing things is fully borne out by the marriage of his youngest daughter, Contessina, who in March 1490, at the age of twelve, had already entered into one of the most prominent of the Ridolfi households – influential backers of the Medici house. Another daughter, Luisa, died at the age of eleven, but had already been engaged.

In this trajectory of ambition, Lorenzo's daughter Maddalena

(b. 1473) brings us to his crucial relations with Pope Innocent VIII and the spectacular climb up the Church hierarchy of Lorenzo's second son, Monsignor Giovanni. Here too we encounter Giulio, the murdered Giuliano's illegitimate son, whose rise in the world was entwined with Monsignor Giovanni's career.

Born in secret in the months before the April Conspiracy, the illegitimate Giulio was brought to Lorenzo's attention by the child's godfather. In action that smacks of purging sin and offering prayer for Giuliano's soul, Lorenzo marked Giulio out for holy orders and tenaciously pursued an ambitious goal for him. Before the child was twelve, thanks to his uncle's string-pulling, he had begun to acquire a scatter of Church incomes, including those of the rich priorate of Capua, awarded by the King of Naples. The talented Giulio would then cling to his first cousin, Cardinal Giovanni, attain in his turn a cardinal's hat, and become Pope Clement VII in 1523.

Salvation and Glory

GIULIO'S CAREER WAS made possible by Monsignor Giovanni's ascent. This story began in 1486, when Lorenzo set out to court Pope Sixtus's successor, Innocent VIII (1484–92), and then swiftly felt his way toward an enterprise that would be the salvation and glory of the Medici. At the time, Lorenzo appeared to have everything against him at the Roman Curia. While having pretended neutrality in a recent war between King Ferrante and Pope Innocent, he had put Florence squarely into the King's camp, largely from fear of the papacy's military power and its common frontiers with Florence in the south and southeast. In addition, Florence and Genoa were divided by a sharp dispute over the coastal fortress of Sarzana – they each claimed it – and the Pope was a proud native of Genoa. When in need, however, Lorenzo was never without the faculty that had won the day for him in Naples – his diplomatic wiles. In sustained diplomacy, he was a powerful letter writer, one of the founders of modern Italian prose. And princes knew that when he had to, he could deliver Florence. Why else would the heads of the Orsini clan offer Alfonsina to Piero de' Medici, if not on the assumption that Florence itself came with Lorenzo's heir? The Medici were getting something of course, but so too, by now, were the Orsini. Florence was a frequent employer of armies, and the Orsini were front-line soldiers, as well as priests intended for the heights of ecclesiastical authority.

The growing amity between Lorenzo and Pope Innocent was nurtured in a secret correspondence, during the so-called Barons' War between Rome and Naples. By the beginning of 1487, the two men were so fully in agreement that Innocent seemed 'to sleep with the eyes of the Magnificent Lorenzo', and they now reached agreement on a marriage between Franceschetto Cibò, the Pope's illegitimate son, and Lorenzo's daughter Maddalena. In the middle of these proceedings, the Florentine ambassador to Rome informed Lorenzo that Pope Innocent had been so utterly won over in his dealings with the Florentine *maestro*, that he wanted papal policy to depend on Lorenzo's advice. The ambassador's letter wound up by saying: 'The conclusion is that you may as well think of yourself as pope.' A mad and happy exaggeration, to be sure, but it catches the flavour of relations between the Vicar of Christ and the statesman cum poet and connoisseur who seemed to reign in Florence.

What lay behind this amazing amity? In Lorenzo's designs, it was one thing, one child, his eleven-year-old son Giovanni, tonsured since the age of seven and being schooled to take his place one day as a prince of the Church. To this ambition the cherished Maddalena (her mother's favourite) had to be sacrificed. Lorenzo pretended that Innocent had pressed for the marriage, that he could not refuse from fear of alien-ating the Holy Father, and even that he had agreed to it for the sake of Florence. How so? Florentine relations with curial Rome had been warlike for too long, and everyone knew, Lorenzo said, 'how naturally this city inclines toward the Church'. He would worry about the girl, but the deed had to be done. He simply took for granted that the honour and survival of the Medici required it; they had been after a cardinal's hat for years. Consequently, at the age of thirteen (May 1487) Maddalena was formally engaged to Franceschetto ('Little Francis'), who was twenty-four years older, small, 'fat, boring, perpetually drunk', and a crazy gambler. In her fourteenth year (January 1488), with a dowry of 4000 florins, which would include the Pazzi Palace, she finally went to Franceschetto, now the Count of Anguillara, and they consummated the marriage. Seven months later, through the restored Medici Bank in Rome, Lorenzo made a loan of 30,000 florins to Pope Innocent.

From this point on the business of the boy priest, Giovanni, sprang to life. When the Pope seemed to drag his feet about the coveted red hat, Lanfredini, the Florentine ambassador, stood by in Rome to nudge him forward. Lorenzo, in the mean time, also courted cardinals, especially the influential Ascanio Sforza, brother of the lord of Milan, with an eye to getting them too to work on Innocent. In a letter to Cardinal Sforza, Lorenzo claimed to hold honour more dear than life itself, but he was writing specifically about the cardinalate for Giovanni. 'And if this desire of mine should not be realised, I don't know that I would be content to go on living. In brief, I commend to your Reverend Lordship the honour of this republic and mine, calling on the same urgency that I would use with God for the salvation of my soul.' Lorenzo knew how to bandy words, but he also believed in Christ, his soul, and the force of prayer.

At the end of 1488 he heard at last that Giovanni's promotion was imminent. On 19 February certain age requirements were set aside for the thirteen-year-old Giovanni. Six days later, in the chapel of the Medici Palace, major orders were conferred on him. On 27 February, though never having studied legal texts, he was awarded the doctorate in canon law. On the morning of 19 March, Pope Innocent created five new cardinals, and Giovanni was one of them. This sensational news was rushed to Lorenzo in Florence, reaching him the very next day. But owing to the scandal of Giovanni's age, Innocent stipulated that the promotion had to be kept a secret for three years. To no avail. Lorenzo was beside himself with joy; those around him spread the news, and Florence erupted in celebration, the announcement signifying an honour for the city too. Employing his usual arts, Lorenzo was able to mollify the Pope over the Florentine betrayal of the secret, though it was a secret that had no chance of being kept, because policy for the good of the Medici house required that such a thing be known at once and even trumpeted. Five months later the Medici Bank paid 95,000 florins into the coffers of the Apostolic Chamber. The sum was a loan with a large measure of bribe;

and it is likely – Rome being what it was – that simony monies also went into Cardinal Sforza's purse.

The two fathers-in-law, citizen Lorenzo and the Holy Father, made an odd pair, but they were now naturally drawn together even more closely. Lorenzo's letters to him turned at times into bold primers of advice, and his influence with the Pope became the common knowledge of all Italy. When seeking favour at the Roman curia, even princes now looked to him for help. Lorenzo was cutting a new figure: he seemed to become an unrivalled mediator and the peninsula's great power broker.

In his final years, accordingly, although suffering from asthma and tormented by acute gout, arthritis, stomach and kidney ailments, Lorenzo began to exercise his power over Florence more like a dictator, while the elite of aristocrats around him saw themselves pushed or drifted into the role of servitors. The other leading officials and secretaries, new men such as Niccolò Michelozzi and Ser Giovanni Guidi, were already servants and subject to his temper tantrums, whims, and sharp words. Frequently on the move in the countryside, as he journeyed from one Tuscan health spa to another and dispatched directives to the governing bodies back home, he began to take seriously the ceremonial love language of patronage, even though knowing well, as in his own relations with foreign princes, that the appropriate verbal tribute was a required ritual. That is, Lorenzo now longed to believe that 'his' men and 'friends' – parvenus and aristocrats alike – truly loved him because of everything he had done for them in the doling out of office or favour, and perhaps too, therefore, because of what he was. In effect, he was asking for that gift of affection and allegiance that princes expected from subjects – a startling expectation. In letters, poems, and doubtless to his face, citizens had often referred to Cosimo de' Medici as 'saint', 'god', and 'beneficent father', but the cunning old banker had not been taken in by such metaphors. Lorenzo, however, had been differently reared, brought up really to believe in his exalted status.

When it happened, therefore, that the ruling councils back in Florence differed with the policy views that he had sent on to them by letter, he was likely to slide into sarcasm about their superior statecraft, 'so much [of their] love and loyalty do I know'. On one occasion he threw out, 'When I go more than ten miles out of the city, the love and loyalty of friends soon comes to an end.' This – love and its accompaniments – was what he longed to have, to be able to count on; and if it vanished when he turned his back, then he, the generous and wise Lorenzo, was obviously dealing with a band of ingrates, namely, all those aristocrats who insisted on having independent views and who could not tear the republic out of their garrulous and vain hearts.

For all the physical pain and melancholy of his last years, he had completed his appointed mission. He could exult in it. Little Giovanni was a cardinal. Yet he could not possibly have seen that his achievement was imbued with the ghost of the Pazzi and the April Plot, since, as Guicciardini observed, he had transformed these dangers into a triumph that far surpassed what would have been possible in ordinary circumstances. Moreover, again as a legacy of 26 April 1478, there was the imposing sight of the man, surrounded by his armed escort, as he left or entered the city with his caravan of aides, friends, and servants – an image made all the more memorable or haunting when infused with awareness of the fact that he was ailing and often in pain.

In reworking his *Commentary*, he looked back to his love verse and vanished youth with a circuitous nostalgia; but in the last rewriting (1490–91), and particularly in the new prologue, he added a Platonic defence of love, a change intended to dignify and elevate that early passion of his. The lord of Florence was staking out a claim, as if sensing that Savonarola, with his powerful religious message, was already around the corner – and indeed he was. Lorenzo himself had summoned the charismatic friar to Florence in 1489, persuaded to do so by the brilliant thinker and petty prince, Pico della Mirandola, a resident in the city.

Meanwhile, Lorenzo had time to think about Cardinal Giovanni and to worry about the future of Maddalena, Pope Innocent's new daughter-in-law. In letters to the Holy Father, he pleaded with him 'to be a Pope', to provide Franceschetto with a financial settlement that would give the couple the means to live in decorous comfort. As it happens, Innocent also had an illegitimate daughter and a granddaughter, Peretta, whom he had married to a rich Genoese merchant, so that she apparently was living in high bourgeois comfort. But Franceschetto and Maddalena proposed to live as aristocrats, from landed income, sinecures, and if possible taxes. In the end, surprisingly, Innocent made no arrangements for the couple;

papal feuds in the Marches and Romagna were all tied up; and after Lorenzo's death, Maddalena would be forced to seek help first from her elder brother Piero, then from the younger one, the Cardinal. Here was a rich young cleric, for whom Lorenzo had scoured Europe in search of benefices, pressing even the Lyons and Rome branches of the Medici Bank to assist him in his dogged search. Awarded Church livings by princes as far away as the kings of France and Naples, our rich pluralist Giovanni, even before his elevation to the red, was to have the income from twenty-seven different benefices, including a canonry in every Tuscan cathedral: all a testament to Lorenzo's far-flung connections.

In the joy and wonder aroused by Giovanni's promotion, Lorenzo reacted by saying that this was 'the greatest honour ever conferred upon our house' and 'the greatest thing our house has ever done' – greater than their exploits as international bankers, and even greater than their brilliant seizure of power in Florence. Yet this judgment, for all its emotional coloration, turned out to be icily perceptive. Little more than twenty years later, in September 1512, a group of Medicean aristocrats, relying wholly on Cardinal Giovanni's political weight, but with the alleged support of a neighbouring Spanish army, overthrew the revived Florentine republic and at once restored the Medici. Pope Julius II – one of Pope Sixtus IV's 'demonic' nephews – now applauded the Florentines for their good behaviour. Cast out again in 1527, yet once more by a wave of republican fervour, the Medici this time had a pope, none other than Giulio, the murdered Giuliano's bastard son, who had been catapulted to a cardinalate in 1513. And by whom? By first-cousin (ex-Cardinal) Giovanni, elected Pope Leo X in the very same year. Giulio in turn, as Pope Clement VII (1523–34), used an alliance with the Emperor Charles V and his besieging army to engineer the destruction of the last Florentine republic in 1530. When the gates of the defeated city opened to receive the victorious commanders, the Medici marched in behind them, never again to be put out. Lorenzo the Magnificent, not the Neo-Platonist but the politician, had seen far and had seen clearly: Maddalena's happiness was a laughable price to pay for two Medici popes and the Medici dukes of Tuscany.

The Odour of Sanctity

IF IN A strain of popular opinion, the genie in Lorenzo's ring linked him to dark mysteries of a non-Christian sort, he himself was perfectly orthodox, steeped not only in Plato and a good stretch of the Latin classics, but also in Scripture and St Augustine. In the last two years of his life, he wrote a sequence of nine sacred lauds, all meant to be sung, and a religious play, *The Representation of Saints John and Paul* (February 1491). Sensing that he was incurably ill, he turned to embrace spiritual and penitential themes. Until his final weeks, however, even in his piety, he remained a vastly complex, slippery, and contradictory man. While believing that the political power of the papacy was a tragic curse for Italy, and that high clerical Rome was 'a cesspool', he yet desperately wanted a cardinal in the family and offered a daughter – in the parlance of the day – to the bastard of a pope. Apart from a note of atonement, there was ambition even in his choice of a career in the priesthood for Giulio, Giuliano's illegitimate son, and all because Lorenzo – reasonably enough, perhaps – put the earthly destinies of the Medici family above everything else.

The clash between his piety and his worldly passions was never so elegantly articulated as in his famous letter of March 1492 to his son Giovanni, just before the young cardinal finally set out on his baptismal journey to Rome. On the one hand, Lorenzo sees Rome as 'the sink of all evils'. On the other, he believes that 'God has wondrously made you a cardinal', despite the fact that he, Lorenzo, had paid for the honour and pulled every conceivable string to have it. He takes for granted that most cardinals are driven by vice and base ambition, but cannot relate this given assumption to the fact that most of them ascended to their exalted rank just as Giovanni had, by nepotism or by the most political and mercenary of all means. He urges Giovanni, once the youth is settled in Rome, to live 'a saintly, exemplary, and honest life', thereby raising a kind of shield against the faces of the many 'inciters and corrupters' who will strive, 'in view of your age . . . to make you slip into that same ditch into which they have fallen'. In this preternatural enterprise, Giovanni is urged to have the force equal to all 'the virtue now lacking in the College [of Cardinals]'.

Fig. 13 Bust of Cardinal Giovanni de' Medici, ascribed to Antonio de' Benintendi.

Alas for his father's wishes, however, for as Pope Leo X, Giovanni (Figure 13) would be the mirror of his place and time: a simonist and a nepotist who put Church office up for sale and feathered the nests of relatives with the goods of the Church. As he put it in a letter to his brother, the Duke of Nemours, 'God has given us the papacy . . . let us enjoy it.'

It only remained for Lorenzo to end his life in the odour of sanctity, and in this, as he lay dying, he disappointed no one in solicitous attendance. Friends, family, and servants — all those around him — marvelled at his piety and came to see him as all but bordering on sainthood, the real and bizarre foil of his powerful genie. Poliziano said that he was seen ardently kissing 'a silver crucifix, set with costly pearls and precious stones'. On the day he died in April 1492, one witness reported to first secretary Michelozzi: 'If only you knew Lorenzo's words and ways in his final hours, both with Piero [his son] and with various Churchmen, his words concerning matters of the soul, and how well he readied himself [for death], your heart would burst.' In a letter written nine days after his death and again to Michelozzi, another of Lorenzo's aides and attendants wrote:

> I urge you to be patient, and I remind you that if Lorenzo helped his native city in life, he could not be helping it any the less in paradise. This city should glory greatly in having such a protector near God, where he must be [our advocate] or no one else is. . . . His death was altogether in keeping with his life. He made his confession, and he took the sacrament with such devotion that those who were present claimed never to have seen a more devoted and Christian sight.

The sacred lauds of Lorenzo's final period, movingly composed by a man in the vicinity of death, look back to the mysticism of thirteenth-century Umbria and fourteenth-century Siena. He prays for release from this wretched, dark, and vain world, so that he may be joined to Christ through love, through the blood of the Cross, and live forever.

CHAPTER FOURTEEN

The Bottom Line

WITHIN A YEAR of Lorenzo's death, some of the aristocrats who had facilitated his widening seizure of power began to turn against his son Piero, who struck them as being too unsubtle and incompetent to occupy his father's place. Always in touch with the leading local men, foreign ambassadors quickly detected the signs of this defection, in an Italy that was already uneasy about King Charles VIII of France, who was openly preparing to march an army into the peninsula, to unseat the Aragonese King of Naples. In view of a potential French claim to the Duchy of Milan as well, Ludovico Sforza, the Milanese lord, had turned to a feverish diplomacy, as he cast about to protect himself. When King Charles crossed the Alps in August–September 1494, at the head of 30,000 men and a formidable artillery train, fear and division possessed Italy's princes and ruling elites.

In this anxious setting, Piero de' Medici set out for the French camp and a meeting with the King, who was to pass through Tuscany and proposed to spend some days in Florence. With much of the city's political class already out of sympathy with Piero, his unwarranted concessions to the King, including the foolish surrender of the fortresses of Pisa and Sarzana, suddenly turned the government and its advisors angrily against him. He had acted without their mandate. Returning to the city on 8 November, Piero and an armed escort attempted to enter the Palace of the Lord Priors on the 9th. They were firmly turned away. That evening he fled from the city, together with his two brothers.

He was never to return. His departure was the signal for a revolt against the whole experience of Medicean 'tyranny', and in the popular fury that followed, a crowd of rioters rushed to the houses of Lorenzo's closest collaborators, setting fire to some of them. One of the first 'villains' to be caught and tried by the Eight, and then hanged from a window of the main criminal court, was Antonio di Bernardo Dini. This man had worked with Lorenzo for years, both among the Seventeen Reformers, a powerful (but dodgy) commission, and as the most important official in the offices of the Monte. He was certainly one of the chief accomplices in his master's theft of public monies.

Within weeks of the Medici flight from Florence, nearly 100 exiles had been recalled to the city, to rejoin their families, to rejoice, to reclaim property, and to offer their help in the rebuilding of the republic. But first of all – indeed a mere four days after Piero's flight – the Lord Priors 'freed [from exile] and exonerated all the descendants of Messer Andrea di Guglielmino de' Pazzi', that is, all the conspirators of 1478 and their offspring. They were now free, even welcome, to return to Florence; and their right to hold Florentine public office was restored. Ten weeks later (25–26 January), referring directly to the events of 26 April 1478, the new government enacted a bill which alleged, in the exordium, that Francesco and Messer Jacopo de' Pazzi had acted 'out of zeal for the liberty of the people and city of Florence', and stated that all the other members of the family, knowing nothing about the plot, had been unjustly condemned. The bill authorises the Pazzi and their descendants to work through an *ad-hoc* commission of five men, with a view to taking legal action against the 'many' citizens who had acquired sequestered assets, goods, or property from the Pazzi Syndics by means of false or fraudulent credit claims. In some cases, such property had been sold 'for less than half of the just price', and this too is to be made good. Although it went without saying, the measure also invites the Pazzi to display their coat of arms again; and their prominence at Easter, as associated with the sacred-fire cart, is of course resurrected.

Despite the presumed infamy of the April Plot, feeling against the Medici, and hence for the Pazzi, was so strong that the foregoing bill was approved in the two legislative councils by a vote of 151/63 in one and 113/47 in the other. Many of the votes against the measure were probably cast by men who were either overly compromised with the Medici or were possible defendants in future legal action by the Pazzi. Suffice it to add, in this connection, that the Pazzi were already in litigation by early January 1495: looking back to 1478, they had lodged a claim of more than 1400 florins against the Lyons branch of the Medici Bank.

In more general terms, the recent unconstitutionality of Medici power enabled lawyers for the surviving Pazzi to argue that Lorenzo and the Eight had illegally despoiled the Pazzi of their wealth, because in law he had been nothing more than a mere citizen, for all his political importance. Consequently, the assault on the Medici in April 1478 had had nothing to do with the crime of lese-majesty, as had sometimes been alleged.

Having a keen recollection of Medici marriage ties with the lordly Orsini, and cognisant of the political dangers of such alliances, the new republican government also brought in a law barring all citizens, male or female, from marrying into princely or 'baronial' families, unless the outsiders happened to be Florentine subjects. The penalties for such a marriage carried a fine of 'a thousand large florins' and stripped the offending family – father, brothers, and sons – of the right to hold public office.

The question of Lorenzo's theft of public monies was fully aired, and a commission of leading men, having studied the relevant Monte accounts, decided that Lorenzo had purloined 74,948 florins. This was the sum now set against the sequestered Medici estate. Whether or not the figure was accurate, however, is another matter, not only because the question was so deeply contentious at the time, but also because the top Monte official under Lorenzo, working hand and glove with him, had been able to make his account entries in such a way as to disguise the track of theft. Even today there is disagreement among the experts regarding both the ways of Lorenzo's fraudulent operations and the stolen sums.

Meanwhile, the Dominican friar Savonarola, resident in Florence and preaching, but not yet in his fiery mode, now stepped up his fervour and managed to join his vision of Christianity to the collective ideals of republicanism. His message began to smack of something 'democratic'. Alarmingly for the most conservative of the old elite, he won the enthusiastic support of most Florentines. The republic sprang to life, and for the next three years a note of religious passion inspired Florentine politics and the pace of constitutional change. Giving rise to animated and even fierce debate, the emotional climate of this political interlude was to reach levels of intensity that were almost unparalleled in the history of Florence.

Poliziano's *Memoir of the Conspiracy* carries many echoes of the infamous and impoverished patrician of Julius Caesar's day, Catiline, and his conspiracy against the Roman state: echoes that go back to Cicero and Sallust. Since all virtue in the *Memoir* belongs to the Medici, the traditional name for the April Plot, 'the Pazzi Conspiracy', has always cast this family into an evil light, both because of stemming chiefly from Poliziano and carrying the shadow of the Catilinarian conspiracy.

In recounting this history, I know that I have seemed hard on the Medici and sympathetic to the Pazzi. The truth is that it may be an illusion to imagine that such a story can be told – if it be told with conviction – without appearing to take sides. And anyway, for all their best efforts, historians tend to take sides. But there was something else at work in my representations. Since the historical record has always been stacked against the Pazzi, with events being seen in the light of the supposed brilliance of the Medici, it seemed to me proper and almost obligatory to try to restore a balance, all the more so in a time like ours, when 'acts of terrorism', such as explosive political murders, are likely to abort rational argument. We can never afford to have the end of reason.

Whatever the title given to the event, Pazzi Conspiracy or April Plot, when reasoning about it for the long term, we soon realise that it should not be made a framework for condemning or applauding either the Medici or Pazzi families. The whole episode reached far beyond them, out to the city's propertied families, to the nature of its political organisation, and deep into the Florentine past and future.

In cultural and political vivacity, from about 1260 up to perhaps 1530, Florence was the most exceptional city in Europe. Neither Rome nor Venice (not to speak of Paris, London, or any German city) had produced writers on the scale of Dante, Petrarch, and Boccaccio; and no other city had given rise to a school of painting that could begin to match the achievements in Florence. Poetry and the short story flourished there, as nowhere else in Italy; and so too did the revival of classical literature, associated with a line of brilliant names now known mainly to scholars.

Two of the greatest political and historical thinkers ever, Machiavelli and Guicciardini, came directly out of Florence — more specifically, out of the keen republican debates that followed the flight of the Medici in 1494. The analytical language of their writings and many of their ideas carry the distinctive stamp of those years.

There was a genre of Florentine writing, *ricordanze*, which had no equal elsewhere in Europe. It was a kind of family account book and personal memoir, with the latter often being introspective and richly reverberant. Florentines, moreover, were astounding record keepers. This is why theirs is the only Renaissance city that has lent itself to socio-logical study in depth.

Both all around and *in* this large activity of reason and imagination, there lay a vibrant society that was relatively flexible, for all its continual capsizing into oligarchy. Men climbed socially through the system of guilds; and when the guilds began to lose their authority around 1400, petty tradesmen and others continued to climb — although mainly, it is true, if they were already the possessors of a family surname and managed to get themselves into the circuit of public office. They might bear a grand name, but be down at heel, down on their luck, ignored, and even despised by those who were socially above them. At some time in the recent past, their immediate families had lost out financially; descendants then struggled; a few might end as the 'shame-faced' poor; and yet it was always possible to make a comeback. They could rise again, marry 'up', buy back the old family mansions, and bring along, in their wake, more humble relatives.

For about 300 years, ever since the twelfth century, the people of Florence had fought to be their own political masters. To do this, they had waged wars against emperors, popes, aspiring tyrants, and neigh-bouring cities. Within their wide circle of walls, civil wars had been chronic in the thirteenth century: Florentine citizens had fought factions and oligarchies, powerful clans, parties, mobs, and armed elites. But through all their anxieties and forbidding conflicts, right through to the sixteenth century, the need and the demand to talk politics, to plunge into political debate, and to take group and community decisions persisted. Of course this discourse waxed and waned; but when it was banished, it soon collected force for a more animated return.

Here, in many ways, was the key to Florentine republicanism: in the insistence on talk about taxes, public office, war, elections, civic leaders, and everyday laws — in short, talk about politics. And here was the greatest threat to the Medicean oligarchy, as lucidly noted by Guicciardini when speaking of the barriers to Lorenzo's ambitions. He singled out Florence's 'being, above all, a city given to freedom of speech and full of extremely subtle, restless spirits'. Money and the most eminent families, to be sure, tended to rule; but many influential citizens had modest fortunes, and they often teamed up with other men in order to mount and carry decisions against the big oligarchs and plutocrats. The dedication to trade, work, public office, and — let it frankly be said — the practice of taking advantage of others, whether of one's own workers and peasants or of neighbouring cities: these dedications gave rise to a pragmatic view of life, a readiness to accept social and political mobility, and to a stance that looked toward more searching horizons. Here were the conditions that fostered the exploratory note and widened the scope of Florentine painting, ideas, literature, and everyday anecdote.

It came about as almost something natural, therefore, that rotation through public office (short office-terms) should hold the centre of Florentine government and politics. Men longed for their turn in office, where they could cast their votes and either speak or be true participants in a vital flow of speech and discussion. In this 'small empire', however, as Guicciardini also noticed, honours were limited; and of the major ones there were never enough to go around, or at least not enough for men like the resentful Rinuccini, who believed that he was deserving of high office 'by right of birth'. It followed that throughout the history of republican Florence, the opposing defenders of 'tight' and 'wide' government fought a tug-of-war. There was a never-ending rivalry between, on the one side, influential citizens from the eminent families, moved by the desire for close oligarchy, and on the other, lesser citizens whose presence in government brought many more voices into 'city hall', thus giving the direction of communal affairs a wider social anchorage.

In our terms, the differences between them may seem trifling: each side remained committed, really, to a form of oligarchy. But in Florentine and Renaissance terms, the disparity was enormous. In a city of not more than 45,000 people, it was the difference between having some forty to seventy citizens who would more or less rule, and a government, on the contrary, in which the chief men, even while dominating the top offices, would have large legislative councils, with changing constituencies of many hundreds of men, actively watching them and, ultimately, fully in control. It was a question of contraries: of several hundred men (at the most) versus several thousand, of a republic in which the *res publica*, the public thing, was either in few hands or in many. The larger of these constituencies included petty shopkeepers and ambitious artisans, small landowners, attorneys (*notai*), and shame-faced citizens from families that had once been prominent: all men of a little substance and property yes, but with a different take on things, as we now say, and with their eyes fixed on the public purse, on questions of war and peace, on the law courts, and on the flow of legislation. Never mind that they too might be propelled by selfish or partisan aims. The point is that they stood outside the charmed circle of the inner oligarchy; and looking on from there, from another standpoint, they could defeat the more unpopular and inequitable policies of the bosses, or even block their election to office. In addition, when moving outside the government palace, once they had a voice *in* it, their views would help to lend strength and respectability to the popular culture of the age; and the high culture would not remain immune over the longer course.

Medicean government began as yet another attempt by one political faction to break the pretensions and push of another. In the course of the struggle, however, excessive authority came to be lodged in Cosimo de' Medici's activity behind the scenes — lodged there by the very leaders of the Medicean party, Luca Pitti, Tommaso Soderini, and others, and by the circle of citizens who orbited contentedly around them. For some time the actors themselves could not see what they were sacrificing over the longer term, and could not know the outcome. They were too close to the action, a piecemeal usurpation, even as it led to a species of tyranny, the fullblown form of which was still in the future.

Lorenzo's marriage to the handsome Clarice Orsini, an act of princely ambition, signalled a break with the past, a turning point; and in that strongly patriarchal society, it could only have been a decision taken by Lorenzo's father, with suggestions from Cosimo before he died in 1464.

Worried about the Medici Bank and the political future, they were beginning to see the need for a fundamental shift in policy: they wanted guarantees of decisive support from abroad. What other meaning could Florentines attach to Lorenzo's alliance with powerful soldiers and princes of the Church? By the late 1450s, with so many Florentine exiles abroad and even more secret enemies at home, Cosimo and his son Piero had seen that they must hold on to power at all costs or go down in ruin, pulling scores of other families down in their wake. Old in the one case and seriously ailing in the other, they groomed the gifted Lorenzo to take power, and he needed little prompting.

The 'rebels' of the 1460s – Girolamo Machiavelli, Agnolo Acciaiuoli, Dietisalvi Neroni, Niccolò Soderini, and others – saw the shape of an emerging tyranny, but they were outflanked by Cosimo and Piero, who were fighting first of all for their own wealth and status, whereas the rebels had more amorphous ends in mind, namely, to break the political controls of the Medici and to bring more men into government. Cosimo, Piero, and Lorenzo could move much faster and strike more decisively, precisely because of their tangible ends and immediate resources.

Again and again in his clash with Lorenzo, by letter, bull, and word of mouth, Pope Sixtus denounced him as a 'tyrant' and urged the Florentines to cast him out, to resume their republican freedoms, and to bring the Pazzi War to a quick end. He had nothing against Florence, he insisted. All the trouble resided in one evil and arrogant usurper. Had this man not scorned – and worked to frustrate – papal policies in the lands of the Church? Get rid of him, and all would be well.

What Pope Sixtus wanted, no doubt, was to bind Florentine foreign policy to his own plans for central Italy. This policy, however, had nothing to do with Lorenzo's expanding tyranny at home, which was a different matter altogether. Aimed, therefore, directly at this point, the Sixtine pitch against him was an appeal to the mute, bullied, and resentful opposition in Florence. And Lorenzo had good reason to be afraid. On the eve of his rushed departure for Naples, with the domestic opposition against him turning bolder, he himself referred to 'the common opinion' in the city that he was the sole reason for the hated Pazzi War.

Ever since 1434, political debate in Florence had been increasingly circumscribed, or simply shut down, although there were occasional outbursts, ending in the *coups* of 1458 and 1466. From the moment of his father's death, Lorenzo's goal had been to concentrate authority around himself and his chosen friends. The special council or group of Seventy crowned the success of his proceedings. Established five weeks after his victorious return from Naples, they were his hand-picked oligarchy, all in one body. Circumventing the Florentine constitution by rising above the Lord Priors and the three legislative bodies (the *Cento* included), the Seventy owed everything to Lorenzo and therefore revolved around him. Inevitably, too, the feared Eight were now able to move more recklessly in their pursuit of political 'criminals'.

As posed by the Mediceans, the greatest danger to republican government lay in their determination to hold power permanently, in a movement, however, that was always passing it ever more fully to one man — an emerging prince. In this process, all other contenders or would-be peers had to be identified with treason and removed from the political scene. Now the possibility of political change was terminated, and real debate in the public forums, even among aristocrats, came to an end. This necessarily meant a deepening of big-boss patronage, of trimming and yea-saying, and of corruption that spread out to the law courts, to offices of all kinds, to tax levies and graces, and to the flow of private legislative bills.

Around the city, meanwhile, alert political citizens were not prised away from their uneasiness. The April Plot and Lorenzo's troop of personal guardsmen cast sinister shadows. As late as 1480, even the local reinterpreter of Plato, Marsilio Ficino, is alleged to have feared for his life, because of his friendship with at least two of the plotters, Archbishop Salviati and Jacopo Bracciolini. Many citizens moved in an atmosphere of resentment and caution; and we glimpse some of the elements of this state of mind in Rinuccini's secret *Dialogue on Liberty*, which converts the attendant anxieties into fury and melancholy. For Rinuccini knew, and could see it in himself, that 'ambition' would flourish, even as political liberty languished; that in their opportunism, too many men would pass over to serve the tyrant, in order to serve their own careers, families, and purses.

Lorenzo himself undoubtedly reacted with fury to the charge that he was a 'tyrant', hence lawless by definition. He had to try to believe in the legality, or at least the rightness, of his political place in the republic. This attitude fully explains his use of spies in the tracking, arrest, and execution (1482) of the courageous humanist, Cola Montano, who in all likelihood was not involved, as alleged, in the plot of the three 'traitors' of 1481. Cola's real crime, in Lorenzo's eyes, was that he had penned a Latin 'Oration' to the rulers of the neighbouring city of Lucca, a mini-republic, denouncing the Medici and the Florentine boss as treacherous tyrants. It was a vitriolic attack, and to Cola's horror – he later claimed in his confession – it had then been rushed into print and circulated, sometime after the April Plot, by the Bishop of Sarno, Antonio de' Pazzi, and by one of Pope Sixtus's great favourites, the soldier and jurist Lorenzo Giustini of Città di Castello, one of the Magnificent Lorenzo's most uncompromising enemies.

Despite Rinuccini's assault on Lorenzo in his *Dialogue*, the republic was far from dead, as demonstrated by the flight and exile of the Medici, and the vigorous revival of republican government in 1494–95. In response to a popular demand for a 'wide' republic, one of the first acts of the new (in part 'Savonarolan') regime was the creation of a mighty legislative body of about 3500 men, the Grand Council, which remained the constitutional foundation of the new republic until 1512.

Was it the case, however, that the social foundations of the city's republicanism, with its essential reliance on shifting family blocs, had been so rotted by the Medicean collusion of the distinguished houses that the republic would be unable to survive? Unable to sideline collaborators, or to gather the group forces to resist the blandishments and arms of two Medici popes? There can be no conclusive answers to these questions, and so it certainly cannot be flatly held that the death of the republic was inevitable. In the study of the past, here with regard to Florence and more generally speaking, it is perhaps never a wise thing to shut out possibilities by putting historical process and reality into a locked box of inevitabilities. We should always hold ourselves ready for surprises.

Current scholarship has pressed a raft of charges against Lorenzo: in particular, his highjacking of Florentine foreign affairs, manipulation of the government debt, tampering with the law courts, purloining of public monies, filling key offices with his cronies and clients, debasement of the coinage, and even the highhanded imposition of undesirable marriages. But if these were facts, it was also a fact that they were made possible by the Medicean system of government, which depended upon the compliance and cooperation – whether freely given, bought, or coerced – of sizeable numbers of the principal citizens and families. The foundations of this system, moreover, predated Lorenzo. He came along, picked up what he found, and ran with it brilliantly. His creatures, the jumped-up men, represented nothing other than their patron. Take him away, and they would all vanish from public life, because they had no standing whatsoever in the recognised political class and would have been removed from office. As it was, even his son, the untalented Piero, could not stand up to a crisis and stem the ensuing republican tide.

The Pazzi Conspiracy was the turning point in the path of Lorenzo's usurpation, not only because the immediate fears aroused by it enabled him and his friends to seize a commanding measure of power, but also because its bloodshed underlined desperations. With a leader of such talents, and given his oligarchy's chokehold on key office, it required war or a successful act of terrorism to overthrow Lorenzo, his cronies, and his creatures. The old ruling patriciate could not do it of its own volition: this route – winding its way through politics, councils, and electoral tactics – was already too difficult, too cluttered and twisted by procedures that the Mediceans had corrupted. Caution and devious light-handed violence were now the rule. It seems fair to say that there was nothing very selfless or high-minded about the Pazzi. But if they had managed to capture the government palace, and to hold Florence for a day or two, their *coup* could have been completed only by enlisting the help and buoyancy of the city's anti-Medicean families and feeling. In this rescue, they would have been swept into a powerful current of republican reforms, leading to the swift expansion of the political class.

For all his remarkable qualities, or really because of them, Lorenzo was the one man – if history can ever be so finely narrowed – who put the Florentine republic on the edge of an abyss: first by disseminating fear and promises, then by knowing how to exploit that fear in his clever recruitment of the ambitions of citizens. And as he worked to make Florentine public authority the possession of the Medici, his constant claim was that the good of Florence and the good of the Medici family were one and the same. He even came to believe it.

NOTES

These notes provide sources and more detail. They start with a page number, followed at once by the first words of a paragraph on that page. All names and abbreviations may be squared with entries in the Bibliography. The sign f. = folio; ff. = folios.

CHAPTER ONE
CONSPIRACY

7 *The assassins wrote to.* On Lorenzo and 1488: M. Pellegrini, *Congiure*, 25–40. *With its cluster of.* Populations: Larner, *Lords of Romagna*, 209–19; Zaghini, 'La popolazione', 257–61; and Martines, *Power and Imagination*, 230.

8 *Count Girolamo was tumbled.* On Caterina's jewels: Breisach, *Caterina Sforza*, 89. Pope Sixtus and Riario: Pastor, *History*, IV, 231–57. The land tax: Graziani, 'Fra Medioevo ed età moderna', 245–6, in Vasina, *Storia di Forlì*. *These slippery circumstances.* Romagnol society and politics: see two entries under Larner in the Bibliography.
As local noblemen. Quotations: Pasolini, *Caterina*, I, 197. Chronicle sources: Cobelli, *Cronache*, 303–41; Bernardi, *Cronache*, 229–71.

9 *Five days later.* Cited letters: Fabroni, II, 318–25; and Pasolini, III, 111–15.

10 *Ten days later.* On Caterina and the Orsi plot: Breisach, *Caterina*, 96–124. *Frightened by the prospect.* Letter of 29 April in Pasolini, III, 129–30. *When Caterina took.* Breisach, 113–18. Quotation: Cobelli, 337–8.

11 *What the mere facts.* See Chap. 13; and M. Pellegrini, 33–4, 48–50, on Lorenzo and Pope Innocent's plans for his son; also Pastor, *History*, V, 240, 265–70.

12 *Seven weeks after.* On Galeotto Manfredi, see M. Pellegrini, 100–15. *If the lands of.* Conspiracies: Fubini, *Italia*, 220–52.

13–16 *Just before the commencement.* Texts for this conspiracy: Corio, *L'Historia*, 830–8; Verri, *Storia*, Chap. 18. Studies: Casanova, 'L'uccisione'; and Belotti, *Olgiati*. Bona's letter and report of the theologians/canonists: Pasolini, III, 30–3.

17 *Pandemonium erupted, just as.* Belotti, *Olgiati*, is the best modern study; see also Ilardi, 'Assassination'.

18 *The Duke's body was.* Published in 1477, the Latin poem by Paveri Fontana, Cola Montano's bitter enemy, is given by Belotti, 114.
The ducal government's frenzy. Quotation: Belotti, 141–2.

19 *Olgiati, Visconti, and Franzone.* The ghastly execution: Belotti, 127–8.
Given the primal importance. On eating the ringleader: Belotti, 138.

20 *The Santo Stefano protagonists.* Cola Montano's fortunes: Lorenzi, *Cola Montano*; and Belotti, 34–50, 167–76.

21 *The Roman conspiracy.* Basic texts for this conspiracy: Miglio, 'Viva la libertà'; Giulari, *Prose*; Alberti's account in Watkins, *Humanism and Liberty*, 107–15; Cessi, *Saggi*, 65–128; and Pastor, *History*, II, 215–39.
Born to a line. Quotation, in Pastor, II, 219.

22 *Like many other educated.* Italian anticlericalism: Dykema and Oberman, *Anticlericalism*; and Martines, 'Raging Against Priests'. Cessi, *Saggi*, 65–128, denies that Porcari's 1447 speech verged on high treason.
Already in touch. For the plot's outlines: Pastor, II, 215–39; and Cessi, *Saggi*.

CHAPTER TWO
SOCIAL CLIMBERS

25 *It began with the.* Scholarship on marriage: Martines, *Social World*, 57–62, 199–237; Klapisch-Zuber, *La maison*; Molho, *Marriage Alliance*; Fabbri, *Alleanza matrimoniale*; Kuehn, *Law, Family*; Dean and Lowe, *Marriage*.

26 *In 1467, like any.* Lucrezia's letters: Tornabuoni, *Lettere*, 62–4; Maguire, *Women*, 129–32. Cosimo sought a red hat for a Medici: Fubini, *Italia*, 80.

28 *To add to the.* On the Orsini: Litta, *Famiglie celebri*, IV.

29 *Lucrezia's older contemporary.* Martines, 'A Way of Looking', mainly on Alessandra. See also Gregory, *Selected Letters*, 1–20.
In a letter of 20. Letters cited: A. Strozzi, *Lettere*, 106–8, 119–23.

31 *A long passage from.* Marco's letter is in M. Parenti, *Lettere*, 93–5.

33 *What to say about.* On brokering marriages in Florence: Fabbri, 139–54.

34 *'Social Climbers' I have.* For differences within the Venetian nobility: Finlay, *Politics*, 59–96, 196–226; and Queller, *The Venetian Patriciate*.

35 *Which is not to say.* On families in decline: See Dei, *Cronica*, 86–7, 90–1.

36 *In the course of.* On the Pazzi family: my Chap. 4, and Litta, *Famiglie celebri*, IV, 'Pazzi di Firenze', Table vii.
By the time Piero. Piero's relations with Tranchedini: Phillips, *Memoir*, 16–17. Medici marriages: Pieraccini, I, 49–75, 95–140, 157–284. Lucrezia's dowry: Tornabuoni, *Lettere*, 3. In the fourteenth century, eminent families often broke with 'magnate' kin, changed surnames

and armorial bearings, and took legal 'commoner' status.

37 *In their ascent from.* What follows is distilled from Brucker, 'The Medici'. Sznura, *L'espansione urbana*, treats the thirteenth-century land market in Florence.

38 *The banker Giovanni.* De Roover did the classic study of the Medici Bank. Holmes, 'How the Medici', adds a note on Giovanni di Bicci.

With a genius for. Martines, *Social World*, 353–78, lists the top 1200 Florentine taxpayers of 1403 and 1427. De Roover, 374, sees Florence as Europe's financial capital and introduces Lorenzo's claim regarding Giovanni.

39 *Political faction was more.* Remarks on Palla Strozzi and the Panciatichi family: based partly on Conti, *L'imposta*, 344–8; also Dei, *Cronica*, 86. D. Kent, *Rise of the Medici*, 179–80, notes Panciatichi marriage links with various leading families.

As Lorenzo was to. Lorenzo's observation: in Fabroni, II, 42.

On the death of. Gutkind, *Cosimo*, remains a valuable biography. On the larger name and myth: Brown, 'The Humanist Portrait'.

He was schooled in. De Roover, 10–20, 109–16, treats usury, interest, and exchange. The subject wants more research. See L. Armstrong, 'The Politics of Usury'. De Roover, 74, on Cosimo's Milan holdings and his 1457 tax returns. Despite Bullard, *Filippo Strozzi*, obscurity surrounds the true profits of papal bankers.

40 *Cosimo certainly felt.* Brucker, 'Economic Foundations', 9–10; and De Roover, 108–41, 374. Goldthwaite, 'The Medici Bank', in *Banks, Palaces* stresses the 'individual' over 'family' ownership of banks. On Sforza's debt: De Roover, 141.

For all Cosimo's talents. Maguire, *Women*, 23–4, touches on Piero and accounting. See De Roover, 358–61, on Piero's takeover of the bank in 1464.

41 *The story begins.* The war with Milan: Brucker, *Civic World*. Taxation: Molho, *Florentine Public Finance*; and Conti, *L'imposta diretta*. Martines, 'Forced Loans', highlights anxieties and targeted taxation.

This was Florence. The best accounts of Florentine politics in the 1420s and early 1430s follow: F. Pellegrini, *Sulla repubblica*; Brucker, *Civic World*, 425–500; D. Kent, *Rise of the Medici*; and the constitutional study by Fubini, *Italia*, 62–86.

42 *In the spring of.* De Roover, 54, on the flight of Cosimo's capital.

43 *Soon, 106 men were.* Exile figures: D. Kent, *Rise of the Medici*, 355–7; Rubinstein, *Government*, 18; and Dei, *Cronica*, 53. Drawing on average household sizes, Dei's count of 500 seems more accurate than the 300 of another contemporary.

The original builder of. The crisis of 1458: Rubinstein, *Government*, 88–135.

44 *The moment for the.* Martines, *Lawyers*, 485, on Girolamo Machiavelli. For the citizens dispatched to their villas and those disqualified: Rubinstein, *Government*, 103, 108; also Dei, *Cronica*, 65–6; and Cambi, *Istorie*, I, 361–2.

45 *Lorenzo de' Medici that.* As a twelve-year-old patron: *Lettere*, I, 3–5.
In 1460, Girolamo. Machiavelli's second arrest: Buoninsegni, *Storie*, 127.
Lorenzo was to go. When on the Sforza payroll as informers, Acciaiuoli and Neroni worked via the Milanese ambassador in Florence. Rubinstein, *Government*, 128, notes the practice of holding official meetings in the Medici Palace.

46 *In 1463, the year.* On Acciaiuoli and Neroni, see Gutkind, *Cosimo*, 125–6, 128, 162–4; Rubinstein, *Government*, 134; and Clarke, *The Soderini*, 38–94.
From this point on. The 1466 crisis: Rinuccini, *Ricordi*, c–civ; Municchi, *La fazione*; Pampaloni, 'Fermenti', a fine study in three parts; and Gori, 'La crisi del regime'. See also Rubinstein, *Government*, 136–73; and Phillips, *Memoir*, 222–59.

47 *Seeing the writing on.* Quotation: Dei, *Cronica*, 69.
Both sides were seized. Events here may be tracked in Rubinstein, 160–4. See Pampaloni, 'Nuovi tentativi', 578, for Acciaiuoli's words of 30 August. On Piero and the archbishops: Clarke, 'Sienese Note', 50.

48 *The city teemed.* Quote from Gondi's *Ricordanze*, in Ridolfi, *Gli archivi*, 87.

49 *Piero had ordered.* On the mounted Lorenzo: Clarke, 'A Sienese Note', 47.

50 *Now that the republican.* The poet: Romano, in Massèra, *Sonetti*, 146.

51 *Contrary to popular belief.* The genius of politics in Italian Renaissance cities: Martines, *Power and Imagination*, Chap. 9.

51–53 *In their campaign.* The seven points are gleaned from many sources, but the best one-volume primer is Rubinstein, *Government*. See also Ninci, 'Techniche'. The penalty for tendering an 'exposed' bean (item 6) was four to five gold florins per infraction (25 *lire*), payable by the ballot taker too. Ballots (beans) were meant to be concealed by the hand: F. Pellegrini, *Sulla repubblica*, xv. Point 7 is my own extrapolation, reasoning from literary sources as well: see Martines, 'Corruption'.

CHAPTER THREE
PROFILE: MANETTI

54 *Politics is life itself.* Guicciardini's words: in his *Opere* (*Dialogo del reggimento di Firenze*), 275, spoken by the interlocutor Bernardo del Nero.

55 *Merchant and banker.* Sources for Giannozzo's life: Vespasiano, *Le Vite*, I, 485–538 and II, 515–622. Some of his writings: Wittschier, *Giannozzo*. Several studies: Martelli (1989), 'Profilo ideologico', and 'L'esilio di

Giannozzo'; also Field, *The Origins*, 64–71; and Connell, 'The Humanist Citizen'. Giannozzo as Latin orator: Vespasiano, II, 579.

56 *Domiciled on the far.* On the Manetti: Martines, *Social World*, 131–5, 176–8.

57 *Giannozzo stepped into.* His career in office: Martines, *Social World*, 176–90. *Although politics often went.* Giannozzo's remark to Cosimo: Vespasiano, II, 583. Cosimo's gross understatement: De Roover, 74.

58 *Even if we halved.* On confiscatory taxation: Conti, *L'imposta diretta*, 303–18. *What exactly had Giannozzo.* Capponi's retort: Vespasiano, II, 569.

59 *In the years when.* On Luca Pitti: Vespasiano, II, 601.

60 *Giannozzo's Latin style.* See Martelli, 'Profilo' (1989) and 'L'esilio'.

61 *Written in the 1450s.* The letters are in Wittschier, *Giannozzo*, 45–8.

CHAPTER FOUR
THE PAZZI FAMILY

62 *When the Christian warriors.* The Pazzi family: Litta, *Famiglie celebri*, IV, 'Pazzi di Firenze', vii–ix; also Davidsohn, *Storia*, I–IV, as on the 'sacred fire' legend, I, 1067–8; Saalman, *Filippo Brunelleschi*, 211–34; and Herzner, 'Die Segel-Imprese'.
In proof of their. On the Pazzi Palace: Moscato, *Il Palazzo Pazzi*.

63 *The Pazzi were happy.* A big warrior clan, they split into two lines around 1200: the Val d'Arno Pazzi remained Ghibellines, partisans of the emperor. Florence's Pazzi became mighty Guelfs, followers of the papacy, and threw their lot in with the 'Black' (Guelf) faction in Florence. See Davidsohn, *Storia*, I, 878, 1067–8; II, 338, 419, 483, 801; *Forschungen*, III, 42–3, 67, 69, 143; IV, 242–3, 248, 264, 373. On the two Pazzi in hell: Dante, *Inferno*, XII, 137–8, and XXXII, 67–9. On the mob and arson: Brucker, *Florentine Politics*, 368.
Since the Pazzi. Knighthood in Florence: Salvemini, *La dignità cavalleresca*.

64 *Despite their feudal past.* Pazzi engagement in banking by about 1250 is touched on by Davidsohn (above), and Sapori, *Studi*, 1046.
At the beginning of. Lists of the city's top taxpayers *c.* 1400: Martines, *Social World*, 351–65.

65 *But Andrea di Guglielmino.* Saalman, 441–2, published Andrea's *popolano* petition. Presence in Barcelona: Melis, *Documenti*, 284.
His contacts were to. Andrea and Pope Eugene: Jacks, Caferro, *The Spinelli*, 196. The knighting: Salvemini, 145. Saalman, 231, on bank deposit.
Andrea's wealth, as reported. All information regarding Andrea's wealth is culled from his tax returns of 1427: ASF, Catasto, 57, ff. 1450r–90r, pagination top right; and Catasto, 80, II, ff. 586r–93v. Molho, *Florentine*

Public Finance, 181, lists the Medici and Pazzi war loans.

67 *In the absence of.* Data on galleys: Mallett, *Florentine Galleys*, 46, 58, 81–2, 88–9, 158, 212. Florin shipments: Dei, *Cronica*, 98.

68 *Over the course of.* Venetian estimate and Cambini profits: Tognetti, *Banco Cambini*, 147, 149–53.

69 *In trawling through Andrea's.* Spallanzani, 'Le aziende', presumes the government's argument for unlimited liability. Goldthwaite, 'The Medici Bank', in his *Banks, Palaces*, cleaves to Spallanzani, suggesting that the different Pazzi firms were spurious fronts for a single company. For De Roover, 77–86, each Medici partnership was a different legal entity, separate from other Medici firms. Pazzi partnerships (*ragioni*) were identically organised. Emancipation of sons: Saalman, 217.

70 *Andrea's tax returns.* Criss-cross investment: ASF, Catasto, 57, ff. 1470–3.

71 *The location of Andrea's.* For details on the parish churches and the chapels in S. Pier Maggiore: Paatz, *Die Kirchen von Florenz*, III, 171; IV, 690; VI 634–5, 637. Davidsohn, *Storia*, II, 338, n. 1, shows the Pazzi already well established in the area in the early thirteenth century.
Like all Florentine men. Herlihy and Klapisch-Zuber, *Les Toscans*, 245–6, 251–9, disclose the extent to which Florentines had bought up Florentine Tuscany.

72 *In tax returns completed.* For the facts in this paragraph: ASF, Catasto, 478, I, ff. 8r–22v, top right.

73 *In the 1440s.* Unlimited credit for the Pazzi: De Roover, 91. The Pazzi and papal funds from Germany: Esch, 'Überweisungen', 301, 309, 327, 350–7, 373–4.

74 *The death of Messer.* Notice of the brothers' division into separate households, plus the data on their Monte shares and properties: ASF, Catasto, 682, ff. 908r–12r. 913r–16v, 917r–31r; also Saalman, 222–3, 442–4.
Messer Andrea obtained. Taxes over ten years: document in Saalman, 444–5.

77 *The new reports list.* Succeeding textual material: ASF, Catasto, 828, ff. 544r–50v, 551r–60v; and Catasto, 829, II, ff. 516r–24v.

78 *The scale of Pazzi.* Luca Pitti item: Goldthwaite, 'Local Banking', 33, in his *Banks, Palaces.*

79 *In 1469, Messer Jacopo.* The 1469 returns: ASF, Catasto, 927, II, ff. 491r–6r, 504r–8r; and Catasto, 928, II, ff. 29r–33r.

80 *In the early 1460s.* On Guglielmo and Nasi: Tognetti, *Banco Cambini*, 299.
The Pazzi had companies. De Roover, 91, 94, 164, 282, 310, 315, 335.

81 *In 1474, when Pope.* De Roover, 164, although the papal alum monopoly did not pass to the Pazzi Bank until June 1476.
If we look back. Guglielmo's son in Bruges: Holmes, 'The Pazzi Conspiracy'.
After Andrea's death. On tales and trickery: the tales in Martines (1994).

CHAPTER FIVE
PROFILE: SODERINI

83 *As Lorenzo de' Medici's.* On Tommaso Soderini: Clarke, *The Soderini*, and her summary essay, 'Lorenzo de' Medici and Tommaso Soderini'.
Already a bedrock. Lorenzo's letters to Sforza: *Lettere*, I, 50–1, 52, 54–5, 63–4, 127–8; II, 68–75, 123–7.

84 *Hewing close to.* Facts here: well documented by Clarke, *Soderini*, 14–64.

CHAPTER SIX
ENTER LORENZO

88 Sources: *Lettere*, I–V; Valori, *Vita*; Fabroni; Rochon; Rubinstein (1966); Soranzo, 'Lorenzo'; Fubini, *Italia*; Frantz; A. Strozzi, *Lettere;* M. Parenti, *Lettere*.
The April Plot drew. The Prato insurrection: Ammirato, *Istorie*, V, 379–80; *Lettere*, I, 122, 155–6. Other designs against Lorenzo's life were reported by many sources, among them ambassadors, Rinuccini, Medici agents, and Cola Montano.

89 *Men born into the.* The witness and quotation: Valori, *Vita*, 46.
His education for formal. Lorenzo at ages five and ten: Rochon, 73–4. The hunting poem: *Uccellagione di starne* (aka *La caccia col falcone*).
Lorenzo was educated. Lorenzo's early patronage letters: *Lettere*, I, 3–6. As broker and patron: Salvadori, 'Rapporti personali'; F.W. Kent, 'Lorenzo . . . Amico'. Del Piazzo, *Protocolli*, establishes the torrent of letters.

90 *In 1463, now fourteen.* See Rochon, 74–7; *Lettere*, I, 14–16; Rubinstein, 'Lorenzo de' Medici', 44.
Less than a year. Rochon, 77–9; *Lettere*, I, 18–20.

91 *The next three years.* Of numerous literary studies, see Orvieto, *Lorenzo*. On his love verse: Martines, *Strong Words*, 99–100. The translation is from 'Io seguo con disio quel piú mi spiace': Lorenzo, *Opere*, I, 152, lines 1–4, 9–11. The Petrarchan echoes are striking.

92 *On 3 December 1469.* Soranzo, 'Lorenzo', 44–7; Rubinstein, 'Lorenzo', 41, and *Government*, 174–5; and Martelli, 'La cultura', on Colleoni plot.
A report to Borso. The frontline oligarchs: Giannozzo Pitti and the jurist Domenico Martelli. Ambassador's report: Cappelli, *Lettere*, 250.

93 *Lorenzo now came up.* Giuliano's unhappiness: *Lettere*, I, 398–9. Lorenzo was nineteen when married by proxy: Rochon, 98–9.

94 *The budding Florentine lord.* Trip to Rome to collect Clarice Orsini: Rochon, 98. The Pazzi in verse of the period: Orvieto, *Lorenzo*, 20; Rochon, 91, 455; Perosa, 'Storia di un libro', 104–5.

In September 1475. Pazzi Priors: ASF, Priorista Mariani, bobina 2, f. 185r.

95 *Years before the April.* Lorenzo's talks with the Milanese ambassador in the 1470s, noted in *Lettere*, I–II (esp. II, 68–75, 123–7), reveal his attitude toward the Pazzi, then echoed in Poliziano's joke about Renato Pazzi: Dempsey, *Inventing*, 101–2. On sharp-tongued Florence: Martines, *Strong Words*, Chaps. 2, 7, 8, 10.

The problem of the. On the Milanese ambassador: Soranzo, 'Lorenzo', 44–5; Lorenzo in *Lettere*, I, 48–55, notes (Dec. 1469); and Buser, *Beziehungen*, 443–4.

In the winter of. Lorenzo's campaign to impose stricter controls in 1470–71: Rubinstein, *Government*, 176–94. Bribery: since top Florentine politicians were at times openly in the pay of princes, they would have had few qualms about corrupting 'lesser' men at home. The practice was well known in Venice.

96 *Meanwhile, as disclosed.* Action against Jacopo de' Pazzi: Rubinstein, *Government*, 185; Fubini, 'La congiura', 225–6. Niccolini-Pazzi marriage, *Lettere*, I, 39.

97 *Yet the curious thing.* Jacopo's position is noted by Soranzo, 'Lorenzo', 52; though for Fubini, *Italia*, 93–5, 241–3, he was already in the anti-Medici camp in 1470. Rubinstein, *Government*, 192–3, on the three Pazzi *polizze* (name billets).

The nepotism of Pope. Imola purchase: *Lettere*, I, 443–6; II, 476; and Fubini, *Italia*, 276, n.74. The Duke of Urbino and Lorenzo Giustini also lent money for Imola. On Salviati, see Hurtubise, *Une famille*, 54–7.

98 *That the Pazzi were.* Patronage letters for the Pazzi: Del Piazzo, *Protocolli*, 15, 35, 500, 501, 504, 506, 507, 514, 524. The mule-train affair: *Lettere*, I, 485–92.

99 *In July 1474.* For the contents of this paragraph: *Lettere*, II, 52–3, 66–8, 74.

Worse was to come. Salviati's appointment is treated by Fubini, *Italia*, 97–101. Lorenzo's illness: *Lettere*, II, 49, n.1. Sixtus on Lorenzo as citizen and merchant: *Lettere*, II, 124, n.4; and Brown, *The Medici*, 216.

100 *I beg you to get.* This and the next quotation: *Lettere*, II, 57–61, 68–75.

101 *This and the preceding.* Bullard, *Lorenzo il Magnifico*, 43–79, makes Lorenzo all but media-conscious of 'his image'.

102 *Lorenzo added that he.* Lorenzo's words and Salviati's reply: *Lettere*, II, 73.

103 *The Salviati case was.* The horse incident: *Lettere*, II, 123, n.2.

Did the Pazzi have. Fubini, *Italia*, 287–8, 318–22, on Antonio Pazzi (doctor of decretals), the Sarno dignity, and the mission to France.

The truth was. The ambassador's words: *Lettere*, II, 115, letter of 24 August.

104 *Lorenzo was naturally stung.* The ambassador's words: *Lettere*, II, 118–20.

They are the source. Quotation: *Lettere,* II, 123–5.

105 *But the Duke of.* The Pope's concessions and Lorenzo's words to the ambassador: *Lettere,* II, 126.

106 *Yet all the while.* On maintaining appearances: the astonishing hypocrisy of Lorenzo's letter of 28 December 1475 to Pope Sixtus, *Lettere,* II, 142–4. *Meanwhile, Lorenzo and the.* See *Lettere,* II, 144, on the alum contract, and 126–7, 276, on disinheriting Beatrice Borromei.

107 *Of the several mysteries.* On conformism in Renaissance cities, especially at Florence: the essays in Martines, *Renaissance Sextet.*

I suspect that the. Andrea ran a Medici firm: Hurtubise, *Une famille,* 48. Garbero Zorzi, 'La Collezione', 189–90, on Sforza's Florence visit. D. Kent, *Cosimo,* highlights Cosimo's piety, patriotism, and good intentions: see Martines, TLS.

108 *If a mild and then.* Chellini, *Ricordanze,* 183: Ficino 'sta per ripetitore cum Piero de Pazzi' (Oct. 1451); also Vespasiano, *Vite,* II, 309–20, on Piero de' Pazzi.

All the same. A. Strozzi, *Lettere,* 59–62, letter of 15 March 1462.

109 *Yet Alessandra's son-in.* Marco's comments: M. Parenti, *Lettere,* 50–1 (Piero's grand entry), 77, 90, 116, 153, 180, 197, and elsewhere. Florence knighting: Salvemini, 147.

It was after this. Quotations here: A. Strozzi, *Lettere,* 59–62.

CHAPTER SEVEN
APRIL BLOOD

111 Sources for this chapter are: Poliziano, *Della Congiura*; P. Parenti, *Storia,* 12–20; Landucci, *Diario,* 17–21; F. Strozzi, 'Ricordo', in Capponi, *Storia,* II, 520–3; Valori, *Vita,* 107–16; Guicciardini, *Storie,* Chap. IV; Machiavelli, *Istorie,* VIII; plus material in *Lettere,* III; Ammirato, *Istorie,* VI, 1–16; Fabroni, *Laurentii,* I, 58–77; Roscoe, *Life,* I, 173–232. For English translations of Poliziano and Landucci see Bibliography. Perosa's notes to Poliziano are fundamental. Essential studies: Frantz, *Sixtus IV,* 174–259; Fubini, *Italia,* 87–106, 220–326.

That year 26 April. Florentine confraternities: Henderson, *Piety and Charity.* For parish churches and other religious buildings: Fanelli, *Firenze,* 10, 28–9, 58.

116 *The signal for.* Only the sentence against the plot's ringleaders cites the elevation of the Host as the signal: ASF, Podestà, 5160, f. 52v.

118 *Unknown people.* Distances throughout are based on my own estimates.

119 *In view of his.* The palace's inner layout: Rubinstein, *Palazzo Vecchio,* 18–24.

122 *One of the diarists.* Giusti, BNCF, Ms. II. II. 127, f. 122v. Dr Rita Maria Comanducci kindly brought this source to my attention.

126 *On Monday, the 27th.* Quotation: Poliziano, *Congiura*, 45, Perosa's notes.

128 *In the late afternoon.* Sources: Landucci, 17–21; Machiavelli, *Istorie*, VIII.

130 *It was afterwards claimed.* On Jacopo's body: Poliziano, 58–9; Landucci, *Diario*, 21–2. Poliziano's 2nd edition suppressed his assertion about the sun.

132 *Within a day or two.* Point in Roman law: Cavallar, 'I consulenti', 337, n. 76.
The Priors and the. See Chap. 11 for the sources. Landucci, 22, noted the Zecca auction. The finer details are my own extrapolation.

133 *On 23 May.* I checked the law in ASF, Provvisioni, 169, ff. 24v–26v. It is in Fabroni, II, 112–15; and Roscoe, I, Appendix XXIII, 62–5.

134 *The bar against.* Florin emblazoning rights: Jacks, Caferro, *The Spinelli*, 23.
There was yet another. On the terror of bankruptcy: Martines, *Strong Words*, Chap. 6. Defamatory painting: *Consorterie*, 159–60.

135 *None other than the.* Botticelli: ASF, Otto, 48, f. 35v; also, *Consorterie*, 159.
The sentence against. As early as the autumn of 1478, Lorenzo moved to protect the marriage rights of his sister Bianca's children: *Lettere*, VIII, 30, n.3. Her son Cosimo Pazzi continued to receive his Florentine cathedral stipend: AOSMF, Deliberazioni, II, 2, Reg. 5 (1476–82), f. 45r–v.
Botticelli's defamatory pictures. Vasari, *Vite*, III, 234–5.

CHAPTER EIGHT
ASSAULTING THE BODY

138 *The fierce civil wars.* On this early period consult: Jones, *The Italian City-State*, 333–650; and Martines, *Power and Imagination*, Chaps 3–8.
Up and down the Italian. Laws of the period stipulate higher penalties for bloody assault: e.g., *Statuta . . . Florentiae*, I, 323, 325–6; *Aegidianae constitutiones*, 288; Ascheri, *L'Ultimo Statuto*, 304, 330–2; *Statuti ... Udine*, 47–8; see also Pullan, Chambers, *Venice*. 87–104. Following are some particular studies: Ruggiero, *Violence*; Chambers, Dean, *Clean Hands*; Gundersheimer, 'Crime and Punishment'.

139 Quotations: 'I am he', in Giustinian, *Laudario*, I, 374–5; and Lorenzo, *Opere*, II, 138–9, line 35.
Every city had its. Decrees, chronicles, and diaries often refer to execution sites: see Edgerton, *Pictures*; Rondini, 'I Giustiziati'; and Fineschi, 'La rappresentazione'.

140 *In Florence around 1400.* Sources for this paragraph: Molho, Sznura, *Alle Bocche*, 167–8; Landucci, *Diario*, 181.

When a murder was. Busechino: Molho, Sznura, 82–3.

140–1 *Capital punishment in the.* Sanuto, *Diarii*, VI, col. 53. On the second case, from the year 1513: Pullan, Chambers, *Venice*, 89–90.

141 *But ordinary executions.* Confraternities: Black, *Italian Confraternities*; Weissman, *Ritual Brotherhood.* Eisenbichler, 'Lorenzo', treats Florence's Black Company. Fineschi, 'La rappresentazione', maps the itinerary of the Florentine march of death.

142 *But the dry outlines.* Edgerton, *Pictures*, 138–46, 192–8; and Martines, *Strong Words*, 42. Landucci, *Diario*, 4–5, for the Gherucci girl and counterfeiter. On perjury and forgery: *Statuta . . . Florentiae*, I, 336–7, 341; and *Statuta . . . Papie*, rubric 37.

143 *What exactly did the.* Roverbella's poem: Text, Martines, *Strong Words*, 42–4.

144 *If Florence had staged.* May 1503 incident: Rondini, 'I Giustiziati', 226; and Landucci, *Diario*, 255–6.

Over the fifty years. The averages here are based on Edgerton, *Pictures*, 231–8, and Gundersheimer, 'Crime and Punishment', 110–13.

145 *Was it the case.* On eating the assassins: Belotti, 138. Violence of mercenaries: Caferro, *Mercenary Companies*; Covini, 'Alle spese di Zoan Villano'; Albini, *Guerra.*

In papal territory one. See *Cronaca della città di Perugia*, 415.

147 *Driven by a burst.* The best overall work on Florentine religious customs: Trexler, *Public Life*. Add Martines, *Strong Words*, 37–81; and Galletti, *Laude spirituali.*

148 *Like every other city.* Material in Brucker: *Renaissance Florence*, 172–212. Giambullari's poem: Galletti, *Laude*, 256.

Since religious views. Martines, *Violence*, treats political violence. The revenger's poem is in Corsi, *Rimatori*, 928. The word 'bastardi' is not in the original, but it jibes perfectly with the 'feel' and sense of the poem.

CHAPTER NINE
A SOLDIER CONFESSES

150 *The plot is best.* Montesecco's confession: Capponi, *Storia*, II, 510–20. Since my translation keeps the confessional sequence, Capponi's pages will not be cited.

151 *Dated 4 May 1478.* The Count's secret chamber: *Lettere*, II, 469.

Montesecco confessed. On the Pazzi palace in Rome: Pastor, IV, 302, note.

152 *When the confession was.* Fubini, *Italia*, 87–106; and his *Quattrocento*, 235–82, provide a background for the plot.

154 *He was born about.* On Salviati: Hurtubise, *Une famille*, 54–8.
When the young Pietro. On Salviati and Sixtus: Bizzocchi, *Chiesa*, 174, 214, 264–5; *Consorterie*, 172–5; and Pastor, *History*, IV, 294–6.
Now everything changed. On Salviati: Fubini, *Quattrocento*, 268–70, 291.

156–7 *In the mid 1460s.* Quotations: Fubini, *Italia*, 83–4; *Lettere*, I, 105; II, 201, n.3.

157 *Machiavelli, instead.* Machiavelli, *Histories*, 327; Guicciardini, *Storie*, 34.

159 *Can it be said.* Essential items on Pope Sixtus: Pastor, *History*, IV, 198–296; Litta, *Famiglie celebri*, IX; Weber, *Genealogien zur Papsgeschichte*, I, lxxxv–lxxxvi, and 336–41; Miglio, *Un pontificato*; Lombardi, 'Sisto IV'; Di Fonzo, *I Pontefici*. On his nepotism: Shaw, *Julius II*, 9–50. A 'shameless celebration', in Clark, *Melozzo*, 21. I am grateful to Professor Barbara Hallman for putting me on to Weber's book.

162 *The fleeting image here.* Guicciardini, *Storie*, 33–4.

165 *Although unnamed in.* On the Duke: Clough, 'Federigo da Montefeltro'.

166 *The soldiers, Giovan Francesco.* For Italian local militias: the revisionist study by Jones, 'The Machiavellian Militia'.

167 *Citing a claim by.* P. Parenti, *Storia*, 18.

168 *The one man of.* For the Bracciolini family: Martines, *Social World*, 123–7, 210–14. On Jacopo: Bausi, 'Paternae Artis Haeres', and 'Politica e cultura'.

169 *As time and more.* On Baroncelli: Valori, *Vita*, 139; Ganz, 'Paying the Price', 250; Fubini, *Quattrocento*, 258, 270, 285; and Grunzweig, xxxii–iii.

171 *At the end of.* Thomas James: *Lettere*, II, 469.

CHAPTER TEN

RAGING: POPE AND CITIZEN

174 *An outstanding debater.* On Pope Sixtus: notes for page 159. Weber, *Genealogien*, I, lxxxvi, suspects that Leonardo, Duke of Sora, was actually the pontiff's son.

175 *The drama itself.* Lorenzo in Rome, October 1471: *Lettere*, I, 352–5.

176 *With papal troops.* Lorenzo for Luigi Pulci, Fabroni, II, 24.
For Lorenzo, at least. On the Pazzi War and its consequences: *Lettere*, III–IV, with notes and commentaries; Frantz, 260–351; Guicciardini, *Storie*, 39–48; and the bull of excommunication in Roscoe, *Life*, I, Appendix XXVI, 68–75.

177 *On 12 June.* Lorenzo's meeting with citizens: ASF, Consulte e Pratiche, 60, f. 159r–v; Rubinstein, 'Lorenzo', 57.

179 *In any war of.* Quotation: Perosa, notes to Poliziano, *Congiura*, viii–ix. For the two decretals: Bizzocchi, *Chiesa*, 267.

A scornful letter to. Letter: Di Benedetto, 'Un breve di Sisto IV', 376–8. The *Florentina Synodus* is in Roscoe, I, Appendix XXVII, 75–98. The epigram: in *Lettere*, II, 71, n.7

180 *Mocking, angry, jeering.* On Becchi's diatribe: Frantz, *Sixtus IV*, 238–59. On Becchi himself: Grayson, 'Gentile Becchi'.

181 *This diatribe against.* On the *Excusatio*: Fabroni, II, 167–81; and Brown, *Bartolomeo Scala*, 84–7, 158–9.

182 *Recently arrived in Italy.* Three printings of the work: Perosa's notes in Poliziano, *Congiura*, viii, xvi–xvii.

Although conducted chiefly. Florentine anti-clericalism: Martines, 'Raging'.

183 *Yet the churchman's savage.* Anonymous poem: Flamini, 'Versi', 315–30.

184 *A second poem.* Poem for Lucrezia: Flamini, 'Versi', 330–4.

Lashing out at the. Lucrezia's verse: Tornabuoni, *Poemetti sacri*.

The Medicean regime. Anonymous jottings (March 1479): Brown, 'Lorenzo and Public Opinion', 77, n.56. Vettori family: R. D. Jones, *Francesco Vettori*, 3.

185 *In a letter of.* Letter: in *Lettere*, II, 269.

186 *The crisis peaked.* Grain prices: Tognetti, 'Problemi di vettovagliamento', and Brucker, 'Economic Foundations', 5–6.

187 *When the young duke.* Journey to Naples: *Lettere*, IV, 391–400; Pontieri, *Per la storia*, 170–88; De Angelis, 'Lorenzo a Napoli'. Gifts: Ammirato, *Istorie*, VI, 46.

190 *Spreading quickly through.* Letter to the Priors and the Pope's fury: *Lettere*, IV, 268, 292, n.2. The anonymous scribble: Rubinstein, 'Lorenzo', 63, n. 62.

Until the spring. Papal demands: *Lettere*, IV, 33–4; Ammirato, VI, 34.

191 *Ferrante was notoriously.* Expense and quotation: Valori, *Vita*, 119–20.

193 *One of Lorenzo's greatest.* On his nose and sense of smell: Valori, *Vita*, 46. Letter to Piero: *Lettere*, VIII, 68–79.

Ferrante kept Lorenzo. Anxious tidings: Guicciardini, *Storie*, 52.

194 *On the very day.* Quotation: *Lettere*, IV, 336.

196 *No more had to be.* The embassy to Rome: Ammirato, *Istorie*, VI, 49.

CHAPTER ELEVEN

THE PAZZI CURSED

197 *Florentine political leaders.* For background to dissent: Martines, 'Political Opposition'. On Perugia: *Cronaca della città*. Bologna was less explosive:

Ady, *The Bentivoglio*. Even Mantua could skid out of control: Chambers, Dean, *Clean Hands*.

Created in 1378. On the constitutional status of the Eight: Martines, *Lawyers*, 135–6, 410–11; Antonelli, 'La magistratura'; Zorzi, *L'Aministrazione della giustizia*; *Consorterie politiche*, 151–76. Lorenzo in the Eight: ASF, Otto, 48, f. 2r (proceedings for May–Aug. 1478). The two men rarely attended meetings and soon resigned.

The Eight who took. The Eight's dispatch of spies: ASF, Otto, 33 (May–Aug. 1473), ff. 3r, 3v, 10v, 35r. On *tamburi*: Otto, 221, ff. 6ov, 100r. Rewards: Otto, 224, ff. 72r–v; 221, 6ov.

198 *When the April conspirators*. Quotes: ASF, Podestà, 5160, f. 52r. The Eight routed major decisions via the Podestà: e.g. ASF, Otto, 50 (Nov.–Feb. 1479), *passim*.

199 *By executing him*. As Montesecco's confession refers to no other Pazzi, this poses the possible innocence of the others. The Eight's new code: *Consorterie*, 153.

Since the case against. Seizing merchandise on the high seas: *Consorterie*, 169–70. Auctions: Landucci, *Diario*, 21, 22. Dowries: Kirshner, 'Pursuing Honor'. Personal and household effects: ASF, Otto, 48, ff. 6v, 15r.

200 *By 23 May*. The bill against the Pazzi: ASF, Provvisioni, 169, ff. 24v–26v. The vote: f. 26r–v. Stripping them of their Easter privileges: BNCF, Magl., 127, f. 98, 'Carro del fuoco sacro che per la Casa de Pazzi il giorno del Sabbato Santo si conduceva alla chiesa di S. Gio. batista e alle case loro, non si faccia piu per detta Casa de Pazzi ma per i Consoli di Calimala.' I owe this reference to Dr Luca Boschetto.

201 *In the autumn of*. The poem: Flamini, 'Versi in morte'.

As grabbing the property. Town criers were a common feature of the urban landscape. ASF, Otto, 48 (May–Aug. 1478), omits the summons to Pazzi debtors. Though unrecorded, the Eight ordered citizens to submit lists of all their arms: see Giusti, BNCF, Ms. II. II. 127 (14 May). My claim about Pazzi debtors is indicated by practice in ASF, Capitani, 74, ff. 117r–118r, documenting the search for all property belonging to Frescobaldi, Baldovinetti, and Balducci, the conspirators of 1481.

202 *Orders went out*. See ASF, Otto, 58, ff. 67v–70r, showing the Eight (7–15 June 1481) in pursuit of the accounts and debtors of the three 'traitors' of 1481, all executed on 6 June. The Eight's acts are studded with notices of business records. ASF, Otto, 221, f. 224r, even shows that in Jan. 1490 an important account book was stolen from the Merchants' Court itself (the Tribunale di Mercanzia).

A special office in. Acts of the Tower Officials (terribly faded): ASF, Capitani, 77, I–II. Claims advanced by Rinuccini and Renato's widow:

Capitani, 77, I, ff. 6or, 350r–v. The second largest dowry (8500 florins) went to a Bardi girl in the Acciaiuoli family: Ganz, 'Paying the Price', 241. An Appiano 'princess' entered the cadet Medici branch with 10,000 'large [full value] florins'. See below, note for p. 240.

Although there is. Lorenzo reserves Renato's house: Del Piazzo, *Protocolli*, 55. Maddalena's dowry: Hook, *Lorenzo*, 171.

203 *Did any of Piero.* Lorenzo and his cousins: Fryde, *Humanism*, 143–57.

The surest proof. Meddling in the Pazzi estate: Del Piazzo, 50, 51, 54, 111; and Grunzweig, *Correspondence*, xxxiii, on Ranieri da Ricasoli, dispatched to Bruges.

Meanwhile, something had. The act on the Pazzi Syndics, 22–4 December 1479: ASF, Provvisioni, 170, ff. 100r–102r.

204 *Of the six Syndics.* Source here: ASF, Balie, 38, ff. 1r–4r.

The Syndics began work. On this and the following items: ASF, Balie, 38, ff. 4v–5r, 5v–11r, 11v–12r, 12v–13r.

205 *Taking two years.* References to Renato, his brother, and property sales: ASF, Balie, 38, ff. 19r, 21v, 27r, 29v, 30r, 31v. Legal counsel for the archdiocese of Pisa contested the sale of Guglielmo's part of the property: ASF, Balie, 38, ff. 27v–28r.

206 *Early in 1481.* On Pazzi saline investments: ASF, Balie, 38, ff. 92r–97v.

207 *A witness to the.* On the Venetian lady: ASF, Capitani, 77, I, ff. 350r–351r; ASF, Balie, 38, ff. 98r–105v.

In the four years. Frick, *Dressing Renaissance Florence*, broaches the remarkable market value of upper-class clothing.

208 *The Syndics closed.* For the pressure of the Syndics on Guglielmo and the Pazzi prisoners: ASF, Balie, 38, ff. 106r–108r, 109r–111r.

It looks very much. Literature: Martines, 'Corruption and Injustice', 377–86.

Francesco de' Pazzi. Quotes: Dante, *Purgatorio*, XVI, 96; *Inferno*, III, 1–3.

209 *Once the cursed Pazzi.* The two Pazzi bishops: Poliziano, *Congiura*, 83–4; Buser, *Beziehungen*, 472–5; *Lettere*, II, 115, 119–20; Lorenzi, *Cola*, 58–9; Litta, *Famiglie*, IV, 'Pazzi,' table vii. Andrea di Giovanni became Sarno Bishop in 1482.

But the Eight were. The Eight's penalties and restrictions: ASF, Otto, 221, ff. 1r, 3r, 17v, 81r, 87v (exile at age eleven); 224, f. 3r; and *Consorterie*, 162–5. Some exiles had to report weekly.

210 *Were Medicean suspicions.* The 1481 plot: *Lettere*, V, 226–8, and notes; *Consorterie*, 162–5. On Acciaiuoli and Altoviti, plus the claim against Guglielmo: Lorenzi, *Cola*, 62, 66, 76–7, 80–2. Soderini and his property: ASF, Capitani, 74, ff. 117v, 123v, 124v, 127r, 130v.

211 *In the process of.* The inventory: ASF, Capitani, 74, ff. 137r–139r.

Something else, very. The five wedding chests: Callmann, *Apollonio*, 79–80.

CHAPTER TWELVE
PROFILE: RINUCCINI

214 Sources, this chapter: Rinuccini, *Ricordi* and *Dialogus de libertate;* Giustiniani, *Alamanno Rinuccini* and *Lettere ed orazioni;* Martelli, 'Profilo ideologico' (1985). Watkins, *Humanism and Liberty,* 193–224, offers the *Dialogus* in translation. *Citizen Eleutherius, a devotee.* This setting opens Rinuccini, *Dialogus.* *They settle down.* Next a summary of *Dialogus,* 272–3, 277–9, 282–8.

215 *Eleutherius replies with.* The ensuing material: *Dialogus,* 293–8, 299–302. *The most articulate.* Quotations: Rinuccini, *Ricordi,* cxxviii; *Dialogus,* 273.

216 *The Rinuccini family.* A family history: Rinuccini, *Ricordi,* the introduction by Aiazzi; and Martines, 'Nuovi documenti'. *Alamanno's father inherited.* A large fortune: Martines, *Social World,* 110–12; and Giustiniani, *Alamanno,* 14–16.

217 *But politics – and Plutarch's.* Quotations: Martines, *Social World,* 347; Giustiniani, *Alamanno,* 145, n.6. *In 1469, Alamanno's net.* Tax returns: ASF, Catasto, 912, f. 14. *Arrested at one point.* Arrested and pardoned: ASF, Otto, 58, ff. 12v, 77v.

218 *His memoirs and the.* Giustiniani, *Alamanno,* 24, 114–17, 130, 157. *On the occasion of.* The clash with Lorenzo: Fubini, *Quattrocento,* 108–22; and the friendly letters, Giustiniani, *Lettere,* 216–18.

219 *The fact that he.* Favouring the Medici: Martelli, 'Profilo' (1985).

CHAPTER THIRTEEN
LORENZO: LORD AND CITIZEN

221 *On a morning in.* Ambassador's account: Cappelli, *Lettere,* 305.

223 *Up to the mid.* Strange occurrences: Guicciardini, 73; Valori, 143–4; Masi, 16–17; Landucci, 63–4; Rinuccini, *Ricordi,* cxlvi. Reactions to Lorenzo's death: Brown, 'Lorenzo and Public Opinion', 61.

224 *Well, but why.* Lorenzo's art collection: Wackernagel, *World of Renaissance Artist,* 254–8; Garbero Zorzi, 'La collezione'; Beck, 'Lorenzo il Magnifico'. *Turning into a bloodbath.* Quotation: Guicciardini, *Storie,* 37–8.

225 *Lorenzo, however, was.* Quotation: Rinuccini, *Ricordi,* cxlvii.

226 *Within weeks of his.* Rubinstein, *Government,* 197–202.

227 *Yet even as Lorenzo.* Quotation: Rubinstein, *Government,* 201, n.1.

228 *Lorenzo's correspondence took.* Del Piazzo, *Protocolli,* calendars many thousands of Lorenzo's letters, some 1900 of which survive: Ricci, Rubinstein, *Censimento.* On letters to him: F. W. Kent, 'Patron–Client Networks', 290–2.

His correspondence shows. Love in the workings of patronage: Martines, *Strong Words*, 13–36.

229 *In relations with Milan.* Sforza debt and the quotation: De Roover, 141, 273. Lorenzo's meetings with Galeazzo Maria: Rochon, 73–87, 202–8. On the artillery train: Mallett, 'Diplomacy', 236.

230 *Letters between Lorenzo.* Lorenzo as client: see notes for page 83.

231 *Lorenzo himself was.* Lorenzo to Ferrante: De Angelis, 'Lorenzo a Napoli'.

232 *His easy public style.* In the 1480s Lorenzo had meetings with ambassadors in the cathedral. Arms ban: ASF, Otto, 48 f. 3v; 221, ff. 1r, 3r. His armed escort: Otto, 48, f. 9r; 50, f. 39r; 67, f. 5r. On Salvalaglio and drawn swords: Cambi, *Istorie*, II, 65, 67. Soldiers around him in 1472: Corazzol, *Corrispondenze*, 296.

233 *Lorenzo's new image.* Merchants' Court: Astorri, 'Note sulla Mercanzia'.

234 *His unconstitutional status.* On Lorenzo's web of clients: Bruscoli, 'Politica matrimoniale', and notes for page 89. His confraternities: Sbregondi, 'Lorenzo'.
   Alamanno Rinuccini claimed. See Rinuccini, *Ricordi*, cxlvii. Supports mercenaries: Lettere, VII, 8–9; Corazzol, 254.

235 *Guicciardini emphasised.* On this emphasis: Guicciardini, *Storie*, 79. Lorenzo, marriage broker: Bruscoli, 'Politica matrimoniale', 347–98.

236 *Already in serious troubles.* Bank in crisis: Valori, 121; De Roover, 366; Fryde, 'Lorenzo . . . Finances', in his *Humanism*. Lorenzo's money needs: *Lettere*, III, 38, 124–6, 143, 153–4, 161, 165, 174, 175–82, 249.
   Reliable contemporaries asserted. Theft: Cambi, *Istorie*, II, 54–5; P. Parenti, *Storia*, I, 198; Rinuccini, *Ricordi*, cxlviii–cxlix.
   It is hard to. Palace costs: Goldthwaite, *Building*, 167, on the Strozzi Palace. Brenda Preyer confirms my Medici estimate. University costs: I calculate a low of 25 florins yearly, though rich young men with servants could spend far more. See Martines, *Social World*, 117; and *Lawyers*, 90. My workers' payroll is extrapolated from Goldthwaite, *Building*, 347–8, 436–9, and a working year of 260 days.

237 *While it cannot be.* On the sum of Medici outgoings: Fabroni, II, 42.

238 *For all his disguised.* On plots: Corazzol, 453 (called off); Lorenzi, *Cola*, 59–62, 67–8, 76–7, 80–1; Cappelli, 254–5, 303, 309. The hermit's feet: Landucci, 36–7.

239 *In their climb to.* The marriages of the Medici family have been traced by Pieraccini, *La stirpe*, I, 49–75, 95–140, 157–284. On the Medici Archbishop of Pisa and his 1500 men: Clarke, 'A Sienese Note', 50; Bizzocchi, *Chiesa*, 233–4.

240 *Once the Medici had.* Match with the Appiano lords: Bruscoli, 'Politica', 356.

For this crucial match. Alfonsina marriage and dowry: Fabroni, II, 316, n.2.

241 *The remaining Medici.* Marriages: Pieraccini, I, 215–43. Bruscoli, 'Politica', 365, gives different marriage dates for Lucrezia and Contessina.

242 *Giulio's career was made.* Lorenzo's relations with Pope Innocent: Picotti, *Giovinezza*, 160–234. His epistolary prose: Bessi, 'Lorenzo letterato', 101–6. *The growing amity.* Lorenzo's secret correspondence, and what the Florentine ambassador said: Bizzocchi, *Chiesa*, 343–4; and M. Pellegrini, 'Innocenzo VIII', 7.

243 *What lay behind this.* On Maddalena: Pieraccini, I, 233–40. On Franceschetto: Hook, *Lorenzo*, 171; and Falconi, 96.

244 *From this point on.* Lanfredini in Rome, nudging the Pope: Picotti, 176–7. Lorenzo's delaration to Ascanio Sforza: Falconi, 96–7. *At the end of.* Of the stages in Giovanni's promotion to the cardinalship: Picotti, *Giovinezza*, Chap. 3; Palmarocchi, 'Lorenzo'; and Falconi, 96, on the 95,000 florins of simony. Brown, *Bartolomeo Scala*, 108–9, n.137, notes that Lorenzo lent Sixtus 30,000 florins in July 1488 and 95,000 in August 1489. Were they mere loans?

245 *The two fathers-in-law.* Lorenzo and Pope Innocent: Lorenzo, *Scritti*, 659–71. Lorenzo's ailments: Martelli, *Studi*, 198, 205. *When it happened.* For the quotations here: Martelli, *Studi*, 198, 205.

246 *In reworking his Commentary.* Martelli, *Studi*, 51–133, is the outstanding study of Lorenzo's revision of the *Comentario*. *Meanwhile, Lorenzo had time.* Letters to Innocent: Lorenzo, *Scritti scelti*, 660–2; Moreni, *Lettere*, 5–34. Giovanni's benefices: Picotti, 67–159.

247 *In the joy and wonder.* What Lorenzo said: Lorenzo, *Scritti*, 671–5. Background to 1512 and 1527: Stephens, *The Fall*, and Butters, *Governors*.

248 *If in a strain.* The lauds: Lorenzo, *Laude*. Performed by a religious confraternity, the play is in Lorenzo, *Opere*, II, 71–115. *The clash between his.* Letter to Giovanni: Lorenzo, *Scritti*, 671–5.

249 *It only remained for.* Letters to Michelozzi: cited in Martelli, *Studi*, 222, and in his 'Il Cristianesimo di Lorenzo', 90.

CHAPTER FOURTEEN
THE BOTTOM LINE

251 *He was never.* The houses of Lorenzo's henchmen burned, Dec. 1494: Cerretani, *Storia*, 207–8; P. Parenti, *Storia*, 152. On the Seventeen Reformers: Brown, *The Medici*, 151–211.

252 *Within weeks of the.* Act of 13 November: ASF, DSCOA, 96, f. 92r. Bill of 25–26 January: ASF, Provvisioni, 185, ff. 53r–54r. I owe my knowledge

of these references to the generosity of Professor Osvaldo Cavallar.

Despite the presumed. Claim against the Lyons branch: Merisalo, *Le collezione*, 5, 81–2.

253 *In more general terms.* On legal argument for the Pazzi in 1495: Cavallar, 'Il tiranno', and 'I consulenti'.

Having a keen recollection. The new bar on princely marriages: ASF, Provvisioni, 185, ff. 40v–41v.

The question of Lorenzo's. The purloined sum: De Roover, 367.

256 *Here, in many ways.* Quotation: Guicciardini, *Storie*, 74.

260 *Lorenzo himself undoubtedly.* Cola's Oration: in Lorenzi, *Cola*, 132–44.

Current scholarship has. See above all the work of Brown, Astorri, Bruscoli, and the authors of *Consorterie*.

BIBLIOGRAPHY

Abbreviations

ASF	Archivio di Stato, Florence
AOSMF	Archivio del Opera di Santa Maria del Fiore, Florence
ASI	*Archivio storico italiano*
BNCF	Biblioteca Nazionale Centrale, Florence
Capitani	Capitani di Parte Guelfa: numeri rossi
DBI	*Dizionario biografico degli italiani.* Rome, 1960–
DSCOA	Deliberazioni dei Signori e Collegi, ordinaria autorità
Otto	Otto di Guardia e balía: periodo repubblicano
Podestà	Atti del Podestà

Acton, Harold. 1979. *The Pazzi Conspiracy.* London.

Ady, Cecilia M. 1937. *The Bentivoglio of Bologna.* London.

Aegidianae constitutiones cum additionibus carpensibus. 1571. Venice.

Albini, Giuliana. 1982. *Guerra, fame, peste. Crisi di mortalità e sistema sanitario nella Lombardia tardomedioevale.* Bologna.

Ames-Lewis, Francis, ed. 1992. *Cosimo il Vecchio de' Medici, 1389–1464.* Oxford.

Ammirato, Scipione. 1853. *Istorie fiorentine.* 7 vols. Turin.

Armstrong, Lawrin. 1999. 'The Politics of Usury in Trecento Florence.' *Mediaeval Studies* 61: 1–44.

Ascheri, Mario, ed. 1993. *L'Ultimo statuto della Repubblica di Siena (1545).* Siena.

Astorri, Antonella. 1992. 'Note sulla Mercanzia fiorentina sotto Lorenzo dei Medici'. *ASI* 150: 965–93.

Bausi, Francesco. 1988. '"Paternae Artis Haeres". Ritratto di Jacopo Bracciolini'. *Interpres* VIII: 103–98.

——. 1989. 'Politica e cultura nel Commento al "Trionfo della Fama" di Jacopo Bracciolini.' *Interpres* IX: 64–149.

Beck, James. 1993. 'Lorenzo il Magnifico and his Cultural Possessions'. In Toscani, *Lorenzo.*

Bernardi, Andrea. 1895. *Cronache forlivesi dal 1476*. Ed. G. Mazzatinti. Bologna.

Bessi, Rossella. 1992. 'Lorenzo letterato'. In Cardini, *Lorenzo*.

Bizzocchi, Roberto. 1987. *Chiesa e potere nella Toscana del Quattrocento*. Bologna.

Black, Christopher. 1989. *Italian Confraternities in the Sixteenth Century*. Cambridge.

Breisach, Ernst. 1967. *Caterina Sforza: A Renaissance Virago*. Chicago and London.

Brown, Alison. 1961. 'The Humanist Portrait of Cosimo de' Medici, Pater Patriae'. *Journal of the Warburg and Courtauld Institutes* XXIV: 186–221.

——. 1979. *Bartolomeo Scala, 1430–1497, Chancellor of Florence*. Princeton.

——. 1992. *The Medici in Florence: The Exercise and Language of Power*. Florence.

——. 1994. 'Lorenzo and Public Opinion in Florence'. In Garfagnini, *Lorenzo*.

Brucker, Gene. 1957. 'The Medici in the Fourteenth Century'. *Speculum* 32: 1–26.

——. 1962. *Florentine Politics and Society, 1343–1378*. Princeton.

——. 1969. *Renaissance Florence*. New York.

——. 1977. *The Civic World of Early Renaissance Florence*. Princeton.

——. 1994. 'The Economic Foundations of Laurentian Florence.' In Garfagnini, *Lorenzo*.

Bruscoli, Francesco G. 1997. 'Politica matrimoniale e matrimoni politici nella Firenze di Lorenzo de' Medici'. *ASI* 155: 347–98.

Bullard, Melissa M. 1994. *Lorenzo il Magnifico: Image and Anxiety. Politics and Finance*. Florence.

——. 1980. *Filippo Strozzi and the Medici*. Cambridge, London, New York.

Buoninsegni, Domenico. 1637. *Storie della città di Firenze*. Florence.

Buser, B. 1879. *Die Beziehungen der Mediceer zu Frankreich während der Jahre 1434–1494*. Leipzig.

Caferro, William. 1998. *Mercenary Companies and the Decline of Siena*. Baltimore.

Callmann, Ellen. 1974. *Apollonio di Giovanni*. Oxford.

Cambi, Giovanni. 1785–6. *Istorie*. 4 vols, Ed. I. Di San Luigi, in *Delizie degli eruditi Toscani*, XX–XXIII. Florence.

Cappelli, A. 1863. *Lettere di Lorenzo de' Medici*. In 'Atti e Memorie delle RR Deputazioni di storia patria per le provincie modenesi e parmensi'. I: 231–320

Capponi, Gino. 1930. *Storia della Repubblica di Firenze*. 2 vols. Florence.

Cardini, Franco, ed. 1992. *Lorenzo il Magnifico*. Rome.

Cavallar, Osvaldo. 1997. 'Il tiranno, I *dubia* del giudice, e I *consilia* dei giuristi'. *ASI* 155: 265–345.

——. 1999. 'I consulenti e il caso dei Pazzi: *Consilia* ai margini della *in integrum restitutio*'. In *Legal Consulting in the Civil Law Tradition*, 319–62.

Cerretani, Bartolomeo. 1994. *Storia fiorentina*. Ed. Giuliana Berti. Florence.

Cessi, Roberto. 1956. *Saggi romani*. Rome.

Chambers, David S., and Trevor Dean. 1997. *Clean Hands and Rough Justice: An Investigating Magistrate in Renaissance Italy*. Ann Arbor.

Chellini, Giovanni. 1984. *Le ricordanze*. Ed. M. T. Sillano. Milan.

Clark, Nicholas. 1990. *Melozzo da Forlì: Pictor Papalis*. London.

Clarke, Paula. 1991. *The Soderini and the Medici*. Oxford.

——. 1992. 'Lorenzo de' Medici and Tommaso Soderini'. In Garfagnini, *Lorenzo*.

——. 1988. 'A Sienese Note on 1466'. In P. Denley and C. Elam, eds. *Florence and Italy: Renaissance Studies in Honour of Nicolai Rubinstein*. London.

Clough, Cecil H. 1984. 'Federigo da Montefeltro: the Good Christian Prince'. *Bulletin of the John Rylands University Library of Manchester* 67.

Cobelli, Leone. 1874. *Cronache forlivesi*. Ed. G. Carducci and E. Frati. Bologna.

Consorterie politiche e mutamenti istituzionali in età Laurenziana. 1992. Ed. M. Timpanaro, R. Tolu, P. Viti. Florence.

Connell, William J. 2000. 'The humanist citizen as provincial governor'. In Connell, Zorzi, *Florentine Tuscany*.

Connell, William J. and Andrea Zorzi, eds. 2000. *Florentine Tuscany: Structures and Practices of Power*. Cambridge, UK.

Connell, William J., ed. 2002. *Society and Individual in Renaissance Florence*. Berkeley and Los Angeles.

Conti, Elio. 1984. *L'imposta diretta a Firenze nel Quattrocento (1427–1494)*. Rome.

Corazzol, Gigi, ed. 1994. *Corrispondenze diplomatiche veneziane da Napoli. Dispacci di Zaccaria Barbaro, 1 Nov. 1471–7 Sett. 1473*. Rome.

Corsi, Giuseppe, ed. 1969. *Rimatori del Trecento*. Turin.

Covini, Maria N. 1992. 'Alle spese di Zoan Villano'. *Nuova rivista storica* 76: 1–56.

Cronaca della città di Perugia dal 1309 al 1491: nota col nome di DIARIO del Graziani. Ed. A. Fabretti. 1850. *ASI* 16, 1.

Culture et société en Italie du Moyen Age à la Renaissance. Hommage à André Rochon. 1985. Paris.

Davidsohn, Robert. 1896–1908. *Forschungen zur Geschichte von Florenz.* 4 vols. Berlin.

——. 1956–68. *Storia di Firenze.* 8 vols. Tr. G. B. Klein, *et al.* Florence.

Dean, Trevor, and K. J. P. Lowe, eds. 1998. *Marriage in Italy, 1300–1650.* Cambridge.

De Angelis, Laura. 1992. 'Lorenzo a Napoli'. *ASI* 150: 385–421.

De Roover, Raymond. 1966. *The Rise and Decline of the Medici Bank.* New York.

Dei, Benedetto. 1984. *La Cronica.* Ed. Roberto Barducci. Florence.

Del Piazzo, Marcello, ed. 1956. *Protocolli del Carteggio di Lorenzo il Magnifico per gli anni 1473–74, 1477–92.* Florence.

Dempsey, Charles. 2001. *Inventing the Renaissance Putto.* Chapel Hill and London.

Di Benedetto, Filippo. 1992. 'Un breve di Sisto IV contro Lorenzo'. *ASI* 150: 371–84.

Di Fonzo, Lorenzo, 1987. *I pontefici Sisto IV (1471–84) e Sisto V (1585–90).* Rome.

Écrire à la fin du Moyen-Age. Le pouvoir et l'écriture en Espagne et en Italie (1450–1530). 1990. Aix-en-Provence.

Edgerton, Samuel Y. 1985. *Pictures and Punishment.* Ithaca, N. Y.

Eisenbichler, Konrad. 1992. 'Lorenzo de' Medici e la Congregazione dei Neri nella Compagnia della Croce al Tempio'. *ASI* 150: 343–70.

Enciclopedia dei papi. 2000. 3 vols. Rome.

Esch, Arnold. 1998. 'Überweisungen an die apostolische Kammer aus den Diözesen des Reiches unter Einschaltung italienischer und deutscher Kaufleute und Bankiers. Regesten der vatikanischen Archivalien 1431–1475'. *Quellen und Forschungen aus Italienischen Archiven und Bibliotheken* 78: 262–387.

Fabbri, Lorenzo. 1991. *Alleanza matrimoniale e patriziato nella Firenze del '400: Studio sulla famiglia Strozzi.* Florence.

Fabroni, Angelo. 1784. *Laurentii Medicis Magnifici vita.* Pisa.

Falconi, Carlo. 1987. *Leone X: Giovanni de' Medici.* Milan.

Fanelli, Giovanni. 1973. *Firenze: Architettura e Città*. Florence.

Field, Arthur. 1988. *The Origins of the Platonic Academy of Florence*. Princeton.

Fineschi, Filippo. 1992. 'La rappresentazione della morte sul patibolo nella liturgia fiorentina della congregazione dei Neri'. *ASI* 150: 805–46.

Finlay, Robert. 1980. *Politics in Renaissance Venice*. New Brunswick.

Flamini, Francesco. 1889. 'Versi in morte di Giuliano de' Medici, 1478'. *Il Propugnatore*, New Series II: 315–34.

Foschi, Marina, and Luciana Prati, eds. 1994. *Melozzo da Forlì*. Milan.

Frantz, Erich. 1880. *Sixtus IV und die Republik Florenz*. Regensburg.

Frick, Carole. 2002. *Dressing Renaissance Florence: Families, Fortunes, and Fine Clothing*. Baltimore.

Fryde, E. B. 1983. *Humanism and Renaissance Historiography*. London.

Fubini, Riccardo. 1993. 'La Congiura dei Pazzi'. In Toscani, *Lorenzo*.

——. 1994. *Italia quattrocentesca. Politica e diplomazia nell'età di Lorenzo il Magnifico*. Milan.

——. 1996. *Quattrocento fiorentino: politica, diplomazia, cultura*. Pisa.

Galletti, G., ed. 1864. *Laude spirituali*. Florence.

Ganz, Margery A. 1994. 'Paying the Price for Political Failure: Florentine Women in the Aftermath of 1466'. *Rinascimento* 34: 237–57.

Garbero Zorzi, Elvira. 1992. 'La Collezione di Lorenzo'. In Cardini, *Lorenzo*.

Garfagnini, Gian Carlo, ed. 1992. *Lorenzo il Magnifico e il suo mondo*. Florence.

Giuliari, G. B. 1874. *Prose del Giovane Buonaccorso da Montemagno*. Bologna.

Giustinian, Leonardo. 1983. *Laudario giustinianeo*. 2 vols. Ed. F. Luisi. Venice.

Giustiniani, Vito R. 1965. *Alamanno Rinuccini, 1426–1499. Materialien und Forschungen zur Geschichte des florentinischen Humanismus*. Cologne and Graz.

Goldthwaite, Richard A. 1980. *The Building of Renaissance Florence*. Baltimore.

——. 1995. *Banks, Palaces and Entrepreneurs in Renaissance Florence*. Aldershot.

Gori, Orsola. 1995. 'La crisi del regime mediceo del 1466'. In *Studi in onore di Arnaldo d'Addario*, III: 809–25. Ed. Luigi Borgi. Lecce.

Grayson, Cecil. 1965. 'Gentile Becchi'. *DBI* 7: 491–3.

Gregory, Heather, tr. *Selected Letters of Alessandra Strozzi*. Berkeley, Los Angeles.

Grunzweig, A. 1931. *Correspondence de la filiale de Bruges des Medici*. Brussels.

Guicciardini, Francesco. 1931. *Storie fiorentine*. Ed. Roberto Palmarocchi. Bari.

——. 1953. *Opere*. Ed. Vittorio de Caprariis. Milan, Naples.

Gundersheimer, Werner L. 1972. 'Crime and Punishment in Ferrara, 1450–1500'. In Martines, *Violence and Civil Disorder.*

Gutkind, Curt S. *Cosimo de' Medici: Pater Patriae, 1389–1464.* Oxford.

Hale, J. R. 1977. *Florence and the Medici.* London.

Herlihy, David, and Christiane Klapisch-Zuber. 1978. *Les Toscans et leurs familles.* Paris.

——. 1985. *Tuscans and Their Families.* New Haven and London.

Herzner, Volker. 1976. 'Die Segel-Imprese der Familie Pazzi'. In *Mitteilungen des Kunsthistorischen Institutes in Florenz* 20: 13–32.

Holmes, George. 2001. 'The Pazzi Conspiracy seen from the Apostolic Chamber'. In *Mosaics of Friendship: Studies in Art and History for Eve Borsook.* Florence.

——. 1968. 'How the Medici Became the Pope's Bankers'. In *Florentine Studies: Politics and Society in Renaissance Florence,* ed. N. Rubinstein. London.

Hook, Judith. 1984. *Lorenzo de' Medici.* London.

Hurtubise, Pierre. 1985. *Une famille témoin: les Salviati.* Vatican City.

Ilardi, Vincent. 1972. 'The Assassination of Galeazzo Maria Sforza'. In Martines, *Violence and Civil Disorder.*

Jacks, Philip, and William Caferro. 2001 *The Spinelli of Florence: Fortunes of a Renaissance Merchant Family.* University Park.

Jones, Philip J. 1999. 'The Machiavellian Militia: innovation or renovation?' In *La Toscane et les Toscans.*

——. 1997. *The Italian City-State: From Commune to Signoria.* Oxford.

Jones, Rosemary D. 1972. *Francesco Vettori: Florentine Citizen and Medici Servant.* London.

Kent, Dale. 1978. *The Rise of the Medici.* Oxford.

——. 2000. *Cosimo de' Medici and the Florentine Renaissance.* New Haven and London.

Kent, F. W. 1996. 'The Young Lorenzo'. In Mallett and Mann, *Lorenzo.*

——. 1994. 'Lorenzo . . . Amico degli uomini da bene'. In Garfagnini, *Lorenzo.*

——. 1993. 'Patron-Client Networks in Renaissance Florence and the emergence of Lorenzo as "Maestro della Bottega"'. In Toscani, *Lorenzo.*

Kirshner, Julius. 1977. 'Pursuing Honor while Avoiding Sin'. *Studi senesi* 89: 175–258.

Klapisch-Zuber, Christiane. 1990. *La maison et le nom. Stratégies et rituels dans l'Italie de la Renaissance.* Paris.

Kohl, Benjamin, and Ronald Witt. 1978. *The Earthly Republic: Italian Humanists on Government and Society.* University of Pennsylvania.

Kuehn, Thomas. 1991. *Law, Family and Women: Toward a Legal Anthropology of Renaissance Italy.* Chicago.

Landucci, Luca. 1883. *Diario fiorentino.* Ed. I. Della Badia. Florence.

——. 1927. *A Florentine Diary.* Tr. A. Jervis. London.

Larner, John. 1965. *The Lords of Romagna.* London.

——. 1972. 'Order and Disorder in Romagna'. In Martines, *Violence.*

La Toscane e les Toscans autour de la Renaissance: Cadres de vie, société, croyances. 1999. Université de Provence.

Legal Consulting in the Civil Law Tradition. 1999. Eds. M. Ascheri, *et al.* Berkeley.

Lettere. Lorenzo de' Medici. *Lettere.* 1977–. 8 vols. General editor: N. Rubinstein. R. Fubini, ed. I–II; Rubinstein, ed. III–IV; M. Mallett, ed. V–VII; H. Butters, ed. VIII.

Litta, Pompeo. 1819–88. *Famiglie celebri italiane.* IV. 'Pazzi di Firenze' and 'Orsini di Roma'. Milan.

Lombardi, Giuseppe. 2000. 'Sisto IV'. *Enciclopedia dei Papi* II: 701–17. Rome.

Lorenzo de' Medici. 1955. *Scritti scelti.* Ed. Emilio Bigi. Turin.

——. 1939. *Opere.* 2 vols. Ed. Attilio Simioni. Bari.

——. 1990. *Laude.* Ed. Bernard Toscani. Florence.

Lorenzi, Girolamo. 1875. *Cola Montano. Studio storico.* Milan.

Machiavelli, Niccolò. 1962. *Istorie fiorentine.* Ed. F. Gaeta. Milan.

——. 1988. *Florentine Histories.* Tr. L. F. Banfield and H. C. Mansfield. Princeton.

Maguire, Yvonne. 1927. *The Women of the Medici.* London.

Mallett, Michael. 1967. *The Florentine Galleys in the Fifteenth Century.* Oxford.

——. 1992. 'Diplomacy and War in Later Fifteenth-Century Italy'. In Garfagnini, *Lorenzo.*

Mallett, Michael, and Nicholas Mann, eds. 1996. *Lorenzo the Magnificent: Culture and Politics.* London.

Martelli, Mario. 1965. *Studi Laurenziani.* Florence.

——. 1985. 'Profilo ideologico di Alamanno Rinuccini'. In *Culture et Société.*

——. 1989. 'Profilo ideologico di Giannozzo Manetti'. *Studi italiani* 1: 5–41.

——. 1990. 'L'Esilio di Giannozzo Manetti'. In *Écrire à la fin du Moyen-Age.*

——. 1992. 'Il Cristianesimo di Lorenzo'. In Cardini, *Lorenzo*.

——. 1992. 'La cultura letteraria nell' età di Lorenzo.' In Garfagnini, *Lorenzo*.

Martines, Lauro. 2002. 'Raging Against Priests'. In Connell, *Society and Individual*.

——. 2001. *Strong Words: Writing and Social Strain in the Italian Renaissance*. Baltimore and London.

——. TLS: Review of Dale Kent, *Cosimo de' Medici and the Florentine Renaissance* 12 January 2001: 28.

——. 1999. 'Corruption and Injustice as Themes in Quattrocento Poetry'. In *La Toscane et les Toscans*.

——. 1994. *An Italian Renaissance Sextet*. New York.

——. [1979] 2002. *Power and Imagination: City States in Renaissance Italy*. New York and London.

——. 1974. 'A Way of Looking at Women in Renaissance Florence'. *Journal of Medieval and Renaissance Studies* 4: 15–28.

——, ed. 1972. *Violence and Civil Disorder in Italian Cities, 1200–1500*. Berkeley and Los Angeles.

——. 1968. *Lawyers and Statecraft in Renaissance Florence*. Princeton.

——. 1968. 'Political Conflict in the Italian City States'. *Government and Opposition: A Quarterly of Comparative Politics* III: 69–91.

——. 1963. *The Social World of the Florentine Humanists*. Princeton.

——. 1961. 'Nuovi documenti su Cino Rinuccini'. *ASI* 119: 77–90.

Masi, Bartolomeo. 1906. *Ricordanze*. Ed. G. O. Corazzini. Florence.

Massèra, A. F. 1940. *Sonetti burleschi e realistici dei primi due secoli*. Bari.

Melis, Federigo. 1972. *Documenti per la storia economica dei secoli xiii–xvi*. Florence.

Merisalo, Outi. 1999. *Le collezione medicee nel 1495*. Florence.

Miglio, Massimo, et al., eds. 1986. *Un pontificato ed una città: Sisto IV (1471–1484)*. Vatican City.

Miglio, Massimo. 1979. 'Viva la libertà et populo de Roma'. In *Palaeographica diplomatica et archivistica. Studi in onore di Giulio Battelli*. 2 vols. Rome. I: 381–428.

Molho, Anthony. 1971. *Florentine Public Finances in the Early Renaissance, 1400–1433*. Cambridge, USA.

——. 1994. *Marriage Alliance in Late Medieval Florence*. Cambridge and London.

Molho, Anthony, and Franek Sznura, eds. 1986. *Alle bocche della piazza. Diario di anonimo fiorentino, 1382–1401*. Florence.

Moreni, Domenico, ed. 1830. *Lettere di Lorenzo il Magnifico*. Florence.

Municchi, Alfredo. 1911. *La fazione antimedicea detta del Poggio*. Florence.

Ninci, Renzo. 1992. 'Techniche e manipolazioni elettorali nel Comune di Firenze tra XIV e XV secolo'. *ASI* 150: 735–73.

Orvieto, Paolo. 1976. *Lorenzo de' Medici*. Florence.

Paatz, Walter and Elisabeth. 1940–54. *Die Kirchen von Florenz*. 6 vols. Frankfurt.

Palmarocchi, Roberto. 1952. 'Lorenzo de' Medici e la nomina cardinalizia di Giovanni'. *ASI* 110: 38–54.

——. 1933. *La Politica italiana di Lorenzo de' Medici*. Florence.

Pampaloni, Guido. 1961–62. 'Fermenti di riforme democratiche nella Firenze medicea del Quattrocento', *ASI* 119: 11–62, 241–81; and 'Nuovi tentativi'. *ASI* 120: 21–81.

Parenti, Marco. 1996. *Lettere*. Ed. M. Marrese. Florence.

Parenti, Piero. 1994. *Storia fiorentina I: 1476–78, 1492–96*. Ed. A. Matuci. Florence.

Pasolini, Pier Desiderio. 1893. *Caterina Sforza*. 3 vols. Rome.

Pastor, Ludwig. 1949. *The History of the Popes*. Vols. III–V. London.

Pellegrini, Francesco C. 1880. *Sulla repubblica fiorentina al tempo di Cosimo*. Pisa.

Pellegrini, Marco. 1999. *Congiure di Romagna: Lorenzo de' Medici e il duplice tirannicidio a Forlì e a Faenza nel 1488*. Florence.

——. 2000. 'Innocenzo VIII'. *Enciclopedia dei papi*, III, 1–13.

Perosa, Alessandro. 1943. 'Storia di un libro di poesie latine dell' umanista fiorentino A. Braccesi'. *La Bibliofilia* 45: 138–85.

Phillips, Mark. 1987. *The Memoir of Marco Parenti*. Princeton.

Picotti, G. B. 1928. *La giovinezza di Leone X*. Milan.

Pieraccini, Gaetano. 1924. *La Stirpe de' Medici di Cafaggiolo*. 3 vols. Florence.

Poliziano, Angelo. 1958. *Della Congiura dei Pazzi (Coniurationis commentarium)*. Ed. Alessandro Perosa. Padua. English translations of this work: in Watkins, *Humanism*, and Kohl and Witt, *Earthly Republic*.

Pontieri, Ernesto. 1940. 'La dinastia aragonese di Napoli e la casa de' Medici di Firenze'. *Archivio storico per le provincie napoletane* 65: 274–342.

——. 1947. *Per la storia del regno di Ferrante I d'Aragona Re di Napoli*. Naples.

Queller, Donald E. 1986. *The Venetian Patriciate: Reality versus Myth*. Urbana.

Ridolfi, Roberto. 1934. *Gli archivi delle famiglie fiorentine*. Florence.

Rinuccini, Alamanno. 1957. *Dialogus de libertate.* Ed. Francesco Adorno. *Atti e Memorie dell' Accademia toscana La Colombaria* XXII: 270–303.

——. 1978. *Dialogus.* See English trans.: Watkins, *Humanism,* 193–224.

——. 1840. *Ricordi,* in Filippo Rinuccini, *Ricordi storici.* Ed. G. Aiazzi. Florence.

——. 1953. *Lettere ed orazioni.* Ed. V. Giustiniani. Florence.

Rochon, André. 1963. *La jeunesse de Laurent de Médicis (1449–1478).* Paris.

Rondini, Giuseppe. 1901. 'I Giustiziati a Firenze'. *ASI* 27: 208–56.

Roscoe, William. 1796. *The Life of Lorenzo de' Medici.* 2 vols. London.

Rubinstein, Nicolai. 1966. *The Government of Florence Under the Medici.* Oxford.

——. 1992. 'Cosimo *optimus civis*'. In Ames-Lewis, *Cosimo.*

——. 1992. 'Lorenzo de' Medici: The Formation of his Statecraft'. In Garfagnini, *Lorenzo.*

——. 1995. *The Palazzo Vecchio, 1298–1542: Government, Architecture and Imagery in the Civic Palace of the Florentine Republic.* Oxford.

Ruggiero, Guido. 1980. *Violence in Early Renaissance Venice.* New Brunswick.

Saalman, Howard. 1993. *Filippo Brunelleschi: The Buildings.* University Park.

Salvadori, Patrizia. 1992. 'Rapporti personali, rapporti di potere nella corrispondenza di Lorenzo dei Medici'. In Garfagnini, *Lorenzo.*

Salvemini, Gaetano. 1896. *La dignità cavalleresca nel Comune di Firenze.* Florence.

Sanuto, Marin. 1879–1903. *I darii.* 58 vols. Ed. R. Fulin *et al.* Venice.

Sapori, Armando. 1955–67. *Studi di storia economica.* 3 vols. Florence.

Sbregondi, Ludovica. 1992. 'Lorenzo de' Medici confratello'. *ASI* 150: 319–41.

Shaw, Christine. 1993. *Julius II: The Warrior Pope.* Oxford.

Soranzo, Giovanni. 1953. 'Lorenzo il Magnifico alla morte del padre e il suo primo balzo verso la Signoria'. *ASI* 111: 42–77.

Spallanzani, Marco. 1987. 'Le aziende Pazzi al tempo della Congiura del 1478'. In *Studi di storia economica toscana nel Medioevo e nel Rinascimento.* Ospedaletto.

Statuta de regimine praetoris civilia et criminalia civitatis . . . papie. 1505. Pavia.

Statuta populi et communis Florentiae. 1778–83. 3 vols. Freiburg [Florence].

Statuti e ordinamenti del Comune di Udine. 1898. Udine.

Strozzi, Alessandra. 1914. *Lettere ai figlioli.* Ed. G. Papini. Lanciano.

Sznura, Franek. 1975. *L'Espansione urbana di Firenze nel dugento.* Florence.

Tognetti, Sergio. 1999. *Il Banco Cambini. Affari e mercati di una compagnia mercantile-bancaria nella Firenze del XV secolo.* Florence.

——. 1999. 'Problemi di vettovagliamento cittadino e misure di politica annonaria a Firenze nel XV secolo'. *ASI* 157: 419–52.

Tornabuoni, Lucrezia. 1993. *Lettere*. Ed. Patrizia Salvadori. Florence.

——. 1978. *I poemetti sacri*. Ed. Fulvio Pezzarossa. Florence.

Toscani, Bernard, ed. 1993. *Lorenzo de' Medici: New Perspectives*. New York.

Trexler, Richard. 1980. *Public Life in Renaissance Florence*. New York.

Valori, Niccolò. 1991. *Vita di Lorenzo de' Medici*. Ed. E. Niccolini. Vicenza.

Vasari, Giorgio. 1967. *Le Vite*. 9 vols. Novara.

Vasina, Augusto, ed. 1990. *Storia di Forlì*. II: *Il Medioevo*. Forlì and Bologna.

Vespasiano da Bisticci. 1970–76. *Le Vite*. 3 vols. Ed. A. Greco. Florence.

Wackernagel, M. 1981. *The World of the Florentine Renaissance Artist*. Tr. A. Luchs. Princeton.

Watkins, Renée Neu. 1978. *Humanism and Liberty: Writings on Freedom from Fifteenth-Century Florence*. Columbia, S. Carolina.

Weber, Christoph. 1999. *Genealogien zur Papstgeschichte*. 2 vols. (Vol. 29, 1–2, of *Papste und Papsttum*). Stuttgart.

Weissman, Ronald F. 1982. *Ritual Brotherhood in Renaissance Florence*. New York.

Wittschier, H. W., ed. 1968. *Giannozzo Manetti. Das Corpus der Orationes*. Cologne.

Zaghini, Franco. 1994. 'La popolazione a Forlì nel sec. XV'. In Foschi, *Melozzo*.

Zorzi, Andrea. 1988. *L'Amministrazione della giustizia penale nella repubblica fiorentina*. Florence.

——. 1992. 'Ordinamenti e politiche giudiziarie in età laurenziana'. In Garfagnini, *Lorenzo*.

INDEX